The Hero of the Herd

Also by Dr. John McCormack

Fields and Pastures New
A Friend of the Flock

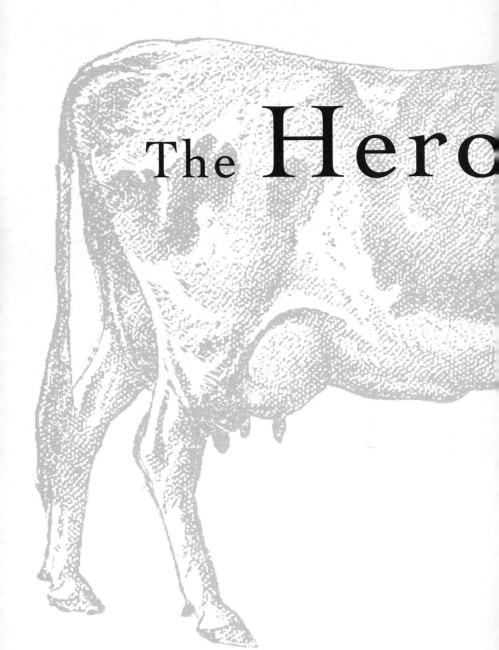

The Herd

of the # Herd

*More Tales
from a Country Veterinarian*

Dr. John McCormack

Crown Publishers ～ New York

Published by Crown Publishers, 201 East 50th Street, New York, New York 10022. Member of the Crown Publishing Group.

Random House, Inc. New York, Toronto, London, Sydney, Auckland
www.randomhouse.com

CROWN is a trademark and the Crown Colophon is a registered trademark of Random House, Inc.

Printed in the United States of America

Design by Cynthia Dunne

Library of Congress Cataloging-in-Publication Data

McCormack, John (John E.)
    The hero of the herd : more tales from a country veterinarian / by John McCormack. — 1st ed.
        p.   cm.
    1. McCormack, John (John E.) 2. Veterinarians—Alabama—Choctaw County Biography.   I. Title.
SF613.M38A3   1999
636.089'092—dc21
[B]   99-23442
                                                                     CIP

ISBN 0-609-60373-6

10 9 8 7 6 5 4 3 2 1

First Edition

This book is for Christine, Dillon, Maddie, and our latest addition, Calli Marie. Mimi and I love you all so very much, and are most appreciative of your love and the time you spend with us.

I never knew grandchildren could be so smart, talented, beautiful, and energetic. I now understand why they are given to younger people.

Acknowledgments

For her tactful editorial assistance and helpful advice, I would like to thank Rachel Kahan of Crown Publishers. And to Rachel Pace, I extend my appreciation for her publicity efforts and keeping me on schedule.

Introduction

By the summer of 1965, our veterinary practice had grown so busy that Jan and I couldn't manage it alone. We often found ourselves laughing, our heads shaking in wonder, at how so much had happened in such a short period of time. It had been only eighteen short months earlier when we drove our loaded U-Haul truck and packed station wagon into Choctaw County, Alabama, not knowing a soul in the entire area, except for Mr. Sexton, the county agent. But he had greased the skids for us, and he convinced us the time was right for a veterinarian to set up a practice in the growing and newly prosperous county, where previous generations had eked out a living from the land, mainly from pine trees, cotton, and an occasional oil well in the south end of the county. In the years before we arrived some had "made a little likker," especially in the one country-stored community of

Fordtown, located in the northwestern area of the county. "Fordtown likker" enjoyed a good reputation among the hard-drinking citizens of the Deep South, many of whom rejected the store-bought and watered-down, bonded, red whiskey. But in the 1950s and 1960s the presence of an agent from the Alabama Beverage Control Board residing in the county had put a damper on the backwoods distilling business. By the time we came on the scene, the moonshining business was on its deathbed.

About 1960 a huge toilet tissue–manufacturing paper mill had been built on the Choctaw County side of the Tombigbee River, a Vanity Fair plant that manufactured quality ladies' lingerie had opened in the town of Butler, and more excellent quality crude oil was being discovered in the Gilbertown area. For the first time in history, a slew of people from "up north" were being transferred into Choctaw County to work in the new and expanding industries. In addition, the secret was out about the county's prominence as a deer and turkey hunter's paradise, which attracted hunters from all over the country. Because it was obviously an up-and-coming county with friendly people and many recreational opportunities, including a new nine-hole golf course, it just seemed like a good place to live and work.

Still, there were a few disadvantages to being the sole veterinarian in town. I was on call all the time, which often cut into the time I wanted to spend with my family, and it was even harder to make time for an occasional hunting or golfing outing, or a rare trip out of town.

Prioritizing emergency calls is a problem, too, when you're the only vet in town. It was frustrating when a frantic Mr. W. J. Landry called, saying his best cow was having difficulty delivering her very valuable calf. Then, just seconds later, Mrs. Miller might be on the phone to tell me that her schnauzer, Rye, had just been hit by a car while making his early-morning rounds. Who do you help first?

With all this going on, trying to keep up with all the latest diagnostic techniques, new drugs, and treatment regimes for all species of animals was impossible. I tried to read my veterinary journals and other literature late at night, but after a long day it was hard to stay awake when reading a dull report from New Zealand about some new sheep dewormer.

I still loved my job, but after a few years I wasn't quite as gung-ho as before. If someone called during Sunday preaching about cows blind with the pinkeye, I no longer bolted from the church house in a dead run. Instead, I returned to our pew and listened to the pastor rant and rave about the evils of working, hunting, fishing, and golfing on Sunday. I would go on the call later. A chronically scratching dog or sneezing cat phone call at midnight no longer resulted in a fast trip to the clinic. Instead, I insisted that it wait until morning. Experience was teaching me that it was also important to relax.

Because of the growth of the practice and Jan's difficult pregnancy in 1965, we added two employees to the clinic staff. Miss Sue was my new office manager, receptionist, and girl Friday. With her can-do attitude, she was ideal for the job. She was also a true animal lover and knew most everybody in town. Sue did whatever it took to make the practice work smoothly, whether that meant cleaning up a pet accident in the waiting room or calmly tending to a big fellow who fainted while I cleaned out Poochie's ears.

The job of kennel boy—or, more euphemistically, "ward sanitary engineer"—was filled by Timmy, a fifteen-year-old who desperately wanted to become a veterinarian. He wanted to learn about animals so much that he had a strange enthusiasm for cleaning out dog cages, sweeping and mopping, and swabbing up after my surgeries. He came in before school and returned early in the afternoon, and he worked on Saturdays, Sundays, and full-time during the summer. Timmy was a very fast learner, especially about what not to do in a veterinary clinic—never dip a Persian cat in dog mange dip, never try to kiss a Chow dog whose manners are suspect, and never, ever, stand behind a two-thousand-pound bull who has loose bowel syndrome and a bad cough. He quickly learned about the dangers of sudden bovine tail-raising movements, and knew to get out of the line of fire.

In addition, Jan's brother, Dick, spent the summer of 1965 with us, helping us with rabies clinics, holding dogs, going on large animal calls, and helping Jan at home with Tom and Lisa. He was a lifesaver for us that summer. Even though I joked about his constant eating and late-sleeping habits, I enjoyed his company, especially our traditional rivalry about whether Auburn or Alabama had the best football team. In spite of being an art major, not the most popular field of study in Choctaw County, Dick fit right in with the University of Alabama "supporters" at the barbershop. Because of his 6′4″, 220-pound size, some were sure he played football for Bear Bryant, and Dick never corrected them.

Those were happy years for my family and my practice, but the 1960s were difficult times for the Deep South. The era of segregation was dying a painful but necessary death, and a centuries-old way of life was being altered in ways that many citizens found unbelievable. Geographically, Choctaw County is in the heart of the Heart of Dixie, but the violence that erupted in places like Selma, Birmingham, and Little Rock seemed like a terrible, faraway nightmare. Fortunately, Choctaw County was spared such brutal confrontations.

It was in the sixties when I realized that everyday humor might just save us all from our ourselves. Scientists and college professors have said that we will live longer and be more creative and healthier by exercising our innards with a good guffaw. I know that my life has been better since I learned to laugh at myself, and being a country veterinarian gave me a lot of opportunities to do just that.

The Hero of the Herd

One

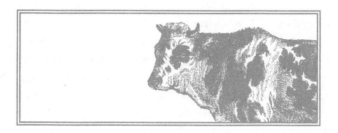

Every Thursday, except for Christmas week, I worked at the livestock sale barn in Livingston, a small town forty-five miles north of Butler. Since there was no practicing veterinarian in Livingston, the neighboring community of York, or even the entire county of Sumter, it didn't take long for the animal owners there to find out there was a vet at the barn every Thursday. Word spread fast, and soon people were calling to ask me to "drop by" and check a cow, test a herd, examine a horse, or treat a pet on my way to or from the sale barn. Some even requested that I come to the house and vaccinate their pets when taking a "break" in the sale barn action. Others found that I usually took lunch at Miss Maude's café, just off the courthouse square, so it wasn't uncommon to wheel up for a bite and see a goat on a pickup truck or a bird dog in a box, just waiting for me to examine them.

In the summer of 1965, Timmy or Dick would usually accompany me on those Thursday visits. Our six-year-old, Tom, was peeved because he was sure he was big enough to be my assistant. His plan was to sit on the vet pen fence and hand me the blood tubes with the big bleeding needles attached—and, of course, lend advice in case the need arose. Naturally, his mother wasn't crazy about the idea, but after much pleading and many sincere promises to be careful, be good, and behave, he was allowed to go "just this once." He neglected to tell her about how he'd be handling those sharp needles and perching precariously on the top board of the fence. But he had been with me on calls before, and he was unusually mature for his age, having already been witness to more veterinary surgery than 99 percent of the county's adults. His very descriptive accounts of several veterinary procedures, including calf and puppy birthings, epileptic seizures in dogs, and how to take a mule's temperature, had already landed him in hot water with Mrs. Minsloff, his kindergarten teacher.

Therefore, just before he started the first grade, we left Timmy and Dick at the clinic with a passel of cleaning chores, and Tom made his first trip to the sale barn. It was great fun to have him along and see his youthful enthusiasm for everything. He especially enjoyed watching for white-tailed deer and wild turkeys along the highway, and constantly asked questions about animals. He wanted to know about the breeds of cattle and the reasons for so many different colors.

"What kind of cow is that, Daddy?" he asked as we buzzed by a pasture full of bovines.

"Which one?"

"The black one."

"That's an Angus. Came from England."

"Why?"

"Well, that's just where her kinfolks originated."

"No, I mean why's she black?"

"Uh, well, that's just the way God made her. He made some of the others red, and some other colors, such as the gray one down there drinking from the pond."

"Why?"

"That's just where they get their water, since they can't drink from a glass."

"Why?"

After a few minutes of "whys" I'd attempt to change the subject.

"What do you want for lunch? I think we'll eat at Miss Maude's today."

"Umm, a hamburger, French fries, an orange drink, and chocolate ice cream," he replied. I should have known. Jan would have suggested the meat loaf, turnip greens, and sweet potato casserole. When I mentioned this alternative menu, Tom made a face and a gagging noise.

"OK, we'll do the hamburger thing, but let's hold the ice cream until we start home, and then we'll stop at the Dairy Queen at York and get one of those big cones," I suggested. This plan met with his approval.

I thought about the week before, when Timmy and I had stopped by the DQ and had each ordered the biggest cone on the list. All went well on the way out of York, but when we hit the county line and I looked over at Tim and saw his lips wrapped around his ice cream, a devilish urge struck me. As a joke, I slapped the bottom of the cone up a little, just as the truck hit a pothole, and the whole glob of half-finished ice cream went flying into Timmy's face.

In my funning around, I had just meant to get a little dab of the ice cream on his chin. Unfortunately, the plan worked a little too well, and Timmy's face, from horn-rimmed glasses to the tip of his chin, was covered in a slowly dripping, cold white mess, speckled with exploded cone parts. A bucket of creek water and a couple of towels helped relieve the stickiness, but Timmy has never forgiven me for that mean trick, no matter how often I apologize. That might be one reason he decided to become a physician's assistant instead of a veterinarian. I guess he hoped he could avoid being tormented by another wicked employer.

This time, when Tom and I parked in front of Miss Maude's place, we saw a German shepherd sitting in the front passenger seat of a pickup truck, its mangy head stuck out a small crack between the window and the top of the door. She was staring intently at the café door, obviously waiting for her master to finish lunch.

"Daddy, that dog's got a bad case of the mange," Tom diagnosed. He was to start the first grade in just a few days, but he was already a pretty good veterinary dermatologist.

"Yep, she does, but what kind of mange is it?" I asked. On many occasions Tom had climbed up on the stool in the lab and peered down into the microscope, excitedly watching a live mange mite crawling over the microscopic field. He also was fascinated by microscopic worm eggs and heartworm larvae as they wiggled in the blood smear.

"I think it's red mange," he said hesitantly.

"Maybe. But why?" Now I was asking the questions.

"'Cause I didn't know there was any other kind."

"There's demodectic and sarcoptic, and maybe even some others. But the sarcoptic kind is real contagious to humans, and if they spend time around places where the dog has been sleeping or they carry the dog around next to their body, it will break out on their skin," I explained. Tom would probably be lecturing on "canine diseases transmissible to humans" at show-and-tell time in school sometime very soon, but I had one thing more to pass along.

"When we go into the café and sit down, look around and see if you see anybody scratching themselves. If they are, they may have it. It might be the owner of this dog."

Tom slowly scanned the small crowd, consisting mostly of Sumter County cattlemen. The Sumter crowd wore cowboy hats, while the few Choctaw Countians had on seed corn caps. I removed the one-page menu from its standard position between the napkin dispenser, the sugar pourer, and the Louisiana Red Hot sauce. The day's offerings were in blue lettering, no doubt from the use of carbon paper. On days when the typewriter wouldn't work, the specials were just scribbled on lined, Blue Horse notebook paper.

"Daddy, look at that man over there with his back to us. He's scratching his side," Tom whispered, pointing to the corner table. "I wonder if that's his dog."

"That's Skeeter Paul. He asked me for some mange medicine a couple of weeks ago for his dog. We'll talk with him after we eat and find out if that's the same one."

Seconds later, Miss Eugenia, the head waitress, was taking our order.

"That's my boy, Tom, Miss Eugenia, and he wants a hamburger with ketchup and mustard, and an order of French fries," I said. "I'll have a pork chop, collard greens, and boiled okra. And corn bread and iced tea, of course."

"What'll you have to drink, young man?"

"I want an orange drink, please, ma'am," Tom answered politely.

While I checked out the crowd, Miss Eugenia took a minute to ask Tom the usual questions.

"Do you start to school this year?"

"Yes, ma'am, next Friday. I'm six."

"Do you have any brothers and sisters?"

"Just Lisa. She's almost four. But my mother is gonna have a little baby any day now!" he stated excitedly.

"Really? Do you want a boy or girl?"

"I'd want a little brother to play with, but a girl would be OK, too." She looked at me and winked, but spared me the same question. I just wanted it over with and a healthy mother and child.

"By the way, Skeeter wants to see you. Something about his dog," she said.

But before she could bring our food, Skeeter had turned and spied us, then headed our way, grabbed a chair, and squawked it up to the end of the table. I noticed he was still scratching his side.

"That mange medicine work, Skeeter?" I asked.

"I didn't use it yet. Old Suzie's lost all her hair and just looks so bad I decided that I'd try to get you to take her back to your clinic and doctor on her until she's cured," he said, still scratching around his belt. "I'm just ashamed for anybody to know I let an animal of mine get in that shape."

"Suzie stay inside or outside?" I asked.

"Oh, she's an outside dog and rides in the back of the truck.

Sometimes I let her get in the front seat, but she gets so close to me she just about pushes me out the door."

"Does she scratch much?"

"Not too much. I'm scratchin' more than she is. Doc, can folks catch the mange from dogs?"

"Skeeter, meet my associate here. This is Tom. What do you think, Tom?"

Tom cleared his throat and declared, "There's one kind of mange that is catching for people. I 'spec you've got it."

"W-what? H-how do you know that?" Skeeter stammered.

"Daddy told me a while ago." The man stopped in mid-scratch and stared at the six-year-old. Then he stared at me.

"Skeeter, I'll take care of Suzie. Now what you need to do is go to your doctor and tell him you think you've got the dog mange. But he won't like it if you say that a vet told you, so say you read it in the *Reader's Digest* or *Ladies' Home Journal.* It's caused by a mite called the sarcoptic mite, and it burrows in the skin and irritates the fire out of you. It's unusual, but I'll bet Suzie's got both kinds of the mange mites on her. They're both bad boys."

Our food arrived presently, and we tried to eat while discussing canine dermatology and how someday there would be veterinary specialists who only see dogs with skin and skin-related problems. I had no problem with my collard greens and other southern delicacies, but Tom only picked at his burger, which caused Miss Eugenia to fuss a little about his appetite. Maybe discussing mange at the dinner table wasn't such a good idea.

"Just talking about mangy dogs made me not hungry," Tom said.

We went outside and took a look at Suzie. Sure enough, she was mostly bald, except for a big tuft of hair at the end of her tail and some splotches scattered randomly over her body. She had the typical odor of a dog with chronic mange, which made diagnosing a full-blown case of the disease easy.

"Tell you what, Skeeter. I'm gonna give you a small bottle of special shampoo that contains selenium. I want you to go to the house, wet her down, pour the shampoo on, lather her up, then let it soak for ten minutes before rinsing her off. Then dry her real good and tie her in the garage on some papers or an old quilt. When I get ready to go home tonight, I'll call and you can bring her over."

"OK. But will that fancy shampoo cure her?"

"No, but it will kill a little of the smell. She has to sit next to Tom all the way home." Tom's mouth gaped open.

"Well, it's either that or you drive and she can sit next to me," I suggested.

"Sure, I'd rather do that," Tom said, deadpan. "Or ride in the back with the worm medicine." He was showing promise as a comedian as well as a budding veterinary dermatologist!

Suzie was a very cooperative dog on the way home. Skeeter had found an old sleeping bag, which we zipped up around the patient, leaving only her head sticking out. She was so embarrassed she hid her head between the seat and the passenger-side door. But when we stopped at the York Dairy Queen, she sat up and looked out the window, causing some strange looks and one very uncouth comment from a high schooler parked there.

"Look over yonder what's in that sleeping bag. I believe that's the ugliest woman I ever saw!"

I stared his way, then waggled a finger as he and his cronies scratched off and disappeared into the humid night, probably headed for the stateline beer joint just minutes away.

Tom ate only half of his ice cream, then gave the rest of it to Suzie. By the time we crossed the Choctaw County line, both my passengers were fast asleep. Everything seemed so peaceful in the truck cab, listening to the wail of the country music singer and the whine of the mud grip tires. But my mind was on Jan and the much-anticipated birth of our third child. I wondered if tonight might be the night. My foot mashed the accelerator down a little harder.

If I had known what was in store for me on Suzie's return trip home several weeks later, I wouldn't have had a peaceful thought in my head.

Two

With Thursday's all-day sale barn and Sumter County duties, calls back home in Butler got backed up, which always made Friday a busy time. I always tried to arrive at the clinic earlier than usual to see what was on the book and get organized. The night before, Tom and I had put our new patient, Suzie, into a large cage, fed and watered her, treated the other patients, than went home and collapsed.

When I arrived on Friday, Timmy was almost through mopping the waiting room, his last morning chore as Choctaw Animal Clinic's resident "sanitary engineer." Local youngsters who wanted to pursue a career in veterinary medicine started out by cleaning cages, feeding the patients, sweeping up, and hosing down and swabbing the clinic floors. From there they learned the easier tasks, such as holding dogs for injections, cleaning ears, muzzling Chows, and bringing dogs to the prep room for surgery.

"Timmy, before you go to school, bring that German shepherd up here. I want to do a skin scraping and worm check on her," I said.

"The one with the mange? That's the worst-looking dog I ever saw!" he exclaimed.

"Yep, that's what somebody said at the York Dairy Queen last night." I saw his lower lip pooch out in a sulk at the words "Dairy Queen." I reckoned he was still stewed about the ice cream deal.

"Can't many people do that," I said.

"Do what?"

"Make their lips do what you just did with yours. Now, I'm sorry about the ice cream. I told you, the devil just took me by the hand. . . ."

"Don't apologize anymore," he said jokingly, "'cause I'm gonna pay you back someday. Remember what Dave Barr Tutt said the other day: 'The sun don't shine up the same dog's nose every day.'"
With that, he disappeared down the hall and into the kennel room.

Moments later, we were staring at Suzie and her severe skin problem. Some portions of her body were completely denuded and infected, streaked with red marks where she had tried to relieve the intense itching by biting and scratching. It reminded me of newly clear-cut pine forest land or a sickly field of grain. We needed to plow up the entire field and plant over.

Timmy took a fecal sample for a worm check and set it up in the lab while I completed my physical examination. Then I smeared mineral oil on several areas of her body and did the skin scrapings to verify the diagnosis.

Looking down into the microscope, I could see plenty of the slowly wiggling, cigar-shaped demodectic mites, and even a few of the scary-looking sarcoptes variety as well. Under the scope, they are straight out of a horror movie, kind of a cross between a crab and a spider, stretching their eight legs and crawling around. I'm sure the sight of these creatures ruined many a late-afternoon appetite.

In addition to the mange mites, Suzie was infested with hookworms, whipworms, and tapeworms, plus a moderate number of fleas. But those were minor compared to the skin problem. The local folklore standard treatment handed down for generations consisted of used crankcase oil and sulfur applied liberally to every nook and cranny on the dog's body. In Choctaw County, this concoction was applied only once, since no sane human soul had ever volunteered to apply a second coat of the greasy mess, and the patient was likely to take off running when the designated farm smearee emerged from the barn door carrying the dreaded oil bucket behind his back. Dogs aren't as dumb as some humans think, plus they have an incredible memory and sense of smell. A normal dog never forgets that initial ordeal with the oil and sulfur, and when later approached by a grinning human with one hand behind his back, departs the scene with great haste.

My treatment wasn't a lot better for the patient. The lindane, chlordane, rotenone, benzyl benzoate, lime-sulfur, or organophosphate medications still had to be applied to the skin, either in an oily base or mixed in solutions that were poured over the patient and worked into the skin. Sometimes, the affected dog was dipped into a fifty-five-gallon drum half full of a properly diluted insecticide.

I had recently heard of a drug called toluidine blue, which when injected intravenously attacked the mites from the inside out. I decided to experiment by using the injections weekly, plus applying various solutions to the body on alternating days. Every Saturday I would get Timmy to bathe Suzie in the selenium-based shampoo, and then we'd start the routine again on Monday. The drugs would hit the mites both internally and externally. In addition, I added a vitamin supplement to her dry dog food, and I gave her a couple of cans of good-quality canned food each day.

After two to three weeks my plan was working. The old hair and superficial layers of grimy skin had peeled away, and new, fuzzy, healthy hair was coming in all over Suzie's body. She seldom scratched anymore, and her personality was becoming more pleasant. The only thing that concerned me was her color. She had turned navy blue after a couple of days of the treatment. Timmy quickly noticed that her kidneys were affected during her morning walk, which caused him to phone me at six o'clock in the morning with the exciting news of blue urine. At first I was afraid that I had made a mistake with the dosage of toluidine blue, but when I rechecked, my figures were correct. Looking farther down the small print text on the little paper insert that came with the new blue wonder drug, there were these words of caution: "Dogs injected with this drug may exhibit a transitory bluish discoloration of the mucous membranes and sclera. There is no cause for alarm."

Four Thursdays later, Skeeter cornered me at the sale barn.

"My dog 'bout cured up, Doc?"

"Uh huh. Still a little blue, but the skin is doing fine," I reported.

"Yes, I've noticed she gets a little down in the dumps from time to time, but don't we all."

"No, I mean the medicine I used turned her blue. She's blue as a violet! But it's nothing to worry about. I'll probably bring her home next week. I just want you to understand that she's gonna look like a different dog. She's gained weight, her eyes look brighter, and her hair is getting shiny."

"But she's blue. . . ."

"Yeah, she's blue, but not for long."

"I hope not. I'd hate for my dog to be running around in blue. That's Auburn's colors."

"You want Bear Bryant red? Then she'd really be hideous." Sometimes I think Alabama citizens take their football way too seriously.

The afternoon before Suzie's dismissal date, I had a message for Timmy. "Timmy, it's really important that you walk Suzie real good in the morning, because I'm taking her back to Livingston tomorrow. Be sure she goes to the bathroom! I've got to stop at Boyd's farm, north of York, to work some calves on the way up and I'll have to keep her in the truck so she doesn't run away. I don't want her messing up my truck!"

The next morning Suzie and I set out at about seven-thirty. As we buzzed north on Highway 17, I thought about the transformation in the dog's condition in five short weeks and how her mental attitude had improved as much as her physical condition. After a few miles, when she put her head on my right leg for some petting, I realized we had grown quite fond of each other.

When I arrived at the Boyd ranch, I unrolled the windows a few inches and said, "Suzie, stay!" She licked her lips as if to say "OK if I must, but I'd rather be running cows!" It occurred to me that maybe I should remove the health certificate books, test charts, blood tubes, and other paraphernalia from the front seat and dash. But as calm as she was, I saw no reason to do so. After all, what could happen in an hour when I was only a couple of hundred feet away?

As we vaccinated and tagged the calves, Suzie would occasionally stick her snout out the open window and bark at farm dogs and cats that wandered too close to the truck. But because of the way the sun was glaring on the truck windshield, I couldn't actually see her. Soon the work was completed and Mr. Boyd and I talked about the cattle market as we neared the truck.

"Doc, your windshield looks muddy. Is something wrong with it?" he said.

"No, I don't think so. . . ." But when I approached the hood, I knew something had gone terribly wrong. With hands over our noses and mouths, Boyd and I stood transfixed for a few seconds, both wondering what the next step should be.

Apparently, Timmy had forgotten to take Suzie for her walk that morning, and she had answered nature's call in a big way inside my beloved truck. Then, in her nervousness, she had walked and run around from passenger window to driver's window dozens of times, then had stomped all over the dash, windshield, steering wheel, instrument panel, and finally, the rear window and gun rack. There was not a square inch of the truck interior left untouched or unsmeared. The stuff had even been forced into the crevices between the seats and onto the brake pedal. The once-important papers and numbered blood tubes were totally trashed beyond recognition, and the mirror was browned out. What wasn't covered with brown animal excrement was covered with a blue-tinged liquid. Oh, how I wanted to be somewhere else at that moment, perhaps somewhere far away like New Guinea—or at least a clean library, reading a very clean book about clean air and beautiful mountains.

"I heard the phone ring, Doc," said Boyd, hurriedly making tracks toward the house. "There's the water hose down by the well house."

Suzie was going crazy, sticking her nose out the window and yapping, her hind end going back and forth a mile a minute, obviously pleased with herself for doing such a fabulous job of fertilizing my truck.

I retrieved a long piece of hay twine from the back, held my breath and looped the twine over the filth-covered dog's neck, opened the door, and quicky changed the twine to my other hand. Suzie immediately showed her gratitude by jumping up on my chest and raking downward, which helped to clean some of the objectionable material from between her toes. When she nuzzled my face I gave up, resigning myself to the fact that I, too, would have to be hosed off. Finally, I was able to get her tied to a persimmon tree beside the pump house, then I located a second hose, which, when connected to the first, was long enough to reach the truck. I wrapped an old T-shirt around my face, covering my nose, and started to hose out the truck interior. After several minutes of superficial cleaning, I got into the flooded cab and moved the truck to the side of a hill where the water would drain out better.

"Timmy did this on purpose!" I mumbled to myself. "He knew that Suzie would mess up this truck if he didn't walk her this morning. This is a heck of a price to pay for ruining his ice cream cone."

An hour later, the truck was spotless—but not odorless, Suzie had been reshampooed, and Boyd was still hiding in the house. I had secreted myself behind the tractor shed, stripped down, and hosed myself off with the icy water from the deep well, then I donned a spare pair of coveralls. I was pleased with myself for not getting angry. After all, the poor dog wasn't to blame.

Skeeter almost didn't recognize his dog at first, she was so changed from the hairless animal of before. But when she jumped up and started licking his face and whimpering, he knew. "She don't even smell no more, Doc!" he declared. I wondered if there was something wrong with his nose. "She looks great, just a little blue in the gums. I'm gonna tell ever'body around here what a good mange doctor you are!"

"Skeeter, you do and I'll never forgive you," I said, my head filled with visions of more days like this one.

"Why? You've cured this dog. I did mean to tell you that she has weak bowels and sometimes can have an accident, especially if she doesn't get walked early in the morning. I just forgot. But obviously everything worked out fine."

"Uh huh."

Later, Timmy vowed that he hadn't forgotten to walk Suzie that morning, and that he would never do such a thing to his boss man. But I heard him laughing out loud when he was cleaning the kennels the next morning. There has to be something very, very funny or personally satisfying for someone to laugh while carrying out their duties as a canine sanitary engineer.

Three

It was Friday, August 27, 1965, 12:05 A.M., when Dick and I arrived home, completely exhausted. We had just returned from a thirty-hour shift at the Livingston livestock auction, testing cows, vaccinating pigs, processing feeder calves, and arguing with livestock haulers about health certificates. The heavy runs of early cattle selling had commenced, and I could look forward to many more long Thursdays until late fall.

I knew it was dangerous working such long hours and then driving the forty-five miles home down dark, deer-infested blacktop roads, but there was no other choice. It was what the sale barn and the Department of Agriculture paid me to do. Having a big strong college boy like Dick along that summer was a blessing.

Dick was a student of art at the University of Alabama, and since both Jan and I had attended arch rival Auburn, there was much kidding and many teasing insults about the two schools. One morning I went into Tom's room, where Dick was sleeping, to deliver him some news about his school.

"Dick! Wake up!" I whispered loudly.

"What is it?"

"I just heard on the radio that a tornado ripped through the University of Alabama campus last night."

"Oh no! Was there much damage?" he said, sitting straight up in bed.

"Actually, it did two million dollars' worth of improvements!" I declared. Then I walked out, hands over mouth, trying to a stifle a child-waking guffaw. I knew I was bound to get my comeuppance sooner or later, but it was still satisfying.

I knew the first trip to Chappell's barbershop with Dick would be a treat, and I was not disappointed. At first Chappell and Myatt, the two barbers, thought he was my brother, because we were both tall, wore glasses, and had on coveralls stained with green cow excrement.

"You a college boy?" asked Myatt.

"Yes sir," Dick answered.

"What you gonna take up?"

"Sir?" Dick said. He didn't know what Myatt meant by "take up."

"Wants to know what your major is," I translated.

"Art. I'm studying art," he answered proudly.

There was immediate silence in the shop, except for the snipping of Chappell's scissors and the groan of the country music singer on the radio. Even the other customers waiting to be clipped set the magazines they were perusing aside and stared in our direction.

"What'd he say?" asked the hearing-impaired Chappell.

"Said art, studies art!" yelled Myatt.

"Art? You mean like drawing pictures and stuff?"

"Oh, yes. I especially like modern and contemporary art, as well as ceramics," Dick said.

More silence. No one in that shop had ever been at a loss for words before. To break the silence, I volunteered a suggestion. "Ask him where he goes to school," I said.

"Where?" Myatt asked.

"The University of Alabama!" said Dick proudly. I felt a wave of nausea. If there's one thing that irritates Auburn people, it's when Alabama people put "the" in front of their university, and put extra emphasis on it.

"Oh, I hear they have a first-class art department up there," declared one sitter on my right. "And don't y'all just love modern art?" They all nodded their heads affirmatively.

"Aw, yeah, it ranks right up there with some of them schools in the ivory league," said the guy to my left, scooting closer so he could better see the new hero of the barbershop. "You mean ivy. . . ." But nobody was paying any attention to me. All eyes were on my brother-in-law, and they had no time for anyone else.

"You ought to come back to our little town and set you up a studio right here. If it's one thing we need here is more of the arts, more culture," Myatt stated, staring at me. "I bet we could fix him up a place right here in the back, Chappell. Folks come in here, get a haircut, then go in the studio back there and get 'em a velvet Elvis Presley paintin'. He could make a killin'." I saw Dick shudder at the mention of the velvet Elvis.

"Well, I don't do that kind of thing. . . ." he said quietly.

I knew that the football question would be asked sooner or later. It came sooner.

"Do you play football up there?" Alabama football was big in west Alabama, and Bear Bryant was the ultimate hero.

"Well, I'm not that great of an athlete," Dick confessed. I wished he had lied and told 'em he had actually been spoken to by Coach Bryant. But it might have been more than they could take.

"Well, you're big enough. What are you, six-four, two-twenty? You'd make a great tight end," Chappell declared. "Doc said he played at Auburn, and you're bigger'n him." Dick looked at me and laughed.

"Well, I never said I played with the varsity, but I did play intra-mural ball in vet school. I was the quarterback when large animal played small animal." I saw no need to mention the fact that I only started when the other three quarterbacks had cramped up and couldn't walk.

"Well, we need more good people in this town, and if you're a friend of Doc's, you're welcome here. He's makin' a pretty good vet, but if he'd a been properly educated at somewhere like The University of Alabama, there's no tellin' what he coulda done here," declared Chappell. Everyone had a good laugh at my expense, and I even smiled.

When Dick went back to school in the fall, I missed his help in the practice and our good-natured kidding about our colleges. But the barbershop crowd missed him even more, constantly asking about my smart brother the artist and whether or not he had ever made the team.

⁓

That August night, when we returned from Livingston, Jan was sit-ting uneasily in her chair, both hands caressing her rotund middle. A suitcase sat in the middle of the floor.

"I think it's time to go," she announced softly, as if talking caused labor pains. Then a grimace came over her face, and she tried to double over, but there was no room to bend. Dick stood by the open door, staring openmouthed, obviously seeing a woman in labor for the first time. It was only the third time for me, and even though I knew the process of birthing was essentially the same for humans and the animals I attended, somehow I was instantly nervous. I thought that nine months of mental preparation for the blessed event would have been enough, but it was not.

It had been a tough nine months for Jan. There was not a day when she hadn't been nauseated, and on a couple of occasions Dr. Paul had been so worried that she was in danger of losing the baby that he insisted she stay in the bed. Then, in mid-pregnancy, she was crossing Main Street in the station wagon when another car ran the red light and bashed her and the side of the station wagon into the corner of the new First National Bank building. Thankfully, she was not injured, only shaken. The president of the bank called later and suggested it would have been much easier to get cash if she had just cruised up to the drive-in window. "I'll call Dr. Paul," I announced, trying to remember where we kept the phone.

"No. I've called Mildred, and she said he's already there and will wait for us," she puffed.

"Why didn't you call me at the sale barn so I could have driven faster?" I said.

"I did, but the girl that answered said you'd already gone. If you weren't here by midnight I was going to get Jane to take me. Grab that suitcase. Dick, you stay with Tom and Lisa." Then she went into detail about what they should be fed later that morning, stopping briefly when overtaken by another cramp but still straining out orders through the pain.

Four minutes and five hundred yards later we were walking toward the emergency room of the West Alabama Regional Hospital. Suddenly a wheelchair piloted by a young orderly burst through the door and came to a sliding stop at Jan's side.

"I been watching for you, missy," he puffed. "Dr. Paul said for me to be sure you didn't walk in this hospital. Said you were gonna need all your strength to push that big baby out."

"Big? How does he know?" I asked.

"Yeah, he thinks over ten pounds and—" Another pain hit like lightning. I was thankful she was in the rolling chair.

"Ten pounds? That's impossible! There's never been a baby that big born around here. What about a C-section?"

"Nope, no C-section. I'm having it the normal way."

"Well, I'm glad I didn't know, 'cause I would have been really worried." Dr. Paul appeared in the doorway nervously puffing on his Chesterfield cigarette.

"Take her into the exam room there and let's see where she is," he bellowed. "Nurse, get me some help over here! Get me a line going!"

No wonder he and Jan got along so well—they both loved giving orders! His voice faded away into a muffle as Jan and half the late-night staff disappeared through a maze of doors and hallways. The last thing I saw was my wife's hand go up in a good-bye salute. The nurse bringing up the rear issued the final order.

"You just sit down right there, boy," she snapped, as if I had done something wrong.

I am glad to know that soon-to-be fathers are more involved in the entire baby-having process today than we were in the fifties and sixties. Back then, hospital staff treated us as if we were completely use-less, ordering us around as if we were lazy cotton field mules. After the same treatment on three occasions, I was wondering if there was a required course in nursing school on expectant father bullying.

Ten minutes later, Dr Paul appeared, lit another Chesterfield, and motioned me to follow him outside.

"She's three or four centimeters now," he said, smoke belching from his nose. "I think we'll take her on down to the delivery room now, even though it might take another two or three hours. The baby is pretty good sized, so it'll take some time. You might as well make yourself as comfortable as you can out here, 'cause there's nothing you can do back there except get in the way."

"Yeah, I got that impression from one of your assistants. Do you think she'll need a cesarian?" I asked nervously.

"It'll be close, but she was very adamant about having it naturally. But you know I'll do whatever needs to be done at the time." Then, with a flip of his right middle finger, he dispatched the half-smoked cigarette into the humid August night, where it soon skidded on the pavement and spun out, its glowing end spewing dozens of sparks like wee meteors. As much as I respected and liked Dr. Paul, I won-dered why he smoked so much.

"I made coffee for you in the doctors' lounge. And while you're there, take a shower and find some of Dr. Neville's scrubs. Y'all are about the same size." Then he disappeared, back into the bowels of the hospital.

The events of the last hour had occupied my mind so completely that I had forgotten that I was still clad in my dirty sale barn coveralls. I knew that my appearance and aroma was probably offensive to the sensitive noses of the hospital personnel and that was why Dr. Paul had encouraged the shower and change. I felt like a big shot walking into the empty doctors' lounge and seeing the signs of the other half dozen town doctors and all the niceties afforded them. But as I poured a cup of coffee from the percolator, I reminded myself of the awesome responsibility of those MDs and the even greater demands the public made on their time. I knew my profession was the right one for me.

I had looked forward to the coffee Dr. Paul had supposedly perked, but found it was warm but weak as water. In fact, it was water. The cord was plugged in and there was coffee in the basket, but since it had not brewed I assumed the coffeemaker was out of order. So I showered and dressed up in Dr. Neville's surgical garb, hoping I wouldn't be mistaken for him and asked to treat a heart attack or suture up a wound.

Sneaking out the door, I saw the familiar face of a nurse who visited my office regularly. She was kind enough to spend the next two hours reassuring me, bringing strong coffee, and talking about her poodles. We found out that good Dr. Paul had tried to make coffee for me by using boiling water instead of cold in the percolator. "He's got his mind on babies. Yours is the third one he's delivered tonight." She relayed reports from the delivery room and kept me busy answering her questions about the health of her dogs. About three o'clock she came back with the news that birth was imminent. I was awake, thanks to my strong-brewed coffee, and was nervously sitting on the floor by the big doors when the doctor came out, his mask dangling from his neck.

"Congratulations, fella! You've got a big healthy boy, weighed in at nine and a half pounds," he said.

"How about Jan?"

"She's OK, but because we had a rough time getting him here, I had to knock her out there at the end. Why don't you go down to the nursery and see him before he starts walking."

Moments later I was staring down at the biggest hunk of a baby I had ever seen while a congregation of nurses oohed and aahed over him, saying how much he looked like me and wondering what Jan had eaten that made him so big. His three or four extra pounds made the other babies seem stunted, making me think of a big double-muscled beef calf surrounded by tiny Jersey heifers. I was bursting with pride. As I stood admiring him, I heard the squeaking wheels of a hospital bed coming down the hall.

"Here comes your wife," said one of the nurses.

Jan was lying with several blankets covering her from lips to toes. Her hair was disheveled and her quivering chin gave evidence of the difficult birth and how cold she was.

"Jan, you OK?" It was a dumb question, but it came out anyway.

She tried to open her eyes, but all she could do was elevate her eyebrows. "Got you another boy," she rasped, managing a weak smile. Then she was out again.

A couple of hours later, I proudly strutted out the emergency room doors, heading home for the usual phone calls to parents and friends. As I drove the short distance the sun was peeking over the loblolly pines to the east, signaling a beautiful new day, a new life, and a lot of new responsibility. It was also the morning Tom started the first grade, and I knew that I was faced with the immediate responsibility of getting him into the correct first day clothing.

After taking Tom to school, a very tired Jan and I named the new baby Milton Paul, after Jan's dad and Dr. Paul. Being named after these two great men, we hoped, would help him grow up to be a compassionate, giving person, yet strong enough to move a refrigerator or piano by himself. We wanted him to be happy in his life, versatile, able to easily converse with all types of individuals and make people laugh with his dry wit. I also looked forward to the day when he would be able to whip his Dad in golf.

Paul has exceeded all our expectations.

Four

A few days after Paul's birth, I was headed south to quarantine a herd of cattle with the dreaded disease brucellosis. I was busy thinking about my new little boy when I suddenly realized that the oncoming pickup truck was flashing its lights and weaving all over the blacktop road ahead of me, indicating that it was one of my clients requesting a free roadside consultation or perhaps a kindly stranger advising that a member of the Alabama state trooper force was parked alongside the road just ahead. I immediately eased my heavy right foot off the accelerator. I had probably used that "mission of mercy" excuse to the area troopers one time too many.

The law enforcement personnel in Choctaw County had been very understanding about my speeding because some of them were animal owners and knew that I had good reason to always be in a rush. So when I met them on the road I would smile real big and wave wildly out the window, just like Dad and other elders had advised me when I was growing up.

"Always wave at the police!" Dad said. "Having a good relationship with the highway patrol may not keep you from getting a citation, but it can't hurt."

In fact, Dad had taught me to wave at everybody I met on the road. "Always wave, 'cause it might be Mr. Brown," he always said. "Plus, it's just the right thing to be neighborly." Mr. Brown was the banker in the small town of Ardmore, south of our Tennessee farm. That was good country advice, since every soul I knew wanted to be on good terms with the local banker, just in case.

The local police, sheriff's deputies, and highway patrol would all return my greetings, and some would occasionally hit the siren button and flash their red lights to put an exclamation point on their salutation. They usually didn't run me down for a lecture, except sometimes at night when they didn't recognize my truck.

On this late-summer afternoon the oncoming pickup belonged to Kathy and Waldo King, who were probably headed to town for a bit of excitement, which usually consisted of a short shopping trip at Charlie Hale's IGA grocery store and a big ice cream cone at the Dairy Queen. I knew a lot about their routine because they were not only good clients but close friends as well. As usual, Kathy was chauffeuring her husband, who was comfortably leaning back in the passenger seat with both feet stuck up on the instrument panel, surveying the countryside as if he actually were the king of the county. On the bench seat between them were their two Dalmation dogs, Crawfish and Tadpole, for all the world appearing just as human as their owners. When out-of-town motorists approached their vehicle from the rear and observed the four passengers looking dead ahead, they surely did a double take.

"Imogene, I wish you'd look at them ears on them chaps up yonder in that truck," the driver might say.

"Uh uh. I think that's dogs. Just watch the road, Buford, not every

Tom, Dick, and Harry sittin' in trucks. All your swerving around is making me nauseous."

I new that when engaged in conversation, Kathy and Waldo always tried to talk at the same time, which sometimes made it difficult for me to follow. So even before our trucks were stopped side by side, I started talking, determined to be the first to do so.

"How's Meathead and Bertha?" I yelled, referring to the mentally deficient calf and uncouth sow that I had treated a few weeks earlier.

"Just great! Meathead's dumber than ever, and—" But before Kathy could finish, Waldo was on another subject.

"How's that new boy?

"Oh, he's something else. Almost big enough to wean," I replied.

"Yeah, that's what the paper said." It was great to live in a place where the weekly paper listed the names of all the newborns and had reports from all the little communities in the county. No doubt there would be something in the Toxey community column on Thursday about Waldo and Kathy going to town to get groceries.

"You need to come by and cut those goats one morning," he said before Kathy cut him off.

"Go by the house right now and get you a mess of tomatoes and some okra, because. . . ."

"What makes a dog eat grass? Tadpole eats grass all the time. Ain't that right, Tadpole?" Tadpole looked around, licked his lips, and almost succeeded in making a dog smile crease across his lips. A few head rubs by Waldo was enough for Crawfish to nose Waldo's hand, begging for the same treatment.

"What did calves sell for last week at the sale barn? Reckon I ought to sell these few at the house now or wait until after the first of the year?"

"Doc, remember, we gotta go deer huntin' this fall. Them things are eatin' my garden up."

"We're having revival at church this week. You and Jan come one night if you can. We got a song leader and everything!"

I do enjoy being around people who are excited about life. I was looking from one to the other, then at the dogs, wondering if they too were going to interrupt. I was trying in vain to make a response to every inquiry, but before I could get out a single uh, er, or umm, another query was being transmitted out the window. Suddenly, two long blasts of a log truck's air horn sounded to my rear and I knew the one-sided conversation was over. Being rear-ended by several tons of pine logs was not a good way to cut short a promising veterinary career.

"Gotta go! Call me!" Then I scratched off, mashing the petal to the metal while cautiously observing the jumbo load of logs gaining on me from the rear. Soon I was heading up a long grade and was putting proper distance between my truck and the moving timber.

"I believe I'll take ten minutes and run by there to get some fresh garden produce," I thought. Even though there were just the two of them, every year Kathy and Waldo planted a garden big enough to supply a small army. Many of my clients had large gardens that produced all their vegetables for eating, canning, and freezing, and there was always plenty left over to share with neighbors, the preacher, and their veterinarian.

Moments later I marched into the unlocked house, picked up a couple of large paper bags from the pantry, then whacked off a wedge of pecan pie that Kathy had left on the kitchen table. One of life's medium-sized pleasures is eating a piece of pecan pie, pointed end directed toward the mouth, of course, straight off your crooked-around hand. Soon I was filling the first bag with corn and okra and the second with both ripe and green tomatoes. Jan liked frying the green ones. Then I selected several large tomatoes for a "to go" snack as I made my way farther south. As I drove and dribbled the juice down the front of my dark blue coveralls, I wished for a loaf of Colonial bread and a jar of mayonnaise. Nothing satisfies a country boy like a tomato sandwich dessert after a piece of pie!

The purpose of my call that day was to brand a large "B" on the jaws of several brucellosis-infected cows and fill out a bucket full of government forms, which the owner and I both reluctantly signed.

Most owners disliked but tolerated all my explaining and informing about what had to be done in order for them to collect the small indemnity payment for their having to sell their infected cows as "bangers," which lowered their sale barn value considerably.

"That way both of you will go to the penitentiary if the cattleman doesn't do what y'all have agreed to do in the paperwork," said Dr. Stewart, the area government man who "supervised" all so-called regulatory work carried out by the veterinarians in the area. His threat of prison was a joke, of course, but the government was serious about a herd quarantine, and it took a dim view of cattlemen who didn't abide by the rules banning the exchange of diseased cattle. Even so, I had often used a rather descriptive eight-letter word for all those silly forms. But I needed the work and was forced to put up with such aggravation, even though I was sure all those properly-signed-in-black-ink forms would wind up in some dead file in Montgomery.

It was almost dark as I made my way back northward. I was only a few miles from the King farm turnoff when I caught the reflection of red flashing lights in my rear view mirror.

"Oh no," I groaned. "I must have been speeding when I came through downtown Toxey!"

Toxey was a small community of less than five hundred citizens, and it had a reputation as a no-nonsense kind of place. If you were from out of town, you bought your gas and your cold drink and Moon Pie, didn't give anybody any sass, and then hit the road. I wasn't even sure that Toxey had a regular policeman, but if so, I knew that he would be tough and he would mean business. I pulled over onto the edge of a driveway and stopped, my driver's license poised in my nervous hand.

Seconds later the speeding vehicle passed me in such haste that his backwash rocked my truck back and forth several times. It was then I noticed that it wasn't even the law! It was a pickup truck with one of those little portable, cigarette lighter plug-in jobs that the user popped up on the dash or on top of the car when the notion struck.

Directly behind the lead truck were several other pickups, all with the same kind of puny red light stuck up on top, and all were being driven by Richard Petty wannabes. Two older-model cars that were smoking badly brought up the rear of the column, no doubt placed there because of the truck pecking order.

It finally occurred to me that the parade of vehicles must have been the local volunteer fire department and rescue squad, and they were either practicing for an emergency or headed for an actual emergency. It wasn't a very formal group of volunteers, just a gathering of good guys who wanted to help their neighbors in need. Then I heard the sounds of sirens drawing nearer, and presently a fire truck and a deputy sheriff's car hustled northward. I knew then for sure that something much bigger than a practice run was going on.

I pulled back out onto the blacktop and attempted to catch up to the fire truck. The adrenaline was pumping through my system, and I realized the rush that emergency workers must feel when they are called on to deal with life-and-death situations. A couple of miles later the fire truck was in my sights, and then I saw a covey of brake lights come on and left turn signals activated.

"They must be turning in at Waldo and Kathy's driveway," I said out loud. Then I began to think about all sorts of tragedies that might have occurred. I couldn't see a bright light over where their house was, so I knew the house wasn't on fire. Waldo had high blood pressure and had been in the hospital recently in an effort to get it regulated. Maybe he'd had a heart attack or a stroke. Maybe one of them fell and broke a leg. Maybe it was a false alarm.

With my truck in hot pursuit, the parade made the turn into the long and rocky driveway, but then turned through an open gate that led to the back side of the two-hundred-acre farm. I was somewhat relieved that the problem was not at the house. Dust was flying everywhere from all the traffic, and after a quarter of a mile of hilly driving, the trucks began slowing to a stop near a steep-sided hundred-foot-deep canyon that served as a community catchall site for loads of tree limbs, leaves, and other debris. Men were jumping from their trucks and hitting the dusty earth in a full run, as they trained their requisite lights on the makeshift road. Powerful light beams from "professional type" spotlights and special issue flashlights were being played over the trees, back up the trail and down into the canyon, but from my truck I still couldn't see what all the commotion was about. Men were yelling, two-way radios were crackling, and the eerie on-again, off-again blinking of the multiple emergency vehicle lights through the dusty haze proved that even the blessed quiet of the backwoods Choctaw night is not exempt from emergencies. I quickly hopped out of the truck and headed for the canyon.

"I don't know how the subject fell down in 'nere, but we've got to get him out. You got any ropes? Ten-four," a voice declared over a two-way radio. I quickened my steps when I realized someone had fallen into the canyon. A young woman carrying a four-foot length of rope trotted up beside me.

"What happened?" I asked.

"Waldo fell down into that ravine and he can't get out," she replied, leaving me in another cloud of dust as she dashed away.

"Oh, my goodness, I hope he's not hurt bad," I said, my voice jerking as I jogged faster, wondering what the lady was going to do with four feet of rope. If Waldo was at the bottom of the gorge, four feet of plow line wouldn't be of much help. Not far behind the crowd I heard the insistent, loud bellow of a single cow, which I thought was odd.

Kathy was standing at the edge of the precipice, peering down into the depths of the canyon, and she seemed to be in a relatively calm frame of mind for someone whose husband was trapped and hurt down there. As I made my way over to her position, I caught a glimpse of Waldo standing on the canyon floor, pointing and yelling orders up to a man he was calling Eddie. This made no sense!

"Doc, what are you doin' here?" Kathy exclaimed. "Did you go by the house and get some garden stuff like I told you?" A platoon of rescue personnel was rushing around on her property and she was concerned about groceries?

"I was on my way home from Aquilla and saw all the red lights and commotion, so I just followed 'em over here. What's going on? Is Waldo hurt?"

"No, he's OK. You remember the cow we call Speckle Face? Well, I heard her bawling for her calf over this way when we got home from town a while ago, so I came over here and she was standing on the edge here. Her heifer calf somehow fell over in the gully and can't get out. But she was lucky enough to land on that ledge down there. Can you see her from here?"

In spite of my extraordinary fear of high places, I crept a little closer to the edge and peered straight down. Sure enough, on an eight-by-ten ledge there stood a three-hundred-pound calf, calmly chewing her cud. I heard the cow repeat her message again, but this time the calf answered. I knew Speckle Face was frantic, even if she didn't have a clue as to why this throng of humans was assembled there.

"She looks OK, but how in the world did she manage to fall at just that spot? Any other place along here and she would gone all the way to the bottom. She'd have been a goner," I declared. "What's Waldo doing down in there?"

"He went down the side of this cliff over where it's not so steep, but now he's gonna need help to get out, too. With all this excitement, I'm afraid his blood pressure is acting up."

"You mean this whole crowd came out here just to pull a calf out of a hole?"

"Well, what happened was, I called Eddie to come over here and bring a rope, and the firefighters and rescue people just happened to be having their monthly meeting. Somebody put a message over the radio that Waldo was down in a canyon and hurt bad. You know everybody knows Waldo, and that's why so many folks showed up." It was gratifying that this many citizens would come to help a neighbor, even if they didn't know it was a four-legged animal neighbor.

Eddie and some of the other brain trust were having a high-level meeting at the canyon edge, and they were doing a lot of pointing and hand gesturing. It was obvious that each person involved had his own idea of how to retrieve the victim. Finally, Eddie tied a long rope around his waist and started a backward descent, the other end of the rope secured to a truck bumper. I stayed back out of sight and out of falling distance.

"Throw me another rope!" yelled Eddie from below. A coiled-up length of cotton rope disappeared over the ledge.

After a suggestion or two about what to do from the top and constant chatter about what not to do from Waldo down below, it became apparent that Eddie's plan was to make a halter on the calf with the second rope, then remove the rope from his waist and cinch it around the calf's middle. Then the dozen men up above would grab the two ropes and drag the lucky beast to safety. I could hear the conversation down on the ledge.

"Easy, baby, easy does it. I'll have you back to yo' mama in just a little bit." It was nice to hear such kind and soothing words. "I got his head secured!" But those soft words suddenly became more stern and earthy when Eddie started to work on the rear end.

"Don't you kick me, you miserable idiot! Here I am tryin' to help you and now you're tryin' to stomp me!"

"Uh uh, don't get 'im upset now. Just be easy, take it easy,"

"Awright, all y'all get on there and pull!" came the order from down below. The sounds of powerful grunts and groans filled the night air as the victim was quickly hoisted to the edge of the canyon.

"Pull her way on out here," ordered Kathy. "Or she's liable to go right back in the hole." Speckle Face was making a spectacle of herself, now creeping closer and closer to her offspring, mooing constantly and making sniffing and snorting noises.

"Awright, take the ropes off and let 'er go!" ordered Kathy. The calf scrambled to her feet and trotted to her mother, who conducted a quick nosing exam, and then they walked away as if nothing had happened, the hungry little one trying in vain to suckle a moving target.

All hands, from light holders to the lady with the four-foot rope, walked away from the canyon edge and stared with pride as the pleasant vision of mother and child slowly faded into the darkness of the adjacent grove of pine trees.

The workers basked in their success, and pouches of chewing tobacco appeared from overall pockets while an impromptu critique of the entire operation began.

"This coulda been a human. And we wouldn't have been able to haul a human out like we did this calf," Eddie declared.

"HEY! HEY! What about me?" a faint voice yelled. "HEY!"

In all the excitement everyone had forgotten about Waldo, even Kathy. Several men rushed to the edge and looked down.

"Tell 'im we're gonna leave his ugly self down in there and we're goin' to the house for coffee and pie," exclaimed Eddie, the self-appointed leader of the pack.

When he heard this, Waldo yelled back. "There ain't no pie left, 'cause somebody went in the house while we were gone to town and near 'bout ate it all! So y'all might as well forget about that and get me out of here," he hollered. I said nothing, hoping maybe someone else had taken a bigger piece than I.

"What do you think about it, Kathy?" someone asked.

"Don't make no difference to me," she replied. "If he ain't at the house, it'll be less mess for me to clean up." As expected, the crowd laughed in approval.

Finally, after typical good-natured debating about Waldo's fate, long ropes were tied together and tossed down to the bottom. Minutes later Waldo was standing with the crowd, thanking each and every one of the rescuers for their help and chastising the ones who'd voted to abandon him after the calf was rescued.

"I'm gonna barbecue y'all a pig," he declared. "Just tell me when you want it." I thought that was a nice gesture from the community good guy.

Because the Kings were so adamant that all the animals on their farm have proper names, I was surprised that the fallen calf had not been named.

"I have the perfect name for this calf," I told Kathy.

"Yeah, me, too," she stated. "It can't be anything but 'Gully Bank.'"

"Exactly!" Actually, I was thinking "Canyon Bank," but then I realized there weren't any real western-type canyons in Alabama.

From then on, Gully Bank appropriately hung around another farm bovine we called "Pond Bank," so-named because her cantankerous mother refused to move out of the pond as I delivered her calf. Both animals later became productive and respected members of the herd, and their unusual stories were told over and over at volunteer fire department meetings and country store gatherings. It would have been nice to give the people who rescued Gully Bank a plaque to hang on the wall, but I think they preferred the barbecue.

Five

It was a pleasant Saturday evening in October. The long, hot summer had finally released its muggy grip, freeing us from constant brow moppings with "sweat rags" and the obligatory but irritating conversation opener "Hot enough for you?" It was easy to understand how the South didn't really rise again until blessed air-conditioning became accessible to the masses.

As I motored back to the clinic from a large animal call south of town, I realized that the cool west Alabama air brought back memories of cotton-picking time, making sorghum syrup, and football games. The hint of hardwood smoke in the air was reassuring, reminiscent of my never-ending childhood chore of sawing up and splitting wood for the kitchen stove and our Warm Morning heater. Drinking in the changing colors of the oaks, hickories, and maples randomly sown among the money-making loblolly pines had something to do with my present contentment. I had been blessed with a great spouse and children, whose love and support made living the pleasant experience that it should be, and having good clients who appreciated my efforts made me feel as if it was all worth it.

But to be completely truthful, my elation probably had more to do with the fact that Happy Dupree had just presented me with a big check, clearing up his large overdue account. Few things please a working veterinarian more than timely and sometimes unexpected payment-in-full checks.

I had made an effort to find Happy earlier that afternoon while I was in his area. By a stroke of luck, I had spied his truck at Miss Ruby's store and was soon bounding up the three steps and reaching for the screen door that proclaimed in bold letters "COLONIAL IS *GOOD* BREAD."

"Looky yonder, Ruby. It's supervet, hisself," cried Happy. He was mimicking Myatt, the number-two shearer at Chappell's barbershop. Myatt always called me "supervet," no matter the time, place, or occasion.

"That all you got to do, Happy? Just hang around here and torment Miss Ruby?" Then I remembered my manners. "How're you today, Miss Ruby?"

"Fine, Doctuh. Just enjoying this fall weather."

"Yes, ma'am, I always love this time of year. And I think one reason is that I'm pretty sure that if all goes well I won't ever have to pick any more cotton. You know, where I was raised up, school let out for 'cotton-picking time' for about six weeks when cotton began to open up."

"You're too young to know the first thing about picking cotton, Doc," declared Happy. "Besides, picking cotton is child's play compared to cuttin' paperwood. Gittin' rattlesnake-bit, ticks, poison ivy, chiggers . . ." Spirited arguing ensued about the relative difficulty of various farm chores, including cleaning out henhouses, working in tobacco, and cutting off vine-entangled fence rows. "That reminds me, have you got anything for red mange? Got a dog that's got it on the side of his face."

A few minutes later, Happy and I were standing at the back of my truck, where I was carefully mixing and pouring my special mange medicine into a pint bottle. My big-city colleagues would chastise my dispensing medicine without actually laying hands on the patient and running a passel of expensive tests, but I wondered if all that was necessary in such simple cases. Besides, Happy would have reached for a two-by-four if I had suggested such foolishness. Money was too hard to come by in Choctaw County for such luxuries as "mange profile" tests.

"How about hitting me a lick on that bill, Happy?" I asked as I poured. "I"ve got a clinic payment to make this month."

"How much is it?" he replied.

"I don't remember exactly, didn't you get my statements?"

"I don't pay any attention to envelopes that's got windows on 'em," he declared, and seemed to be proud of it.

A quick two-way radio communication with Sue at the office revealed the total of the outstanding balance, and soon I was filling out a counter check for the entire amount, even though he was shaking his head as he scribbled his signature.

"Thanks, Mr. Dupree. I appreciate your business. If I can ever be of service to you, please call my office."

Happy just shook his head again. "I never thought I'd see the day that I'd spend more money on a vet than I would on a real doctor. I just oughta get shed of some of those animals. They're just a bottomless pit to throw greenbacks in."

"Where you gonna start? How about that pen full of deer dogs? Or you could put Glenda's little lapdog up for adoption," I suggested, tongue in cheek. He looked at me as if I needed to be netted and carried to the asylum in Tuscaloosa.

"You know them dogs are there to stay, boy. Without them, how could I take this high-priced, worrisome veterinarian deer huntin' every fall? But the lapdog can go, so I'll just assign you the job of talking with the womenfolks at the house about that."

"Oh, no," I exclaimed, laughing. "I'd rather clean out a henhouse than mess with that crowd about that Chihuahua!"

Good old Happy! To hear him carry on in his cranky way a stranger would never know that he was one of the world's finest people, with a heart the size of Mobile Bay. There hasn't been but one Happy Dupree, and there will never be another one like him.

~

I had looked forward to this day because of the scheduled football game between Auburn and Tennessee. I was hoping that just once I could sit quietly with my family, have a nice uninterrupted dinner, then watch the game in peace and quiet. Kind of like a normal family might do. Practicing veterinary medicine solo has its advantages, but having emergency duty twenty-four hours a day, seven days a week, was not one of them. I was pondering all this when the two-way radio crackled.

"Mr. Clinch is on the phone," Sue announced. "One of his best cows has been in labor for most of the day and he can see no progress. He wants you to come up there as soon as you can."

Mr. Clinch was one of my best clients, owning some three hundred sows, two hundred purebred and grade Santa Gertrudis cows, a dozen or so coon dogs, a few horses, and best of all, a fine lake full of bass and bream. I often took my fishing gear and tried to remove some of those fish after the vet work was done. The only problem was that his farm was forty-five hard-driving and dusty road miles away to the north in Sumter County.

Well, there went the game. It was almost six o'clock, and by the time I drove the ninety-mile round-trip and relieved the difficult birth, it would be halftime, at the earliest. Maybe I could get home in time to see the second half.

"OK, ma'am," I said. "Tell him to hang up the phone and watch for a cloud of dust. I'm on my way."

The trip to the Clinch farm wasn't too bad of a drive that evening since it was too early to encounter the drunks making their way home from the state line honky-tonks and too late for the road-hogging, pulpwood truck traffic. But while I enjoyed the drive I was wondering if we would have to run the cow down and try to lasso her in the woods.

When I arrived at the farm, Mr. Clinch was nowhere to be seen. Instead, one of his part-time helpers, Mr. B. J. Roach, was sitting on the corral fence. Fortunately, and to my amazement, the cow was penned up in the newly remodeled corral, the old one having been recently demolished courtesy of a couple of uncouth and uncooperative bovines during a deworming episode. I knew that B.J.'s ability to help would amount to zilch, but at least his witticisms would keep me entertained.

"Mr. Clinch, he said to tell you that the cow is in the pen, Mr. Doc," B.J. loudly asserted. I suppose he wanted to be sure that I was aware that the large red cow lying some twenty feet away, two tiny bovine hooves protruding from her rear parts, was my patient.

"What's he doing, B.J.?"

"I think he's over there at the country club with the other big shots watchin' that football game on television," he answered.

"Now isn't that something!" I thought to myself. "Seems like he ought to be out here helping, if this cow is so valuable." On the other hand, maybe it was a blessing that he wasn't there, because he'd just be wringing his hands and trying to tell me what I should and shouldn't be doing.

"How about getting me a bucket of water, B.J." I wondered whether I could hop over the fence and get the calf delivered before he returned.

The patient was an older cow, which was surprising, since most difficult cases are first-calf heifers. She did not offer to get up when I climbed over the fence into the corral, placed the lariat over her head, and made it into a temporary halter. As I was getting the rope fixed over her nose just right, she stood, but still didn't offer resistance, unlike most frisky Brahma-blooded cattle. My first impression, after seeing the two fetal hooves protruding from the proper place, was that she was having difficulty getting the fetal head in the correct position and going in the right direction. Sometimes a larger-than-normal head will be diverted off to one side or the other or downward, or it just won't fit into the birth canal along with both forelegs. In most cases, it isn't a big problem to introduce an arm into the birth canal and get things progressing in the right direction.

After scrubbing up, I made my examination. Sure enough, the little fellow's head was crooked around to the right and lying alongside his body. To check for signs of life, I pinched a toe and touched an eye. Detecting no sign of life made me feel sad.

"My long arms and trusty calf-saver snare are gonna have this thing out of here pronto!" I thought to myself.

"B.J., how about you going over to my truck and turn on the switch so we can listen to the ball game. And you'd better turn the volume up some," I requested.

Just as I introduced the snare to retrieve the head, Auburn kicked off. Getting the snare manipulated into the right spot and over the crown of the head wasn't as easy as I had anticipated. The object of my immediate search was just barely within reach, and just as I thought the snare was secure on the head, a steady tug would cause it to slip off. About the same time of my technical difficulties, the radio announcer informed listeners that an Auburn running back had fumbled the football or the quarterback had thrown an interception. That would add to my frustration and make me feel a little more depressed and weak in the arms.

The cow had suddenly decided that standing and straining against the stupid veterinarian and his long arms was too much for her, so she laid back down in the muddiest part of the corral in order to be more comfortable. Now I was lying on my belly and rocking back and forth in the mud as I tried to accomplish my objective. I had replaced the snare with a sixty-inch obstetrical chain and had looped it around the lower jaw.

"Pull kinda firm on this chain with that stainless steel handle over there in the bucket," I told B.J. "Maybe we'll get somewhere with both us of working together."

He jerked the chain with too much force, and when the loop

slipped off, he went sprawling back into a substantial pile of common barnyard material. He did extract two fetal incisors, though, due to his mighty pull.

"Aw, man, Mr. Clinch is gonna skin me for pullin' them teeth!" he cried. "I shouldn't have jerked so hard."

"B.J., the calf is already dead. It's OK."

When I again tried to get the chain looped on the head, I discovered that the lower jaw I was struggling with contained all its teeth! Only then did I realize that we were dealing with a two-headed fetus. No wonder it wouldn't budge. There was no way the double-headed monster could pass through the canal. She would need a cesarian.

The football game was having its problems as well. According to the announcer, whose voice was fading in and out, it was total war, with many casualties being suffered by both sides. While I prepared the patient for surgery, one player was taken off the field on a stretcher and another wobbled off with a concussion. Yet, the announcer kept going on about what a great game it was.

As the surgery progressed, the radio became more and more staticky, until the broadcaster's voice finally faded completely away and was gradually taken over by a Saturday evening preacher, who wanted everybody within the sound of his raspy and chanting voice to know that old Satan was for sure, and if we didn't all do exactly as he said, we were doomed to the fiery pits down below. But when he gave his own address as the place we needed to send the money, I sort of lost confidence in him. The last thing I heard about the ball game was something about a minor misunderstanding on the field's turning into a major fracas involving both benches, coaches, and some drunken fans.

Finally, I made the incision into the calf bed and the cause of all the poor cow's trouble of the last several hours popped into plain view. B.J. was suddenly cowside, gasping and pointing at the freak calf.

"Whoo-weee!" marveled my pale-faced aide. "I ain't never seen nothin' like this here. Wait'll I tell everbody down at the feed store Monday about this two-headed calf." He would have been really impressed had I told him that the strange malformation was due to an abnormal duplication of cells during the early embryonal phase. But at that moment, my recollection of vet school embryology was severely challenged, so I blurted out that it was very rare, maybe one out of every ten thousand births. Certainly, I had never observed the birth of a two-headed calf before. "Too bad it was stillborn, 'cause you and Mr. Clinch could've sold it to the circus sideshow with the ape man and the alligator woman that crawls on her belly," I lamented with a smile.

All of a sudden B.J. was an expert on bovine obstetrics. He was rattling on and on about the strange event and how "we" had done this or that, and how he figured all along that the cause of the dystocia was some kind of freak. I was suturing as fast as I could, wanting to get into my truck and change the radio station to something besides the irritating, raspy-voiced preacher, who was still begging for money and frequently repeating his address.

On the way home, I tried but couldn't find any stations that were carrying the ball game or reporting scores. But when I arrived home, Jan had a piecemeal report for me.

"So many of the young men seemed to be badly hurt, and there was a terrible brawl that involved both squads. It was quite a game."

"Well, who won, who won?" I asked quickly.

"Oh, I don't know about that," she replied. "I changed channels during that horrible fight and started watching Lawrence Welk."

A few quick calls to some of my Auburn friends gave me a blow-by-blow replay of the game, which was more than I really wanted to know. I could have just waited until the following week and read about the game and the other Saturday evening happening of interest in the weekly paper. I could envision the two pictures on the sports page, a photograph of the big football game fight, and a grainy picture of a grinning B.J. holding up the two-headed calf.

The article would state that Mr. B. J. Roach, head herdsman at the Clinch Ranch, had delivered the freak calf. In his vast experience with livestock birthings, this kind of thing rarely happened, maybe once in ten thousand births. No mention, of course, about the exhausted vet spending his entire Saturday evening wallowing around in the muck of the barnyard. The story also wouldn't mention the fact that the owner was not present to lend a hand because he and his fine lady were all dressed out fit to kill over in the comfort of the country club, sipping on fancy cocktails, dining on prime rib, and cutting a rug to the finest band in west Alabama. But that was just fine with me, since I took all of that into consideration when I made out the bill!

Six

Driving home from the Clinch Ranch that night, my truck suddenly veered to the right at the stoplight in downtown York. I knew it was headed for the Dairy Queen and one of their monster, twirled-high ice cream cones. I wished Tom, Lisa, and Timmy had been with me, because they were huge fans of the DQ's soft ice cream.

"Draw me up one of those whopper cones, please," I asked the young lady at the order window. When she stared at my placenta-stained coveralls and wrinkled her nose, I understood. I should have changed clothes, but at the time I didn't know the truck was thinking ice cream.

"You're that vetran from Butler, aren't you?" she said, handing me a cone piled with enough ice cream to break the Borden Dairy Company.

"Yeah, that's right. I'm that veterinarian," I replied, trying to pronounce the "V" word very plainly.

"What're you doing up here tonight?"

"Been to Mr. Clinch's ranch up towards Emelle, helping a cow have her baby."

"Cool! I didn't know you had to do that."

"Well, you don't usually, but sometimes the baby gets crossed up and needs help. But tonight, the calf had two heads," I declared. The girl's mouth gaped open and her eyes widened. "I had to open up her abdomen and get it out because it was so big." If I had told her I was a native Martian she couldn't have acted more surprised.

"Wow!" she exclaimed, then paused, taking a good look at my soiled clothing. "So that's why you look sort of messy."

"Yep. I'm tired and thought I'd go on home and shower before putting on clean duds. But this truck decided it wanted an ice cream cone."

After a little more chatter and an occasional lick of the cone, I headed south, quietly laughing to myself, just thinking about the tale the teenager would be telling the others next morning at Sunday school. Most of them would have never even heard of such a strange operation. Even some adult farmers had never heard of a C-section when I first arrived in Choctaw County. I had done the first C-section in the area several years before.

It was Easter Sunday afternoon, and I was snoozing on the sofa, when I heard the jingle of the phone. Jan caught it on the first ring.

"Phone, honey. It's Mr. Kent Farris."

Mr. Kent was a tough, independent type, like most of my other farmer clients. He didn't mince words, nor did he like to call the cow doctor without due cause.

"Doc, I need you to come help us birth a calf," he drawled.

The key word in this brief utterance was the word *us.* This meant that all the neighbors had tried their hands at midwifery—or, more accurately, midcowery—as had the kinfolks and even two surprised drunks who had been flagged down as they weaved down the gravel road. All had given up or had become exhausted in their attempts to assist the cow. "How long has she been laboring, Mr. Kent?" I asked.

"Aw, just since yesterday about dinner. I saw her off to herself down by the road, fidgeting and looking around, her tail up in the air." Poor beast, not only had she been laboring for twenty-four hours, but she had bravely tolerated the prolonged internal gropings of well-meaning but unqualified would-be obstetricians.

"Sounds like we'll probably need to do a cesarian on her," I suggested.

"What you talkin' about, Doc?"

If Mr. Kent's knowledge of doctoring cows was the same as some of his neighbors', it didn't go much beyond coal oil drenches, splitting tails for the hollowtail, and smearing hog lard on rattlesnake bites. If he didn't know what a cesarian was, I feared trouble.

The trip through the rolling, pine tree–covered territory took about fifteen minutes. When I topped the hill and looked down at the farm, I could see numerous cars and pickup trucks pulled off on the road shoulder. Drawing nearer, the scene resembled a combination family reunion, Methodist church quarterly meeting, and goat killing. There were farmers wearing overalls and feed store caps milling about, their hands stuffed deep in their pockets, some of them gazing expectantly toward town. Others had spied the vet's truck tearing down the road accompanied by a huge cloud of dust and were excitedly pointing it out to their comrades. I noticed that several observers had already secured an observation post atop the rickety catch pen fence. Most of them had the obligatory cud of tobacco already inside their bulging cheeks, while others were busy trying to mooch a chew from anyone who had a pouch of the leafy stuff out in the open.

As I neared the catch pen, a host of young junior cattlemen raced to see who would be the first to drag open the halfway-fallen-down barbed-wire gap. Farmers who have wire gaps or gates despise having to be constantly opening and closing them. That's why they nearly always have a youngster in the truck with them to open and shut gates.

After parking and pulling on clean (and soon-to-be-retired) white coveralls, I made my way over to the patient, a five-hundred-pound Angus-Hereford cross heifer. This kind of birth was such a common problem I could have predicted that it was going to be a heifer that was bred too early because the herd bull was allowed to run with the cow herd year-round. At her first heat cycle, the heifer would be bred by the bull even though she wasn't big enough to have her baby without assistance. In most cases, it is better to establish a controlled breeding season and keep the bull separate from all the females until a breeding plan has been made. Not only will the females have their calves more closely together, a lot of calving problems will be prevented because the heifers will be bred when they have reached the correct size.

As I made my way over to the patient carrying my lariat, bucket, chains, and calf jack, I could hear the murmurings of the old-timers in the background.

"Ain't never seed no vetnerry with white clothes on before."

"I cudda pulled that calf myself if'n I'd a had them chains and that cumalong thing," said another, rattling the leaves on a pokeweed bush with a spate of Bull-of-the-Woods tobacco juice. I graded his spitting style as very poor, not even coming close to the excellent style some of the ladies exhibited down in the south end of the county.

"He's a big feller awright, but if Unca' Silas can't get that calf, can't nobody!" declared a third, who expectorated in the same manner as his associate, except for suffering even more spillage on his shirt.

"Hi y'all doin'?" I asked.

"Doin' arright, uh huh," was the scattered response.

My cursory physical examination revealed that the heifer was in remarkably good condition, considering what she had been through. Examination revealed a swollen and dry birth canal and the stubs of two amputated forelegs, which were attached to what seemed to be a huge and obviously deceased fetus. I decided not to ask why the forelegs had been removed; I didn't want to hear the answer and the justification.

"Mr. Kent, we've got to take this calf out her side," I stated assertively.

A hush fell over the multitude. A few had heard of such, perhaps in the *Progressive Farmer* magazine, but most had no faith in such shenanigans.

"Who ever heard tell of slicin' a cow open to get a calf?" one whiskered citizen mumbled.

I could hear other comments being offered by other self-proclaimed experts as Mr. Kent and I negotiated a settlement to the problem at hand. I knew that my only choice to save the heifer was to do the surgery, and I was determined to do it. "Tell you what, Mr. Kent. We'll operate on the cow, like I want to do, and if she dies, you don't owe me anything."

"But what if she lives?" he asked.

"If she lives, you give me half interest in her and we'll sell her at the Livingston Stockyard this fall, then split the check."

"OK. Hop to it, Doc."

Putting the heifer down and shaving, scrubbing, and injecting local anesthesia along the incision site were accomplished in short order. With so many spectators looking over my shoulder, making the incision was a dramatic moment—kind of like the kickoff in a football game. I continued my incision down through the oblique muscles, encountering the usual bleeders and clamping them carefully with forceps. Nevertheless, blood was seeping out of the incision. I knew that if there was going to be any fainting or mumblings about "not feeling too good," it would start now. Sure enough, a sudden commotion caused me to turn and look towards the fence.

KA-WHUMP!

Joe Bob (Sinkin') Jenkins had fainted at the sight of the blood and had fallen off the top board of the fence backwards into a growth of briars and pokeweeds. Everyone rushed to see if he was still alive, leaving me alone with my patient.

While they were administering to Joe Bob, I used both hands and arms to delve through the eighteen-inch incision, reflect the omentum anteriorly, then exteriorize half the uterus. It was just too large and heavy to get all the way out, so I stuffed towels around the periphery of the organ and called for Mr. Kent.

"When I make an incision right here in this uterus, you reach in there and grab his hind legs and pull 'em carefully. They're gonna be slick, so hang on tight. As you pull, I'll extend this cut so the uterus won't tear."

A minute later we had the smelly fetus almost removed, just as some of the observers returned cowside.

Bad odors get to some people, and this situation was no exception. Suddenly, the fence was empty and bodies were streaking for the bushes with hands over mouths and with throats making harking, gargling noises. It was as though someone had lobbed a canister of tear gas into the audience. Joe Bob was sitting up, glass-eyed and grinning, picking briars and limbs from his bleeding arms, trying to decide what day it was.

One of my little shortcomings is an uncontrollable urge to snicker whenever big, tough Joe Palooka types start gagging during surgery. Imagine how I snickered that day on seeing twenty or so men and boys heaving and harking, six or eight more trying to remain stoic with faces the color of double-bleached rice, and one unattended zombie knee-walking through the pokeweeds.

With tears streaming down my face and my body shaking with stifled giggles, I finally closed the uterine incision. I had almost finished with suturing the muscle layers when most of the survivors of the nausea attack returned for further observation. Now I was in control of the situation. To them I was one tough dude just because I had not run for the bushes.

"Look at 'im handle them tools," one dry-mouthed pulpwood loader marveled. "He's tyin' knots with them little silver pliers."

"This instrument is called a needle holder, and those over there on the drape are called mosquito forceps," I lectured as if they were first-year veterinary school students.

"Did you learn all this stuff in vet school?" someone asked.

"Naw, he saw it all in pictures in the back of a Captain Marble funny book!" declared Joe Bob, now standing. "That's where my Uncle Carney Sam learned how to be a toxidermist." Everybody had a good laugh, including me.

"How many of these kind of operations have you done, Doc?" asked one of the quicker thinkers.

"Aw, a heap!" I exclaimed, not defining the word *heap*. Certainly, no one wants his cow to be the vet's first.

When the ropes were released, the heifer scrambled to her feet with enthusiasm and tried to run out the open gap. She began to nibble on the grass around the edges of the catch pen. When Mr. Kent fetched a pail of water from the creek, she slurped it all down in seconds.

"Look at 'er. She feels better already!" declared a cowboy. Most of them were on my side now.

"Probably lookin' for a better place to die," drawled his buddy. He wasn't convinced.

While I was cleaning the instruments at the back of my truck, the heifer started to eat some baled hay that Mr. Kent had brought from the barn across the road. He was smiling as he sidled up to me.

"Doc, I got my checkbook right here, so if it's OK with you I'll just go ahead and write you a check today and we'll forget about that partnership," he said. Once he realized the cow had a good chance of surviving, it hadn't taken him long to figure out that my half in the fall would be a lot more than my fee the day of the surgery. "Uh uh, why don't we wait until fall and I'll just get my half then, just like we planned."

"Doc, please let me just go on and pay now," he pleaded.

"OK, are you sure that's what you really want to do?"

"Oh, yeah, it is," he said quickly.

That was hundreds of C-sections ago, but that afternoon at Mr. Kent's place is very vivid in my memory, probably because of the dramatic nausea scene and the fact that a farmer actually begged to pay a bill. I wish I had it on tape.

Seven

Every taxpayer dreads receiving that official-looking, brown, United States government envelope. We all know it's coming; we just don't know when. So when mine arrived, after several years of my being in veterinary practice, I was not surprised. But I still shuddered when I read the return address in the upper left-hand corner that announced "Internal Revenue Service, Mobile, Alabama."

The shudder was accompanied by a cold and tingly chill ascending my achy spine when I jammed my dull pocketknife under the flap and gouged it open. I had felt that same chill only days before, when a bull's goring attempt had missed his mark by a whisker, leaving me with nothing more serious than a scraped buttock and a resolution to be more cautious when running away from a large, four-legged patient with revenge on his mind. It was also the exact chill I had experienced when I had taken my eyes off of crawling baby Paul for a second or two, only to discover he had escaped into the cabinets under the kitchen sink. No harm done, but the scare still haunts me.

"You are hereby notified . . ." the letter began. I wondered why those letters always started out that way, and I made another mental note to look up the word *hereby* in my traveling dictionary. I had stowed one in the glove compartment of my truck, hoping to be able to decipher some of the words my clients used, but much to my disappointment, very few of them could be found in Webster's. The letter went on to inform that I was being audited and my presence would be required in their offices on a specific time and date. I remember the appointed date was a Thursday.

"I can't go down there on a Thursday," I raged. "Don't those idiots know that's sale barn day?"

"Now, honey, just cool down," recommended Jan. "Getting yourself all riled up won't help anything. They're just doing their jobs. You'll just have to get someone to cover for you at the stockyard that day."

"There is no one else. I'm the only one they've got!"

"John, when are you going to learn that you alone can't save the world? You simply cannot do everything by yourself and never ask for help from other people."

"That's not true. You suggested that I hire somebody to help at the sale barn after Timmy and Dick went back to school. So I went by the pool room and hired Ricky, but the first day he had a sinking spell from the heat. Nobody down there wants to do anything but drink cold Cokes and shoot pool."

"I don't believe the pool room should be considered an acceptable employment agency, Dr. John," Sue admonished. Now I was getting the works from two women. "You'd have been better off stopping by the quick loan company. But that's got nothing to do with this IRS problem. You've just got to give up a day and go down there."

"Maybe I'll call 'em and go down there on a Saturday afternoon, or one night," I suggested.

"You know very well that government workers don't go to their offices on Saturday or at night," Jan chided. "Maybe hurricane trackers and FBI guys do, but not IRS types."

"Well, I can't worry about it right now," I said hurriedly. "I've got to go test those cows up at the Norman Lewis place."

I fled the office and kangarooed into the driver's seat, then goosed the accelerator, throwing gravel up against the side of the building as I wheeled out onto the main drag. I knew Sue and Jan were on the two-way telling me to slow down, to quit throwing rocks, and to calm down, et cetera, but all I heard was the up-and-down whining of the engine as it went through it's gears.

"Those IRS idiots!" I ranted to myself. "Here I am out here barely making ends meet by delivering calves, getting kicked and stomped by bulls and mules, wading in mud and manure. Those agents don't have enough sense to know what's going on in the real world. If they would let me be in charge for just one dadgum day I'd get everything straightened out in this country." The last statement was one that I frequently uttered to myself when I was in seething swivets.

Minutes later I realized I was leaning over the steering wheel, my teeth were clenched, and the truck was literally rocketing down the roadway, its two-way radio antenna laid back almost parallel with the truck body since my foot had the accelerator smashed flat on the floorboard. My truck was passing slower-moving vehicles like they were standing still, the impact of the backwash from my excessive speed road-shocking the drivers, causing them to veer off onto the shoulder in a momentary loss of control. In the rearview mirror, I saw the panicky drivers fighting their steering wheels, and the raised fists and rude hand gestures of passengers, their cars and trucks kicking up great clouds of dust and clumps of debris as they ran off the pavement, then fishtailed back onto the pavement across the center line before regaining control. I knew I was supposed to honk out a warning of the impending danger, but I was afraid all the horn tooting would scare them witless.

I did feel ashamed when a church group raking leaves close to the highway right-of-way had their piles disrupted and then blown back into the yards, but I would stop later and apologize, and help them clean up for a couple of hours.

My buddy with the unusual name of English Office was reading an opened letter at his mailbox with his neighbor, their heads bent over in deep thought as I missiled by. When I tapped my horn, they grinned and waved, but they should have grabbed their hats, which were instantly vacuumed off their heads and sent rolling into the pine trees. But they were still smiling and waving as they ran and made grabbing movements for their beloved hats. Obviously, they hadn't received a letter from the IRS.

Moments later, I turned off the main highway onto Indian Creek Road, a narrow trail that had recently been paved with tar and crushed stone. I slowed down, but suddenly, when I topped a small rise, there was Goat, the mailman, and he, too, was in the center of the road, his head focused downward into the front seat, seemingly fiddling with his cards and letters. I felt that cold chill again while I tried to steer and find the horn.

It was fortunate that neither of us was traveling at our usual rates of speed, because the only way to avoid a head-on collision was for both of us to hit the ditches. My truck turned first, and at the last possible moment Goat looked up, wild-eyed, and turned hard into his ditch.

WHAM! BAM! POW! It's always shocking how loud a collision can be, even if it is only a fender bender or a ditch slide-off. Then there was the strange, almost eerie silence, punctuated by an occasional pebble rolling down the edge of a ditch and the light whisperings emitting from under truck hoods, just a normal engine-cooling process, I hoped. Spewing and lots of steam are always causes for alarm.

Finally, doors creaked open and both of us, shaking, tried to slide out. I found it was easier and faster to crawl out the window, but Goat was determined to exit the traditional way.

"Goat, we got to stop meeting like this!" I said, dusting off my pants. "Are you OK?"

"D-D-Doc," he stammered. "You s-s-scared me to d-death. We n-nearly hit h-h-head-on!"

"Yeah, neither one of us was paying attention to business," I said. "Let me call the office on the two-way. Sue'll get John Earl to come and pull us out with his Allis-Chalmers."

I made the call while Goat surveyed the damage. It is always difficult to call in with news of an accident, so I always start off by saying, "I'm OK now, everything's OK." Naturally, that opened the floodgates for rapid-fire questions. Jan got on the air, worried about injuries, and wanted to send J. C. Allen and his high-velocity ambulance, but I convinced her that neither of us was hurt. Suddenly, I realized that I wasn't in a vile, anti-IRS mood anymore. A narrow escape from a serious injury makes one glad to be alive.

Damage was light, but my truck seemed to have received the worst end of it. The right door was scraped up, but it had been dented in a few months earlier, compliments of a wild Brahma yearling on the end of a thirty-foot rope. Goat's car had little more than mud and kudzu vines on the front end.

We sat down on the ditch bank and chatted while John Earl was on his way with the tractor.

"Goat, you work for the government. Have you ever been audited by the IRS?"

"Naw, Doc," he answered. "But two of my brothers have. Did you get one of them bad letters?"

"Yeah, and I need to change the day of the audit. They want me to come in on sale barn day."

"You can change the date, and sometimes they'll even come to you and do it at your house or office. You need to call and ask them. But be really nice when you call and do a lot of groveling, saying complimentary things and all. It might keep you out of jail." I felt the cold chill once again, but I hoped he was joking.

What Goat said made me feel better. If the agent came to my office I would have the home field advantage. There wasn't any reason to panic, I reassured myself, since the IRS people were simply doing their jobs. Surely they meant no harm. After all, I had done nothing wrong.

Finally, John Earl arrived and extracted both of our vehicles. I completed the work at the Norman Lewis place and then headed back to the clinic to make the call to the IRS.

"Good afternoon, Internal Revenue Service," a honey-voiced Southern belle answered when the phone call finally got through. "May I help you?" How nice she was! Surely someone that pleasant had no malice in her heart towards a poor, hardworking taxpayer.

I briefly told her about my problem, and she seemed sincerely interested in trying to help.

"Sir, let me connect you with Agent Jones. He has been assigned as your primary auditor." Within seconds, a gruff, no-nonsense man was barking curtly in my ear. He sounded like a Marine sergeant.

"This is Agent Jones speaking. What is the problem, Mr. McCormick?" I was used to being called "Mr." and at that moment wasn't too keen at being identified as a doctor. He might think I was one of the wealthy M.D.s in town. Of course, when he studied my tax returns he would find out otherwise.

"Well, you have my audit scheduled for Thursday. That's by far my busiest day and . . ."

"Why so busy on Thursday?" he quickly queried.

"I'm the veterinarian-in-charge at a stockyard, and I have to be present for testing and vaccinating cattle and swine. Since I've got to be there every Thursday, do you think we could make it another day of the week? And do you think you could come to my office for the audit?"

There was a lengthy pause, and I could hear the shuffling of paper and the flipping of calendar pages.

"This is somewhat irregular, Mr. McCormick," he stated, "since I seldom perform on-site audits, except in special hardship cases."

I spent the next few moments trying to convince him of the reasons he should come to my office. I told him that I was the only vet in the county, and about the sale barn work on Thursday, and I made sure to mention all the work I did for the animal-owning public. Finally, he spoke.

"Actually, I do have to be in your community two weeks from Tuesday to seize some property from a delinquent taxpayer. I'll just come by your place and get started, then spend the night and finish your books the next day."

I gulped hard when he used the word *seize*. He'd said it with such gusto.

"Yes sir, Agent Jones," I said weakly. "That will be just fine."

"I will need all your tax returns from the past three years, plus all the records of your expenses, and a complete list of property."

"Yes sir, I'll have everything ready, and a clean place for you to work," I said, trying to grovel, just as Goat had advised.

"Oh, by the way, Mr. McCormick," he asked. "My nephew wants to be a vet. Tell me, do you have to go to any kind of school for that, or can you just take it up? He loves to fool with stock."

I felt that cold chill again. . . .

Eight

On the day of the big IRS audit appointment, I was at the clinic before the sun came up, having spent the night tossing and turning. I checked in with Timmy, who was feeding and exercising the dogs, then made my way to the storage room to create a work space for Mr. Jones, the IRS man. I moved supplies around and neatly stacked several cases of drugs, then swept up and placed a card table and chair where he could work undisturbed. I thought if he had a relatively quiet place for his figuring, maybe he would be impressed with my thoughtfulness and have mercy on my soul while he was checking the books.

I didn't know what time Mr. Jones would arrive, but I knew that I was to be his second victim of the day. Since it was possible he would be in a bad mood when he drove into our parking lot, I even found some flowers around the house and set a mixed bouquet on the desk. In addition, I made several orderly piles of all the previous years' income tax returns that he had requested, all my record books and day books, even lined up pencils, pads, and an adding machine neatly beside the flowers. Then I went about treating the patients and answering the phone, trying to delay any appointments until after the arrival of the tax man.

At about 11:25 A.M., and after several fretful hours of waiting and watching the clock, I saw a new, plain black Ford sedan with official-looking United States Government writing on its side creeping down the highway, scanning the animal clinic property. As the car made its slow and careful entrance into a front parking slot, I noticed the driver eyeing my truck, perhaps a little too covetously, and also the cattle-handling chute parked on the north side of the building.

"What would the IRS do with a cow chute?" I wondered to myself. Of course, I knew why any red-blooded Southern male would be envious of a truck. I continued to be concerned about that "seizure of property" he had mentioned earlier over the phone.

"He's here, Dr. John!" called Sue.

"Yeah, I see 'im."

Through the exam room window, I saw the well-dressed government worker look at his watch, then at his odometer, and carefully make an entry into a plain gray ledger book with a black government-issue pen. Next, he rolled up the window on the driver's side, opened and exited the door, then meticulously locked the door, double-checking to be sure it was secure.

"Wow, what a weirdo," I thought to myself, since nobody ever locked their vehicles in Choctaw County, and many didn't even lock up their houses. If you found the front door locked, it meant you were supposed to go around to the back one.

From the trunk, the dreaded visitor retrieved an old and well-used dark gray briefcase, two large manila folders, and an ancient adding machine. After one last quick inspection of his government wheels he started for the office entrance, where I stood, holding the door open and grinning broadly.

"Yes sir," I beamed. "Good morning, good morning! You must be agent Jones. Welcome to Choctaw Animal Clinic!"

"Mr. McCormick, I presume," he announced in a very businesslike manner. I nodded my head in the affirmative, and he timidly grasped my offered hand. I thought it was strange that such a tall, long-footed, tough-sounding, property-seizing man had such a Milquetoast handshake.

"Actually, it's McCormack," I replied. "But I'm thinking of changing that *a* to an *i* to see if I can lay claim to some of Uncle Cyrus's estate," I said, grinning. He stared at me as if I had rabies.

"You know, Mr. Cyrus McCormick, the feller who invented the reaper? Don't you know he left a pile of money that's just waiting in a bank . . . aw, never mind." Now he had his head tilted as he stared, seemingly clueless about my little joke.

"Yes, I'm Agent Jones with the Internal Revenue Service, and I am here to investigate your tax irregularity. Would you direct me to your business office, please." Even in my embarrassment and with my potential upcoming problem, I managed a wry smile and humorous thought when he mentioned "irregularity." To a vet, that word indicates a large bowel problem in an old dog, or perhaps in a horse with sand impaction of the cecum.

"Well, I don't reckon we have a business office as such." I grinned again, still thinking of constipated dogs. "But I have fixed you up a nice place in the storage room, where you won't be disturbed." I proudly led him down the hall and into the room that would be his headquarters—for a very short time, I hoped. Admittedly, it did contain some of my veterinary equipment, assorted junk, drugs, and supplies. I snapped on the desk lamp.

"How's this?" I asked. "You won't be bothered by barking dogs and people coming and going." But my mouth had scarcely shut when I heard the baying of a redbone hound parked in a dog box outside, and the faint yet persistent yapping of a Chihuahua in the kennel room, and we both knew I had told a story. Then he looked up, startled, and turned his left ear toward the east as we detected the increasing racket of the co-op feed truck and its busted muffler as it approached from the south, then rumbled down the hill in front of the clinic, headed for north Choctaw with provisions for hundreds of hungry swine. "Well," he said hesitatingly, and peering around suspiciously. "This is somewhat irregular, but I suppose I can make do with these meager facilities." In addition to being irregular, my facilities were now meager. "I see that you do have all your records right here. Very good!"

"Is there anything I can get for you?" I asked. "I do have a right smart of work ahead of me."

"No, I think not. But don't vacate the area, since it may be necessary to interrogate you at length about some of these records." There he went again, using *interrogate*, another offbeat word that was even scarier than *irregular* or *meager.* I wanted to get away, but I still had one last thing to ask.

"Do you know any Joneses in Nashville? My college roommate was from up there, and his name is the same as yours. Doesn't that *T* stand for 'Thomas'? Just wondered if y'all were kin."

"Don't know him, and I've never been to Nashville," he replied curtly, wiping the desk with a large white handerkerchief that he reeled out of his back pocket. His eyes never met mine as he smeared and rearranged the imaginary dust.

"Well, I was just asking. Y'all are both tall and got big feet." I laughed.

Apparently, Mr. Agent Jones didn't have a sense of humor. Instead, he sniffed the air several times before asking the question "What is that pungent odor in here?"

I, too, sniffed the air, but didn't catch anything unusual, so I just shook my head from side to side.

"It seems to be coming from the vicinity of those parcels over there," he said, pointing into the corner.

"Oh, yeah, that's just some sacks of aureomycin crumbles. And that drum in the corner contains mineral oil, and those buckets there are full of horse vitamins. I just love the smell of a veterinary drug room, don't you?" I thought everybody appreciated the aroma of B vitamins and rumen stimulants.

But he just stared at me and the medicines with his nose wrinkled up. It appeared that he was one big guy who didn't like the unique smell of a country vet clinic.

"Bet you've been to a lot of vet clinics over the years, haven't you?" I asked, still trying to be neighborly.

"Negative. This is my initial case," he confessed, still rearranging the desk. It appeared that in spite of his distaste for the aromas, he was planning to stay for a spell.

"But you have checked veterinarians before," I said.

"Negative. You're the first and only. I don't even own a pet, and certainly not a dangerous horse. I have no earthly idea what you people do. All I know is that you fool with animals."

I was starting to feel chilly again. I had been hoping he would know something about the nature of my work so we could converse intelligently. It looked as if I had some educating to do.

⌒

He broke for lunch at exactly 12:30 P.M., went to his car with brief-case in hand, and ate his lunch in the front seat. I went out and offered cheese, bologna, bread, and an RC cola from the clinic refrigerator, but he declined with a great show of refusal. I am certain he thought I was trying to bribe him with cold cuts.

As he was dining in the comfort of his Ford sedan, I left to make several farm calls. I tried not to worry about the strange man back at the office, but I couldn't help it. I kept having horrible visions of being handcuffed and marched down our front porch steps on the way to the paddy wagon, my wonderful family huddled and sobbing together, peering longingly through the living room curtains. I shook my head to clear those thoughts away and tried to think positively.

"Base to unit one, base to unit one. Do you read?" It was Sue on the two-way.

"Yeah, come on, base."

"Dr. John, the tax man is here and wants to ask you some questions about the records. I'm going to put him on."

"OK." I noticed I was white-knuckling the steering wheel.

"Uh, you there, Mr. McCormack?" Mr. Jones's voice carried over the airways. It was obvious that he wasn't a practiced radio man.

And there was no telling who was listening. I was ashamed that some of my colleagues in Wisconsin and Illinois and other faraway states who were on the same radio frequency would hear my conversation with the IRS man.

"Uh, there are some very odd entries in your record books and receipts that I need to ask you about. First of all, here is where you allegedly paid $120.50 for a calf named Jack. Please clarify."

"Mr. Jones, I don't have the foggiest notion what you are talking about. But I can assure you that I haven't bought a calf named Jack or anything else. Just hang tight and I'll be there shortly. I can't talk very well with you over this radio, ten-four."

As I beelined back toward town, I tried hard to recollect ever buying a calf. I was positive I had never bought a calf any of the years for which I was being audited. There was a calf whose leg was broken in the delivery process because of the calf jack . . .

Then it hit me! Calf jack! Of course. I had bought a calf jack, and he didn't understand the veterinary jargon.

"It's not a calf named Jack," I yelled as I charged through the clinic door. "It's a calf jack."

"What's a calf jack?" was the easily predicted IRS response.

"We use that piece of equipment to assist a cow in labor. Sometimes a cow has been in labor for a long period of time, and she just gives up and quits trying. Then we have to help her by using the calf jack to extract the fetus," I stated.

"All right, that's a sufficient explanation," Mr. Jones replied. "Now I have some other questions. What is the purpose of a squeeze chute?"

After I convinced him that we needed a chute to restrain wild cattle, he asked about several other items. He wanted to know why my gasoline and truck expenses were so outrageous, wanted an explanation of my high drug bills, and even questioned the one vet meeting I had attended the previous year. Several hours later, and much more knowledgeable about veterinary medicine, Agent Jones packed up his gear and started out.

"It has been a pleasure, Doctor," he said, and he actually smiled. "You sure opened my eyes about your profession. I'd like for my nephew to come up and spend some time with you during his summer vacation. And I want to apologize about addressing you as 'mister.'"

"That's just fine. But I'd like to hear the results of your trip up here."

"In about two weeks you will receive a report," he said. "Good day!"

He walked around his plain car, checking every tire and inspecting the body for evidence of tampering or damage, then sat down in the driver's seat, adjusted it, made an entry in his book, went through a several-minute routine of checking every gauge and button before cranking the motor according to Ford's book recommendations. He slowly pulled out into the road, after looking both ways three times, then headed toward Mobile, never looking back or waving. I never saw him again.

I felt good about the audit until the letter arrived three weeks later. When I read it, I had cold chills, hot flashes, and a sinking spell. The biggest problem was improper depreciation of a calf jack, a squeeze chute, and two trucks. In addition, there were several other violations, and they wanted the money I owed them immediately. I'll never forget that the bill was the equivalent of 125 calf deliveries. That's a pretty steep price to pay for some government agent to address you as "Doctor." Thankfully, our accountant helped get the figures straightened out, and the amount we owed was reduced substantially. But from that day forward, it has been difficult for me to communicate with tall Feds who drive plain black cars.

Mr. Jones's nephew never did show up at the Choctaw Animal Clinic. I suspected that he decided to follow in his uncle's long footsteps.

Nine

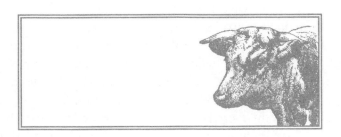

D oc, I need you to come over here and see about a cow that's down and can't get up," said the voice on the other end of the line. It was a cool Sunday morning in February.

It was my friend Clay Boozer, a part-time cattleman, pulpwood dealer, and full-time fan of the Alabama Crimson Tide football team and their legendary coach, Mr. Paul (Bear) Bryant. Clay was a good feller, but his constant carrying on about Alabama football tested the patience of many, and especially an Auburn fan like me.

I got a little background about the cow and then promised Clay I'd be there as soon as I'd stopped to look in on a sick mule.

Downer cows that have been unable to rise for several days suffer from muscle and nerve degeneration, and because they respond poorly to treatment, they are among a vet's least favorite calls. Years ago, a downer cow call frequently meant milk fever, and the affected cow would hop up and walk off after an IV of warm calcium. But some cases are caused by complex metabolic problems for which there is no standard therapy.

Clay's cow was suffering from chronic malnutrition, a common wintertime problem in 1960s Choctaw County. It didn't always mean the cow was underfed. Sometimes she was old and missing teeth, or her teeth were so worn down she was unable to eat properly. "Chronic malnutrition" sounds a lot better to a cow owner than "starvation." Other useful euphemisms include "high trough disease," "internal energy deficiency complex," and "abomasal filling defect." I liked the term "hollow belly," but it could rile some folks to the point of chasing the vet off the premises. Some owners simply don't feed their cattle enough, sometimes because they can't afford it, or sometimes because they don't understand the nutritional needs of the herd during cold weather.

Clay's cow had hidden in the deepest part of the woods, as cows tend to do when they are in trouble, and it was only due to the woods-hunting skills of Lige, Clay's right-hand man, that she was even found. We drove Clay's old World War II jeep down the rutted logging road, then walked another hundred yards among the pines, where the old Hereford-Jersey cow was down and being attended to by Lige, who had gone ahead of us with the tractor, carrying hay, grain, and water. She was eating the grain with hound dog gusto, occasionally taking a large swipe off the half-full pan of feed and eyeing me suspiciously as she chewed, dribbling bits of corn and cottonseed hulls down into the hay.

I knew Lige practiced a little homemade veterinary medicine, although not to the extent of Carney Sam Jenkins. But he helped Clay with his herd and an occasional neighbor who had a cow problem. I knew he was a proponent of the hollertail and hollerhorn theories, whatever they were, but he was also a leading authority on "the Murrah." One farmer had sized up my own reputation as a veterinarian in the community. "Doc's pretty good at calvings, prolapses, and herd work," he bragged. "But he ain't worth a dern on the Murrah. I gen'ly go git Lige whenever one of my cows comes down with the Murrah." As best as I could determine, symptoms of the Murrah included a swollen head and tongue with drainage from the mouth.

"What do you reckon's wrong with this old cow, Lige?" I asked diplomatically, knowing what his response would be. I had started my exam at the rear of the cow and was moving forward.

"I reckon she's got the hollertail, suh," he said almost apologetically. Now I was up to the head, which I grasped in my left arm while I pulled down her lower lip and scanned the area where her teeth once had been. Her incisors were gone, except for the pearl-like nubs which had worn down until they were flush with the gum line.

"How old do you think she is, Clay?" I asked just to see what he would say.

"Aw let's see, Doc," he allowed, trying to think. "I think I bought her at the Linden sale barn the year Alabama played Tulane a night game in Mobile at Ladd Stadium, and she was a yearling at the time. So I guess she's about ten." A true Alabama football fan dates everything in his life to some Crimson Tide football event.

"Look at these teeth, Clay. She's old enough to vote!" I exclaimed. "And look at her condition. She's so thin there's nothing here but skin and bones. Plus she's pregnant with a big calf, which is a huge burden on her since she can't chew properly. She doesn't have a chance."

"But, Doc, I remember you coming over to Aunt Molly's place and treating an old Jersey milk cow that was down. When you gave her that shot, she jumped up and ran off."

"But that was milk fever, not starvation, and it just won't work that way on this cow."

"Lige said she had the hollertail and we ought to split her tail and put salt and pepper in it, but I told him your medicine was better," Clay said. "She's been a good player and I hate to lose her."

"Well, in my opinion, I don't think splitting her tail and putting kitchen table spices in it is gonna get her up. Let's do this. We'll give her some glucose and other IV fluids, then some vitamin injections. If we don't get a first down with that plan, we'll pass a stomach tube and pump gruel and grits into her. If we don't gain any yardage with that, then we'll put the hip lift on her and pick her up twice a day. If we still haven't scored, then we'll punt and you can fire the coach. Does that sound like a good game plan?"

"It does, but I still think we ought to split her tail and . . ."

"We're not gonna do that. Just get that notion out of your mind. That would be unsportsmanlike conduct!"

The treatment was completed, and I left medication for Lige to give. Clay called every other night to report her progress or the lack of it. He always suggested that we consider allowing Lige to perform his tail surgery. Nursing downer cows becomes very frustrating, especially when the cow and the human nurses both lose their spirit and give up. Clay gave up about four weeks after I had first seen the patient.

"Doc, can you come over here and put this old cow out of her misery?" he requested. "I just can't keep on doctorin' her, and I don't have what it takes to shoot her. Can't you give her one of those go-to-sleep shots?" I told him we could.

"Doc, you ain't gonna like this," he confessed. "But Lige kept on and on about splittin' that old cow's tail, so I let him go on down there a while ago and do it."

"Yeah, you're right. I don't agree with it, but she's your cow and you can do what you want with her," I replied.

On the way down the woods trail, I said, "Clay, you've got to understand that we've done everything possible to save that cow and nothing else could have been done that would save her. She was a goner from the start. Don't second-guess the treatment we used."

Finally we completed our rough passage through the rocky pasture and started slowly making our way down the rutty logging trail to where the doomed patient was located.

Suddenly, Clay sprang to the edge of his seat, quickly wiped off his side of the windshield interior, and blinked his eyes.

"D-Doc, do you see what's coming up the trail, or am I seeing a h-haint?" he stammered.

As I strained to look down the trail through the pine and underbrush, I could make out a briskly moving figure. As we both stared, openmouthed, the old cow that had been down and knocking on death's door only a few hours before came marching toward us. She was even smart enough to stay in the center of the road where the footing was less treacherous and there were no ruts. Her gait was stiff, and she occasionally stumbled, reminding me of an old crippled soldier proudly marching during a Veteran's Day parade. I could almost hear the band playing the Marine Hymn as she trudged up the hill and paused briefly in front of my truck as if she were going to salute. Instead, with eyes blinking, she just stared at the two startled figures in the vehicle.

With a switch of her bandaged tail, she stomped by the truck, made her way out into the pasture, and began sampling some of the green stuff.

It hit us at the same instant. The bandaged tail meant Lige had done it! We both turned back toward the trail just in time to see him emerge from a grove of trees, grinning from ear to ear and carrying a half-pound box of Watkin's pepper in one hand and a box of plain Morton's salt in the other. The remnants of an old ragged sheet dangled from a rear overall pocket. He explained what he had done.

After making a liberal incision just above the tail switch, he'd poured copious amounts of his spices into the incision, then wrapped the wound with strips of the sheet. A bow knot adorned the finished product.

"Lige, how did you make her get up?" I asked, trying to mask the shock that was on my face.

"Well, suh," he drawled, "ah jus' done her tail lack ah always do, then urged her to git up. She didn't, so ah whispered in her ear."

"What did you say to her?" Clay asked impatiently.

"Tole her this was Mr. Coach Bear Bryant and that she was supposed to rise an' walk. In a little bit, she slowly started to git up, so I grabbed a holt of her tail and helped her the rest of the way up. She tried to run at first, and nearly fell, so she started walkin' slower."

"Why'd you say that about Coach Bryant?" I asked.

" 'Cause Mr. Clay's all time talkin' so much 'bout Mr. Coach Bear Bryant and how he walks on water and keeps it from rainin' on ball game day. So I reckoned he could easy git an ole cow up off the groun'."

"Lige, will any brand of pepper do?" I asked.

"Naw, sir, it's got to be Watkin's—and be sure you use the plain kind of Morton's. Don't use salt with that old iodine in it." I had heard the same recommendation from Carney Sam and his supporters.

A few weeks later, the old cow gave birth to a fine heifer calf and raised her to weaning age. But the following fall, Clay came home from a football game late one Saturday afternoon and couldn't find her in her usual hangouts. The next morning he and Lige found her in the deep woods, where she had gone to die.

I still don't understand the mechanism involved in getting that old, weak cow to stand. I'm not sure I want to know. But I did learn from Lige and the old cow incident that I should never be so bold as to tell a client that a home remedy will absolutely not work.

Ten

D oc, you sure tell a lot of stories about bulls," declared Waldo King. "How many of 'em are true?" We had just finished deworming his cow herd and were in the barn hall, resting on bales of coastal bermuda hay, refreshing ourselves with iced tea. The cows and their calves were noisily bellowing as they trotted through the just-opened corral gate, each searching through the crowd for its next of kin. Several of the cows turned back and ran toward the gate, mooing, looking and sniffing at every calf they encountered until they finally discovered the one that looked and smelled just right.

Watching the herd "mother up" is always an enjoyable affair. There can be fifty momma cows separated from their calves, but when turned out together they find the correct parent or child in minutes, often in seconds. It doesn't matter if they are all the same color, size, and shape; somehow the cows just know.

"Well, they're all true, of course, and I like telling folks about them. Someday, if I live long enough, I'm gonna write about them. Anyone who deals with bulls on a daily basis knows that crazy things are always happening," I answered. "Remember the day that white yearling bull jumped through the board fence out by the road?"

"Yeah, that's why we named him 'Stupid,'" he declared.

"Naw, that was Little Stupid. Stupid was gone by then," corrected Kathy.

"Yeah, I remember. But, Doc, you told a tale about a broken-legged bull named 'Wheel Chair.' Did that actually happen? Y'all really took him over to the folks' hospital to get that leg X-rayed?"

"Yep, it really happened," I replied. "That man really loved that bull."

There was another owner who loved his bulls just as much. Dr. Brown was a retired M.D. who owned a small herd of registered Angus cattle and spent a lot of time selectively breeding show stock. He worked hours at a time shampooing bulls, curling their hair, and polishing their hooves, preparing for various state and regional shows, and an equal amount of time traveling to and from the show locations. When traveling, his animals were always attired in their fancy red capes in order to keep their coats clean and shiny.

Although her appreciation for their bovines only minimally approached that of her husband, Mrs. Brown assisted in the paper-work on vet days and was always on hand with her well-organized herd records, ready for any ancestry question or information about necessary vaccinations. She even rode with the doctor when it was show time, entertaining herself in the pickup by knitting or some-times reading Civil War books.

The couple amused me because they were so different. While Dr. Brown seemed to relish wearing old overalls, shuffling around in his Sears-Roebuck brogans, a dirty baseball cap askew on his head, Mrs. Brown always appeared to have just stepped from the door of the beauty salon. Her silver hair was always perfectly coiffed, her nails painted bright red and shiny. She carried herself tall like a queen.

Dr. Brown used my services frequently and without hesitation whenever the slightest need arose. He didn't put any faith in the "give-'em-a-shot-of-everything-in-the-bag" shotgun treatments used by some of his neighboring cattlemen, nor did he spend his time fooling with homemade remedies like splitting tails, boring horns, or rubbing a corn cob on the spine for the "tightback." He was a respected medical doctor, and he recognized the difference between man and cow.

One day we were treating a simple case of foot rot on his "best" cow. Of course, like many of my clients, he felt nearly every cow was his "best cow," and according to them nothing but the best cow ever suffered a health problem.

"Dr. McCormack, are you certain that she's got the plain old foot rot?"

"Yes sir, I am," I replied, scraping around between her swollen front claws. "Don't you smell that foot rot odor?"

"Odor? I don't smell anything. Don't you think we should take some X rays and send some blood to the lab? I'm not sure I trust your nose as much as you do."

So, off we went to the folks' hospital for a date with the portable X-ray machine, hoping that this patient wouldn't create as much of a stir as the famous wheelchair bull a couple of years earlier. Luckily, all went well, and the radiographs were made by a technician whose dog had just been treated for heartworms at my clinic. There were no newspaper reporters, gawking onlookers, or irate head nurses to give us any trouble.

After Dr. Brown and I reviewed the pictures and went over the blood work in great detail, he was finally convinced that my initial "diagnosis by nose" was accurate. Not many livestock owners are willing to go to such great lengths or expense to make an absolute diagnosis. Finally, we treated the cow with the appropriate antibiotic and applied foot rot lotion to the swollen foot. Her lameness disappeared in forty-eight hours.

As liberal as he was with the medical and surgical care of his herd, he was overly frugal when it came to transporting his cattle. Instead of hauling them in a long, luxurious cattle trailer, he used an old, side-by-side, two-horse trailer, which was barely wide or long enough to accommodate two adult bulls. He pulled this junky trailer with a ten-year-old, half-ton Ford pickup. Not only was the Ford underpowered, but its suspension system was weak and insufficient for the loads he carried. When he was trailering a heavy load of two cattle, the front end of the truck almost came up off the road, and the rear end almost dragged the pavement. He swayed all over the road, especially if the animals in the trailer shifted excessively or started to knock each other around.

One early-fall morning, this obviously dangerous situation came to a head when Dr. and Mrs. Brown were happily swaying back and forth across Choctaw County on Highway 10, heading toward the Dixie National Livestock Show in Jackson. Their load that day consisted of two huge bulls, Moe and Joe, Dr. Brown's pride and joy. With four thousand pounds or more of live bull flesh squeezed into his small trailer, Dr. Brown was aware that there was little room for the animals to move around or recline. With this in mind, he decided to stop at frequent intervals during their three-hour journey to check on Moe and Joe, and let them walk around if necessary.

Everything went well for the first leg of the trip, but just as the Butler city limit sign came into view, an unusual amount of turbulence, accompanied by shifting and jerking, rocked the vehicle. Getting the truck and trailer off the road and into a wide spot safe for parking was not an easy task because of all the goings-on in the back, but the doctor finally guided the rocking vehicle to a slow stop.

An investigation revealed that Moe had apparently tried to lie down for a snooze. Joe, meanwhile, had also decided to shift to a more comfortable position, using Moe as a soft place to put his extra-large feet. When Moe became uncomfortable with this arrangement, he tried to stand up again, but the more he struggled to get upright, the worse his predicament became. In addition to getting thoroughly raked by Joe's feet, he was also beginning to suffer from excessive rumen bloat from being down so long.

When Dr. Brown found Joe standing atop a bruised, battered, and bloated Moe, he went to work trying to open the jammed door, finally resorting to the use of a sledgehammer. He somehow coaxed the haltered Joe out of the trailer, then led him over to the grass on the right-of-way of the westbound lane and tied him securely to a pine tree.

After considerable begging and much physical urging, it became apparent that Moe was not going to be able to rise without additional manpower. Somehow, Dr. Brown prevailed upon his faithful wife to remain at the roadside site while he rushed to our clinic with a fast-sinking Moe.

It was approximately eight A.M., and I was on the phone and looking out the clinic window when I saw the speeding truck and trailer wheel into the clinic parking lot and come to a screeching stop. A frantic Dr. Brown hopped from the truck and looked over into the trailer, all the while gesturing excitedly toward the clinic and two trucks that had followed him into town. The truck drivers knew if a man left his beautiful wife and a large bull wearing a fancy coat beside a busy road, something serious had happened.

In seconds, I was looking at the terrible sight inside the trailer. The once-beautiful Moe was on his back, feet pointing skyward, his body wedged tightly in between baled hay in front, a broken half partition, and the rear door. He was so filled with gas that he looked like a big, black, round ball. He was skinned up, bleeding from several stomp marks, and his once-beautiful coat was now disheveled, the hair gouged out in several locations. His head was swollen and bruised from his beating it against the floor of the trailer in his efforts to get up.

After a brief discussion, a couple of nylon lariats were looped around Moe's rear legs and every available warm body lent a hand in trying to pull Moe to his feet. Much grunting and tugging followed in the next few minutes, but it was all in vain. The bull was all dead weight, and he did nothing to make the process easier except grunt with each short and catchy breath and occasionally make a half-hearted attempt to struggle. As we stroked our chins and thought up a second course of action, I heard a John Deere tractor coming down the hill. I recognized it as one of the city-owned tractors that was used for digging trenches and laying pipe with its front-end loader. It was exactly what we needed, and not a moment too soon! Like a flash I was in the road, flagging it down and directing the driver into the clinic parking lot. It was improper to use the city's equipment for personal projects, but I was going to use it now and worry about the consequences later.

Dr. Brown was concerned that using a tractor would cause further injury, but since he couldn't come up with a better suggestion and time was running out, he agreed. Mr. Jenkins, the tractor driver, came up with a good suggestion.

"If y'all will let me tie those two rear leg ropes to the bucket in front of the tractor, I believe I can lift him up pretty high and just slide his head out the back."

Using his suggestion, we tied the ropes as he instructed, then with a lifting and reversing action, eased Moe out of his predicament. With several hands helping, we quickly had the dazed bull sitting up. He immediately started belching up large quantities of gas, and even tried to stand up.

"Doc, reckon we ought to draw some blood and be sure he's OK?" Dr. Brown was back in business. "And what about some X rays?"

"Let's just wait and see if he gets up and eats some alfalfa," I suggested.

It was at this point that I heard Mrs. Brown was over on the east side of town, bull-sitting.

"You mean to tell me they're over there on the side of that busy highway?" I asked. Butler, Alabama, has no traffic jams, but there are a lot of cars on the road during our little rush hour. And even though it's a rural town, not many people driving to work have been that close to a bull, especially one dressed in a jacket and standing beside a lady knitting a sweater. I could just see the drivers gawking and traffic backing up.

"I hope they're still there. That's where I left 'em," Dr. Brown declared.

"This I got to see," I exclaimed. "I've got a farm call out that way, so I'm going to drive out there to see this sight when you leave."

"What about Moe?" he asked as the battered bull finally got up without assistance. He stood there, quivering and slobbering.

"I think you ought to go on to Jackson, but leave him here at the clinic for observation. That way we can monitor his progress. I'll get him a room at one of the farms nearby and treat his wounds until you get back."

Five minutes later, I was approaching the site where Mrs. Brown and Joe were waiting. As I rounded a gentle curve, I could see traffic backed up over the hill coming into town and blue lights flashing nearby. I had a good idea why the lights were flashing.

"I'll bet some rubbernecker slowed down or stopped to gape and got rear-ended," I thought to myself.

I whipped off the road shoulder and slowly drove down through the shallow ditch to where Joe stood, tied to a speed limit signpost. A straw-hatted Mrs. Brown sat in her folding chair nearby. He was chewing and she was crocheting, both seemingly contented and unaware of the excitement they were causing.

As expected, just down the road a state trooper made a big to-do of directing traffic around two slightly damaged cars, while a second officer surveyed the fender bender and wrote up his report. The drivers involved hung their heads in embarrassment.

"Doctor!" cried Mrs. Brown, springing from her seat. "How is Moe? Is he all right?"

"Yes, ma'am, he'll be fine. But he's mighty bruised up and is gonna be pretty sore for a while."

One of the burly state troopers headed our way.

"You the owner of this cow?" he asked curtly.

"No, and he's not a cow."

"OK, then, what's your connection with this steer?"

"He's not a steer either. He's a bull, and I'm Dr. McCormack, his personal veterinarian," I replied. I reckoned he was new on the job, or maybe had just been transferred to the Choctaw County area.

"Well, I don't care what you are, you've got to get this animal off this road before somebody gets killed. This ain't no pasture, you know!"

"He can't be moved," I said professionally. I had always wanted to say that, just like they do on those hospital TV scenes. "At least, not until his conveyance arrives. It'll be here shortly." I noticed Mrs. Brown smiling.

He stomped back over to where one of the cars was being hauled off, then started motioning for traffic to move faster. I noticed the two accident victims were now arguing about something, and both were pointing fingers at fenders and bumpers.

"He must have just been assigned here from Big City, USA." Mrs. Brown giggled. "He's gonna have to learn how to smile a little if he wants to make it in Choctaw County."

"How are you making it out here with the bull?" I asked.

"Just fine. But there's been lots of horn honking, yelling, and squealing tires. It's like these people have never seen a bull before."

"I just came by to see if Dr. Brown had actually talked you into standing guard over Joe out here on this busy highway," I said. "That must be a sign of true love."

"Either that, or maybe it's just because he had his ox in a ditch." She laughed.

Dr. Brown arrived presently, so I stayed and helped to load Joe back onto the trailer. Then they were off to Jackson for more adventures.

Moe recovered nicely from his very close call with the grim reaper. I treated him daily for about ten days, until he started trying to pick a fight through his stall wall. Dr. Brown arrived in a brand-new, luxurious, all-aluminum trailer designed for prize cattle. He seemed pleased when I prescribed physical therapy–type exercises for Moe's rehabilitation program.

"You ought to buy your wife a nice present for the way she took care of Joe out there on the road," I suggested.

"Oh, I did," he exclaimed. "I bought her a heifer at the sale in Jackson. Her name is Flo. And I was just wondering, do you reckon she needs some blood work and X rays? . . ."

Eleven

It was at least eleven P.M. when I finally straggled into the house, dog tired. Jan was sitting in the old blue rocking chair softly humming a lullaby to the lightly sleeping baby in her arms as she rocked. Paul was about three months old and was fighting sleep, as usual. After watching her patiently deal with three little ones, I knew why nature had intended for mommas to be children's primary caregivers. She always knew what to do when they cried or hurt themselves, and seemed to possess a sixth sense about what to expect from them, especially if it involved violating bedtime rules, going out in the cold air without proper head cover, or refusing to eat their vegetables.

"Bobby Joe Henley called about an hour ago," she whispered. "One of his big Charolais cows is in labor. He said to just come by and pick him up at the house." The baby stirred in her arms. I waited a few seconds before I whispered back.

"OK. I'll just get a quick bite and go on out there," I replied. "Did he say whether or not he had her up in the barn?" Her grimace told me what I already knew; the cow was still out in the woods somewhere.

"Anything else?"

"No, it's been real quiet. Your supper is in the oven."

I reached down and kissed both of them and tiptoed down the hall, the pleasant aroma of shampooed baby's hair lingering in my nostrils. Tom and Lisa were sacked out, both lying in crazy contorted positions in their beds, oblivious to the real world of late-night calf deliveries and graveyard shifts at the paper mill. Drinking in their innocent beauty in the dim night light always caused me to shake my head in wonder, as I had done every night since they entered my life. As I checked to be sure they were breathing all right, it was hard to believe that just a few hours ago both of them had been going full throttle, their energy levels the envy of both their parents.

Then it was back to the kitchen, where I tossed two pork chops and a couple of wedges of cornbread into a brown bag, then poured a big glass of iced tea before heading out the door. Jan whispered something I couldn't understand, but I had a good idea what her message was.

"Don't you want a plate and a napkin? And be careful," was probably what she'd said, since that's what she always said. Jan is keen on plates and napkins, but seemingly unaware of how difficult it is to eat from a plate while whizzing down the road several miles above the speed limit.

"Someday I'm gonna get tired of all this running all over the county at all hours of the night. I wonder if I could get one of those easy professor-type jobs in a veterinary school somewhere," I thought to myself as I sped over to Bobby Joe's house. "I may just check on that in a couple of years."

Bobby Joe lived in the small subdivision on the opposite side of town, but his thirty brood cows were on his three-hundred-acre, heavily wooded family farm, about ten or twelve miles west of his house, right on the Mississippi line. This created a problem for both of us, since he didn't check on his cows as often as he should have. In addition, he had no corral, just an old, half-fallen-down barn. Every time he had a veterinary problem, a rodeo ensued, with two half-wild cowboys twirling nylon lariats while standing on a truck bumper or hanging dangerously out the passenger-side window.

"Bobby Joe," I had pointedly advised him, "you've just got to check on this herd every day! When these cows are calving, you can't afford to let them go. And another thing! You've got to build a catch pen so that I don't kill myself out here some dark night trying to rope one of your old wild cows."

"I know, Doc, but it's hard to get out here every day. You know, the young'uns have got to be taken to ball practice, music lessons, and then I like to play a little golf after work now and then. Then I have to go huntin' and fishin' a right smart, too." He didn't mention anything about fixing a catch pen. I always wound up getting irritated with him, because with a little time and effort his farm could be turned into one of the better ones in the county, with good water, lots of fine pine timber, and beautiful cattle. Half the people in the county would have given an arm to get that property.

Five minutes after leaving my driveway, I was turning into Bobby Joe's. I drove right into the carport until my two-way radio antenna banged on the eave. Presently, Bobby Joe appeared at the screen door, along with a set of diapered twins and a barking, tail-wagging, terrier-type squirrel dog. The dog was the only one of the three wearing a shirt. I wondered why those kids weren't asleep at that hour of the night and why the dog was clothed.

"Hey, Doc, come on in an let's drink a Cocoler 'fo we go!" he yelled.

"Naw, let's don't take time for that, Bobby Joe! Just bring it with you," I pleaded. "Let's go get this over with. I'm worn out." I didn't even have the energy to finish the second pork chop I had brought along.

"Well, then, let me get a shirt on and make one phone call," he yelled.

"Who could he possibly be calling at eleven-thirty at night?" I mumbled.

The grimy-faced and dirty twins maintained their posts at the screen door, staring at the stranger parked halfway in their carport. The peanut-butter-and-jelly sandwiches they were smearing all over their faces and dropping on the floor, much to the delight of the dog, made them look even more dirty and sticky. I wondered what their hair smelled like.

The dog was acting as if he had not been fed in at least a week. He stood first by one twin, then the other, his eyes staring as if glued to whichever hand contained an askew sandwich. Every few seconds he would quickly lick his chops, waiting for the chance to dive upon a dropped morsel. One careless twin wasn't paying attention to where he held his snack, and in a flash, the greedy dog had snapped it from his grasp and headed for the back of the house, the wailing kid in hot pursuit, his brother right behind. But in just seconds, both twins were back at their stations at the door, mushy sandwiches in their hands, with one sandwich exhibiting some canine dental tracks.

Several more minutes passed, but Bobby Joe had not reappeared. I fiddled with the radio dial and finally located an Ohio radio station playing country music. Then the announcer came on and began trying to sell talking harmonicas. A very talented musician demonstrated how he could make the instrument actually say "momma," "water," and other alleged words.

"What a wonderful harp that thing must be," I said. "If I had it right now, I'd make it say 'Bobby Joe, come on!'" I laughed aloud at my stupid little joke, struggling to stay awake. The stone-faced little kids were not amused as they continued their staring and jelly smearing.

Finally, Bobby Joe appeared at the door, pulling a golf shirt over his head. With a wave of his hand, he dispatched the children back into the house, slipped on a juicy sandwich gob on the linoleum, then hopped down the steps into the carport. Moments later we were rushing out the highway toward the farm, the aroma of grape jelly permeating the interior of the truck.

"Tell me about it," I said.

"Well, Doc, when I was out there late this afternoon deer hunting, I noticed this old cow laying down over there where you shot that eight-pointer last year. She had her tail up, but I couldn't see her doing any straining at all."

"Did you get a rope on her or put her in the barn?" I don't know why I even asked the question, since I knew what the answer was going to be.

"Uh, naw, I didn't have a rope with me. Besides, she's just lyin' there. She won't be a minute's trouble to get a hold of."

Some folks have a hard time learning about bovine behavior. Somehow, a calving cow that is down and unable to rise can make a miraculous recovery when the veterinarian's truck motors up. This resurrection is immediately followed by a thirty-mile-an-hour sprint toward the nearest thorny thicket, cypress swamp, or pine forest, setting the scene for at least an hour's worth of cow chasing and frayed tempers.

"Bobby Joe, I swear!" I tried to say tactfully, "don't you remember what we got into here last winter chasing that old lineback Shorthorn? Remember me trying to head her off with the truck and running into that stump? This truck was in the shop for two days. And that very night you promised you'd fix a place for us to properly handle these cows."

"Yeah, Doc, and I feel real bad about it. But this cow's just a plum pet. I guarantee . . ."

My temper was slowly getting the upper hand, but I was desperately trying to keep the impending explosion at bay. So for the next few miles Bobby Joe and I argued politely about people who expect vets to rope cows in the woods at midnight and also expect it done for little or nothing. About a half mile from the pasture gate, the conversation ceased and there was an icy silence, except for the harmonica-selling guy on the radio.

Seconds later, we turned off on the south side of the road at a gap in the barbed-wire fence. Bobby Joe, tight-lipped, jumped from the truck, wrestled the contraption away from the post, then half dragged and half slung it off to the side.

"Go to the left, Doc," he yelled. "I'll just hang on the back bumper."

I wasted no time in negotiating the vehicle down the rough and holey logging road. Soon, more rusty barbed-wire fence loomed prominently in the beam of my headlights.

"Which way now?" I yelled out the window.

I received no answer, so I repeated the question. This time I heard a faint cry in the distance from where we had just driven. I quickly exited the truck and played the beam of my coon hunter's light back down the trail. Out about fifty yards or so, I spotted a staggering, frazzled Bobby Joe, hobbling in my direction. As he came closer, I could see that his formerly clean golf shirt was now smeared with mud and grass stains, and his pants were ripped over both knees.

"What happened?" I said. I was pretty sure what his answer would be.

"You tho'ed me off back there when you took off so fast," he whined.

"Are you OK? Did you hurt that leg?"

"Aw, I sprained that old knee again." He frowned as he bent over and massaged the knee slowly and carefully.

After considerable moaning, rubbing, flexing of the knee, and several steps of walking practice, he announced that he was ready to continue efforts to locate our patient.

We turned right at the fence and slowly headed the truck down through the brushy trail, going left or right according to his directions. Finally we came to a ten-foot-wide creek guarded by a high bank on the near side and honeysuckles and brambles on the far side.

"We'll have to wade across the creek right here. She's right over yonder on the other bank."

We loaded ourselves down with flashlight, calf jack, rope, bucket, and black bag, then slowly eased over the kudzued bank and into the water. As we waded across the knee-deep stream, I dipped up a half bucket for washing the cow. Once we started up the other side, we were forced to get down on all fours and then crawl on our bellies over a well-used path and through a small opening in the vines. I could tell it was a trail that raccoons and other small wildlife used to get down to the water.

Bobby Joe went first and was progressing satisfactorily in spite of issuing a series of ouches and ohs as the briars jabbed and hooked him in the back through the thin shirt. I shoved the bucket of water and calf jack ahead of me and followed, snakelike, through the crawl space. In less than a minute, I emerged from the brush, scratched from the briars and wet from the sloshing of the now mostly empty bucket.

"She's right over here, Doc," Bobby Joe declared, pointing his flashlight beam toward the base of a large pine tree.

"Where? I don't see any cow." I frowned, moving and searching with the beam of my stronger light.

We made our way to the spot where the cow had allegedly been patiently waiting for us, but there was no sign.

"She was right here less than six hours ago. I'm almost positive this is the place."

"Almost positive! You mean you're not even sure she was here?"

"Well, it looks different at night and—"

"That's your trouble, Bobby Joe, you don't think," I exclaimed, less tactfully than before. "You expect somebody else to come roaring out here and tromp the woods all night trying to find a lost cow that you should have haltered or brought to a catch pen." By that time I had violated the "be courteous to everyone" rule to such a degree that I was hopelessly mired in my own temper and self-pity.

We stared at each other in the dark, each training his light on the other. Our clothes were torn and covered with dirt, mud, and grass stains. My arms were bleeding from the briar scratches, and three-fourths of my body was wet from the encounter with the creek and the sloshing pail of water. At that moment I questioned whether I was in the right line of work. Perhaps it would have been better if I had selected an easier job—like working in a dynamite factory or cleaning out smokestacks.

I was so mad, I could have bitten a tenpenny nail in half. However, I helped Bobby Joe search for our patient by rummaging through thickets and pine-tree tops that had been left by the pulpwood cutters. But after about ten minutes we had not seen the first sign of the elusive cow, nor had we seen any of the remainder of the herd. It seemed that we had walked at least a mile.

"Bobby Joe," I hollered, "this is crazy! We'll never find her tonight. Let's go home."

There was no reply, except for the whine of the wind in the pines. I stood, not moving a muscle, hoping to hear something, maybe a rustling of bushes or the snapping of a twig. Again I yelled, but again heard no answer. I realized I was out there all alone with no idea how to get back to my truck.

I plopped down under a huge pine tree to rest and think, hoping that Bobby Joe might stumble back that way. Confused and disoriented, I had no idea which direction was north. It was cloudy—and more fog was creeping in.

After feeling sorry for myself for several minutes, the anger began to subside and survival instincts began to take over.

"OK," I reasoned, "I know that I'm on the south side of an east-to-west highway, and it's the only highway around for miles. Sooner or later I'll hear a vehicle come along, and then I'll just walk in that direction. When I come to the creek, I'll go downstream until I find where we crossed earlier. No, I'll need to go upstream, I think. No, I'll just go straight for the highway, find the gap, and then come back to the truck." I was still confused, but more confident than I had been a few minutes earlier. I was getting a little concerned that Jan might worry. She knew how long it took me to deliver a calf or do a cesarian.

Soon, I heard the far-off roar of an eighteen-wheeler as it made its late-night run on the lonely highway, so I immediately started in that direction. When I finally intersected with the creek, I challenged the brushy bank, waded across just as before, and continued my beeline trek toward the highway, still carrying my stainless steel bucket in one hand and calf jack over the other shoulder.

Sometime later, I found the highway right-of-way fence line, climbed over, and gleefully ran onto the blacktopped roadway. It seemed like an old friend. Even though I was still stranded out in the middle of nowhere, I wasn't lost anymore. Now I would simply head west and hope that I would come upon the gap entrance, then follow the trail to my truck.

As I walked and worried, I heard the sound of a vehicle coming from the direction of what I hoped was town. When it came nearer, it began to slow down as if it were going to stop.

"That looks like Jan's car!" I said to myself when I finally turned and gazed into the dimmed headlights of the Chevy station wagon.

"John, why are you walking? What has happened to your clothes?" It was Jan! Why was she out here?

"Where's Bobby Joe?" cried another voice, this time from the passenger seat. It was Emma Lou, Bobby's big, muscular wife. "He's gone and got himself lost in the woods again, hasn't he?" She snorted with contempt.

I crawled into the backseat among several children of the two families. Some were asleep in the turned-down third-seat area, but others, including the twins, were wide awake. I noticed that they were eating peanut-butter-and-jelly sandwiches. I wondered if they were the same sandwiches they had been sharing with the dog some hours ago.

While I humbly confessed to our predicament, we motored a half mile or so and turned in at the entrance.

"Go right, Jan," ordered Emma Lou a few yards later. "We'll go up to the old homeplace and ring that old dinner bell. I always do that when Bobby Joe is out here hunting and I need him for something. He'll be here in less than thirty minutes."

Emma Lou pulled viciously on the bell chain, and the bell peeled forth its loud penetrating message into the foggy night. Sleeping children bolted upright in terror from the sudden racket but were soon soothed by the grown-ups in the car.

"Now we'll wait," announced Emma Lou as she sat back down in the car. They explained how Emma Lou had gotten worried about us and called Jan. They decided to come to the farm just to be sure we weren't in trouble. More small talk followed, and someone started to play with the radio. The same Ohio guy was still trying to sell the same harmonica. Apparently, I dozed off, because the next thing I remember was Bobby Joe crawling into the car on the opposite side.

"Doc, you left your switch on in your truck and your battery is dead," he said. "When I couldn't find you I was going to drive the truck up here and ring the bell. I figured you had gotten lost."

"And you weren't?"

"Naw, I was just looking for my cow."

"Did you find her?"

"Oh, sure. She already had the calf, and they're both fine. While I was here, though, I thought I'd do what you said and check 'em all out. I found a calf that's really lame and I thought since you were here, just maybe we could catch him and see what's wrong. He's just a pet . . ."

I don't recall the exact words I used at that point. But they had something to do with him being a thoughtless person who shouldn't own livestock or have friends to abuse. I remember requesting that he find himself another veterinarian because this one had taken his last dose of abuse from Bobby Joe Henley.

We left the truck in the woods and headed home. I would get Raymond Miller, my service station buddy, to go with me in the morning to pick it up. Bobby Joe and I argued all the way to town while our wives sat quietly, their lips pursed.

"Send me a bill if I owe you anything," sneered Bobby Joe as he and his family exited the car at their house.

"You'll get a bill all right," I declared. "Just don't call me again."

"Honey, I've never seen you this angry," Jan said softly. "It's not good for you. You might have a stroke."

Bobby Joe failed to respond to the one-hundred-dollar statement that I sent him. I said nothing, nor wrote nasty notes on the following monthly statements. However, when he opened up a new TV store in Meridian six months later, I was there for the grand opening. After looking around and pricing all the merchandise, I selected a real nice twenty-four-inch set in a beautiful walnut cabinet. I gave my business card to the salesman.

"Please deliver this one to my house," I said. "And tell Bobby Joe to send me a bill if I owe him anything."

They did, and he didn't!

Months later, after building a nice corral and using the services of my veterinary colleagues in Meridian, Bobby Joe asked me to make a farm call. We buried the hatchet that day, and our mini-fracas was never mentioned again. I think he couldn't afford to pay the fees of those "city" vets, who charged by the hour. They must have made good money waiting on Bobby Joe to corral his stock.

Twelve

Buck Hay and family were an outstanding dairy farm family in the county to the north, and were good clients of our practice. Somehow, Buck came into possession of several nice Duroc sows, but he had no place to put them except in a wooded lot that he temporarily used as an overflow pen for weaned heifers. It wasn't long before the sows presented Buck with an immense number of baby pigs, the vast majority of which survived and did well.

Now, as anyone who has ever produced pork knows, there is at least one important veterinary matter that must be attended to before pigs can be sold at the market for top dollar. I'm talking about the castration of the males, which keeps the pork you buy in the supermarket from being tough and pungent with boar aroma. Obviously, it is easier to take care of this little matter when the pigs are small. However, Buck was so busy with the dairy farm that this important swine task was not his first priority, even though I mentioned it to him several times on my visits to the dairy.

"When you gonna cut those pigs?" I asked one day. "They're growing like weeds."

"Aw, we'll do it one day real soon," he replied.

"How about right now? I"ve got a few minutes."

"Can't. Got an appointment to get my hair done."

Of all the dairy farmers I have ever known, Buck is the only one to have a standing appointment to have his hair coiffed. I will admit that his hair always looked nice, it's just that you don't expect to see a real farmer out baling hay or spreading manure with a hair net over his head. I had teased Buck a little too hard about his beauty salon visits, where Mr. LeRoi was his regular hairdresser. He took issue with my kidding one day, so I said nothing further about hair. It was obvious that he enjoyed getting his hair done.

Finally, after a month of November and December rain, we were able to find a day that was too wet, too cold, and too uncomfortable to do anything with cows and crops. It was Christmas Eve when we headed for the porkery with Everett, Buck's muscle-bound handyman, and John, a veterinary student who had dropped by to work with me for a couple of days. I was confident that they would both make good hog catchers and holders, but I wondered if they could tolerate the cold and occasional drizzle that made the thirty-eight degrees seem much colder. Southerners aren't built to tolerate cold weather.

Buck arrived moments later with the feed buckets, yelled two or three times toward the woods, and tossed an appetizer of shelled corn into a couple of the feeding troughs. Immediately I heard muffled gruntings and the sounds of hooves slopping through mud. Suddenly there were hogs of every breed and color heading in our direction, obviously delighted about the possibility of a mid-morning snack. They were all uniform in size, but I was surprised at how large they had become. I counted about twenty-five males, more or less, and I estimated they each weighed 150 pounds. This was not going to be easy. What would have taken twenty minutes four months earlier was now going to take most of the morning. It was obvious that general anesthesia was going to be necessary.

Minutes later, Buck was trying to entice my potential patients into a small catch pen that he had constructed. We formed a human wall, angling out from the pen, then scurried in behind the assemblage with hog wire gates as the hogs scrambled and sloshed through the mud toward the shelled corn Buck was dumping in the wooden troughs. We must have been lucky that morning, because swine are usually too smart to be driven.

"Buck, we let 'em get too big," I declared. "This job's gonna take all morning. You got anything else pushing?" I started to ask about hair appointments but bit my tongue.

"I got pert near all day. Just as long as I get through in time to milk, feed the calves, the dry cows, the heifers, and the bull, then clean up the parlor, put out some rat poison in the feed room, and eat supper," he droned. I was getting exhausted just listening to the list of his never-ending chores.

The plan of action was to put several of the hogs down the narrow alleyway that Buck had built, catch one at a time with a nose snare, inject a dosage of barbiturate anesthesia into an ear vein, then, when the patient collapsed, have the two assistants drag him outside into the lot. Soon we had six large boars lined up side by side and snoring. While Everett and Buck were bringing more patients into the crude anesthetic chamber, John went to work scrubbing up surgical sites with surgical soap and restraining hind legs just in case the anesthesia was too light. A lightly sleeping boar hog shouldn't be kicking his rear legs while the veterinary surgeon is using a sharp scalpel in the vicinity.

In spite of freezing hands and a steady drizzle, the task soon became routine. After each boar was altered, the incision was sprayed with an antibiotic and each patient was injected with an antibiotic and tetanus antitoxin. Of course, our coveralls were wet and covered with mud, and as expected, there was a problem with one hard-core resister. He had apparently decided he wanted no part of the surgical procedure and had somehow evaded capture by scaling the short fence and retreating back down the hill into the swamp, where the mud and mire were the most intense. After several chases back and forth from swamp to pen, the aggravation index of all participants had risen several notches.

Suddenly, a grim-faced Buck beelined toward the escapee, who was taking a much-needed breather in the deepest and gummiest part of the lot. When he came to within about ten feet of the porker, Buck made a flying tackle and landed atop the surprised pig.

The resulting chaos was worthy of national television coverage. The loudmouthed shoat was expressing his sentiments by emitting squealing sounds several decibels higher than those of any of his associates when they were caught. It was enough to wake the dead! In fact, some of the earlier anesthetized patients were shakily raising their groggy heads, eyes half open and tongues lolled out, trying to determine the source of the ear-piercing eruption.

"Hep me! Y'all hep me with this fool!" blubbered poor old Buck. He was spewing and spitting as his open lips scooped up large quantities of hog lot goo. The panic-stricken animal was straining mightily to extricate himself from the grasp of a determined Buck, who was now being dragged helplessly along through the mud. In spite of their giggling, Everett and John piled on the wallowing duo. In the process of trying to jump and run through the mud, I lost both of my knee-high rubber boots.

Trying to hold a syringe full of deadly anesthetic high above my head with one hand and help keep a large swine pinned to the ground with cold bare feet and the other hand wasn't an easy task. However, I was soon able to get the ear cleaned well enough to find an ear vein and make the injection. In seconds the squealer was quiet and sleeping soundly, and then the surgery was completed.

When it was all over, we stood staring at the scene for several moments. Never had I seen such a sight.

There were twenty-seven sleeping pigs, several of whom were starting to come out of their anesthetic trances. A couple actually stood and staggered around a bit, only to go back down for another snooze. The human beings were almost unrecognizable, covered from head to toe in red mud, hog lot excrement, and occasional splotches of blood. Buck's Funk's G Hybrid seed corn cap had flown off his head in the wrestling match and now laid half submerged in a wallow. All that was needed was several fires burning, with smoke slowly spiraling upward, and the scene would have been reminiscent of a Civil War movie, not long after the Yankees had marched through the farmsteads outside Atlanta.

I don't remember who started laughing first, but it wasn't long before we were pointing fingers and chuckling heartily at our appearances. We were also laughing at how ridiculous the entire situation would have looked to a phantom passerby. Grown men wallowing around in the mud with a bunch of swine, then giggling like schoolkids, all done to make some family's breakfast ham and sausage taste better, and nobody even said a thank-you.

Five minutes later, we were hosing ourselves off in the cow holding area next to the milking parlor. We were covered with so much mud, it was like taking a shower with clothes on. I was surprised to see Buck strip down to his Fruit of the Looms. Even they were soaked with mud.

"Buck, this was fun and all, but it would suit me not to go through this again," I said.

"Doc, this won't ever have to be done on this farm again, I guarantee."

A month and a half later Buck sold all the pigs we had worked on, even the sows. After paying my substantial bill, he made a nice profit off the free pigs, but never again accepted any more donations of swine. I was glad because I didn't want to go through another marathon hog castration.

"Some people just aren't cut out to be pork producers," Buck told me later. "And I'm one of 'em."

I suppose he thought getting up at three o'clock every morning of the year and working with dairy cows until eleven o'clock at night was an easier life. Nothing is easy for a farmer.

Thirteen

I t was a few minutes before midnight on New Year's Eve at the VFW Hall. Jan and I were having a great time dancing to an old-time band that specialized in Glenn Miller tunes. The Butler Cotillion Club held dances two or three times a year, and Jan was thrilled when she found out about them. She dearly loves to dance, having inherited the dancing gene from her parents, who were affectionately referred to by their friends as Fred and Ginger. They occasionally made the 150-mile trip down from Birmingham to attend the dances and help with the setup work.

Unfortunately, I was not as fond of dancing as Jan. My parents had been against dancing, probably because they assumed liquor would be consumed at dancing parties. The sinful image of boys sneaking out to theirs cars and trucks and taking swigs from bottles in slim paper sacks had been prominently etched on my youthful brain. All the preachers of my youth ranted regularly about the evils of dancing. At twelve, I didn't understand exactly why, but if the preacher said it was so, it must be the truth, since he seemed to know a lot more about that sort of thing than anybody else. Usually when he ranted about the evils of dancing, he also threw in card playing, smoking, and Sunday baseball just for good measure.

But now Jan and I were the co-presidents of the club, and we had to do much of the work, from getting the band and finding a suitable place for the event to arranging for the snacks and setting up the tables and chairs. Then, after it was all over, we helped take down tables and chairs, clean up, and in case there were participants too beverage impaired to drive, make arrangements to get them home.

As we cavorted with our friends on this night, I heard a familiar voice call my name from the vicinity of the front door.

"Oh, no," I said to Jan, whirling to put my back to the door. "That's Carney Sam Jenkins over there behind me, isn't it?"

"Yep, sure is," she said with a sigh. "Why don't you go hide behind the piano."

But it was too late. He had spied me in the semidarkness and was shuffling our way. He was ill dressed for a big dance, uniformed in a red checkered flannel shirt, khaki pants, engineer's boots, and Funk's G Hybrid seed cap.

"Carney! What are you doing here, boy?" I exclaimed. "I didn't know you were a dancer. Is your missus with you?"

"Evenin', Doc. How're you, Miz Doc. No, but she says howdy," he said as he took off his cap in respect to the lady present.

"Doc, my boy Werner Fred has this old mare we call Dixie, and she's been hurtin' off and on all night. I've been foolin' with her myself, and I just can't get her to respond. Reckon there's any way I could get you to run out there and take a look at her?"

"Has she got the colic?" I asked. He followed Jan and me as we waltzed in place. I wasn't looking forward to sitting up the rest of the night with a very sick mare, but at least I wouldn't have to shuffle my feet around the floor anymore. Jan never seemed to tire of dancing, but my legs began to cramp up after a couple of lóng hours.

"Yeah, that's right, she's been trying to lay down and wallow, and she's bloated up pretty good. I've drenched her with chinaberry tea, turpentine, coal oil, and I've even tried mine and your Choctaw County Colic Cocktail that we mixed up that night at Miss Ruby's place. 'Course, I put the turpentine on her navel first, but it wouldn't draw, so that eliminates the possibility of the kidney colic." It sounded as if he had just about run the gamut on the area's equine home remedies.

Jan was beginning to drum her fingers on my shoulder and her lips were beginning to purse, a sure sign of growing impatience. She didn't care much for the way Carney used me, calling for help late at night after he had already exhausted all his questionable treatments. Even though he was a homemade vet, she felt that he should have to pass state board exams and pay license fees, dues, and malpractice insurance just like her husband. But now, people were staring at the three of us as we half danced and tried to converse above the singer as she neared the end of "The Tennessee Waltz." They all knew exactly what was going on; they just didn't know what species of animal was sick.

"Look, let's go over to that table in the corner, have a glass of punch, and decide what we're gonna do," I suggested. Since Jan's car was in the shop, we had come to the dance in my truck. Now I needed to figure out how she was going to get home and get the baby-sitter delivered to hers.

While Carney and I sipped on our punch, Jan joined some of our cohorts and left us to discuss the sick mare. Apparently, Werner Fred and Tootie Turner had taken Carney's old pickup just across the Mississippi state line and purchased a load of alfalfa hay as sort of a combination Christmas and New Year's gift for Dixie and the other horses. Dixie had probably eaten too much new hay, which was much richer than the old fescue and bermuda grass that she was used to. Now she had a bad case of abdominal cramping at the very least, and perhaps something much worse.

"I've got to go see about this horse," I told Jan. "You can ride home with Loren and Geraldine and they can take the baby-sitter home." It wasn't the first time they had helped us in similar situations. She didn't say a word, but her pursed lips and glaring eyes said it for her.

As I followed Carney out to his place, I thought about all the times Jan and I had missed parties, school functions, church events, and similar happenings because of conflicting animal emergencies. I appreciated the way she understood the nature of our profession, even though she thought that I should do a better job of educating the animals' owners in preventive medicine, and thus eliminate some of the late-night calls.

There was dim light coming from a corner stall in the barn, so I knew Werner Fred was sitting up with Dixie, nervously waiting for his father to return with the doctor.

The mare was lying quietly on the stall floor, Werner Fred kneeling at her head, slowly rubbing the side of her neck. She was covered with sweat lather, her abdomen was bloated, and there were abrasions and large bruises on the poor animal's head where she had been flopping around in pain. The hard clay gave evidence of numerous back-and-forth hoof scars, and the aromas of turpentine, horse sweat, and good alfalfa hay permeated the barn air.

"Daddy, she finally got easy 'bout an hour ago, but now she won't get up," Werner Fred said slowly.

When I examined the patient, I found that her gums were a murky blue-purple, her ears ice cold, her pulse thready and about 120 per minute. She was in deep and irreversible shock, probably from a ruptured stomach or some portion of the intestines. It was all over for her, but how was I going to break the news to her master that she would surely be dead by morning? I looked at Carney and shook my head.

I wondered if somewhere in my training I had missed the information on how to diplomatically deliver the awful news to animal owners that their dog or horse is not going to survive. It is a dreaded and difficult task for me, especially if that owner is a youngster and is unaware how ill the animal really is.

Werner Fred didn't realize the mare had become quiet and apparently easy because of the severe shock. I suspected that Carney knew all along that the mare wouldn't survive, so he came for me to take care of the hard part.

"Carney, would you get me a bucket of warm water from the house?" I asked. I knew he would have to heat the water in a kettle on the stove and then dilute the hot water with hand-drawn well water to make it just right. Actually, I didn't need any water; I just wanted to get him out of the stall so I could figure out how to tell the boy about his dying horse.

"She's been a good old mare hasn't she? How old is she?"

"About twenty," Werner Fred said without hesitation. "I ride her every afternoon when I get home from school."

"Yeah, I see y'all together when I pass by. Werner Fred, I've got to tell you some bad news, and I think you probably already know what has happened to Dixie. The reason she's not in pain anymore is because her organs inside have just given out. She's just too sick to make it, and there's no medicine we can give her that will save her." That explanation was obviously not technically correct, but I felt it was acceptable in the present situation.

The young teenager was tough as nails, but when he looked up at me there were big tears in his eyes. He was trying hard to hold them back in front of me, but his grief was just too much.

"The right thing for us to do now is to give her a shot that will just put her to sleep, then we'll know for sure that she won't suffer," I said slowly but firmly. He was sobbing now, but continued to rub his pal's cold and clammy skin.

"Whatever you think is best, Doc, but maybe I better go and ask Daddy," he sobbed.

"Why don't I go and talk with him, since I need to go to the truck anyway," I said. It was also a good excuse to leave the two together for a few more minutes.

When I stepped up onto the back porch, there sat Carney in an old straight-back chair, staring into the darkness. The tough old buzzard was crying.

"Doc, that's why I wanted you to come out here," he said, his voice quivering. "I just couldn't tell the boy that his hoss was gonna die. You're a heap better than me at tellin' folks real nice like that bad things are gonna happen. You know yourself that boy out there will believe whatever you say." I wanted to tell him the truth, that at such a time I always felt the lack of proper words and wished that someone more articulate could relieve me of that duty. But it wasn't the proper time.

"If it's OK with you, I'll go put her down. You do know what's happened inside, don't you?"

"Yeah, I know. You go do what has to be done. I'll get the neighbors in the morning to help me move and bury her," he said sadly.

"OK, I'll talk to you tomorrow or the next day," I said, walking away. Then I heard him giggle.

"Doc, you look like a dern penguin in that dancin' suit."

"Uh huh, I know it. I better get it off before I get turpentine all over it."

"Or else Miz Doc'll whup me and you both," he said.

Later, with coveralls over the "penguin suit," I drew up the deadly injection into a horse-size syringe, Werner Fred looking on with interest. Then he insisted on helping me inject the overdose of euthanasia solution into Dixie's vein. Within a couple of minutes, she had quit breathing and her heart stopped. The young man broke the silence.

"Doc, thanks for what you did, 'cause I know she's a lot better off now. But I'll always be grateful that she lived here on this farm as long as she did. I bet we've rode together a thousand miles." I'm sure it was more than that, though. Dixie was that boy's best friend.

Driving back home that night, I thought about the role veterinarians often play in dealing with hopeless cases, such as Dixie. More and more, I was learning that my profession was a people business as well as an animal one and that the way veterinarians deal with people has everything to do with whether or not their practices are a success. A kind word, an expression of encouragement, and a heartfelt compliment often mean almost as much as a masterful diagnosis or successful drug therapy. I've tried to remember that when the phone rings at midnight.

Back at the VFW Hall, the cleanup committee was hard at work. Tables and chairs had been stacked, the borrowed ones loaded onto pickup trucks to be delivered back to the church and high school. I grabbed a mop and joined in the fun with the swabbing crew.

"This place smells like champagne," I remarked.

"For some reason, all I can smell is turpentine. I betcha some fool knocked over a gallon of it back in the storeroom," said the mopper next to me.

"Uh huh, I wouldn't be surprised. Why don't I go check . . ."

Fourteen

I t was a cold January morning when I neared the Fowler place in south Choctaw for my second appointment of the morning. On the right side of the road I could see the small, state-of-the-art, barbed-wire corral, which covered an area some twenty by forty feet, complete with the obligatory four-foot-high stump. The corral was about half full with some twenty crossbred Hereford cows.

"This won't take long," I said to myself. "I'll be on my way in an hour." But I didn't see the pickup trucks that were usually there, pulled off on the sides of the road. "Well, I guess they're at the house," I mused.

On the other side of the road was an old but well-maintained gabled house. With such a nice house I wondered why they couldn't have had a better place to work their cows. When I turned into the driveway, there were no trucks, but a fortyish, chunky man almost fell off the steps as he descended from the screened porch. Then he reeled off the yard path into the gray bermuda grass of the lawn as he made his way toward my truck. He was a healthy six-footer, but I realized that he was not nearly as plump as I had first thought. He was wrapped up in so many coats, vests, and other foul weather paraphernalia that he appeared bloated. Then I saw the gallon Coca-Cola syrup jug he was holding with his left hand. He had his fore-finger stuck through the loop at the top, and I knew it must contain some of his own homemade moonshine liquor. I also knew that I was in trouble, because it's not easy to work cattle with a drunk in the way. He fell up against the truck and shoved the jug through the open window, sloshing its reeking contents over both my clothes and the interior of the truck. I remember noticing a dead, or per-haps happily unconscious, spider floating around in the crystal-clear liquid.

"Have a drank!" he ordered, slurring the words. He issued the command with his face not a foot away from mine, but his eyes were trying to focus somewhere in the vicinity of the lower left corner of the windshield. I had been in Choctaw County long enough to rec-ognize that according to the "slur index," he had been hitting the jug for about an hour and a half, which meant he had gotten an early start since it was then about nine A.M. I knew we'd have to work fast before he went down.

"Naw sir, I don't think so. Feel a little cold coming over me this morning," I replied.

"Thish stuff here'll fix you rat up. Drank sooome!" The breath fumes from Fowler and his jug were bothersome, but I reckoned that since I would be hounded all morning until I had a sip, I might as well go ahead and get it over with.

"OK, but let me get out of the truck," I begged. He bumped his head as he backed out of my window.

"Are you about ready to get those cows tested?" I asked, taking the jug and cleaning its mouth with the sleeve of my flannel shirt. I shuddered thinking about what I was about to do, but like it was castor oil, I quickly grabbed the jug's glass ring by my right index finger, heaved it up to my right shoulder, and put my lips close to the opening. I almost gagged when I sniffed Fowler's tobacco juice leavings around the rim.

"Is that your dog over there? Looks like he might have whip-worms," I declared. While he tried to find and focus his eyes on the dog, I clenched my lips together and turned up the jug and held it there until he looked back at me, then I returned the jug to his wait-ing hands. Then he repeated the same motion, only this time several large bubbles wobbled upward through the potent liquid.

"Aaaah," he whispered, some of the juice dribbling off his numbed chin.

"Uh huh," I said, shaking my head back and forth. "That's a good batch." My lips were on fire, perhaps as much from the tobacco as from the liquor. I knew that I'd surely be plagued with a couple of fever blisters from the event. But none of the potent stuff had entered my mouth. It brought back the memory of my first and only encounter with a large swallow of Mr. Kent Farris's liquor several months before, which I was convinced had permanently damaged my poor throat.

"It's amazing what I'll do for public relations," I thought to myself.

Ten minutes later we were standing in the middle of the corral, my well-used lariat in hand, exchanging wary glances with the cows. After a minute or so of stare-down time, I finally let the loop fly, and proudly watched as it encircled the neck of the first cow.

"I'm gettin' pretty good at this ropin' thing," I thought to myself. "Maybe I'll just join up with the rodeo." I must have absorbed some of the white lightning through the sensitive skin of my lips.

I quickly tossed the tail end of the rope over to Fowler, who fum-bled around with it briefly but finally accomplished his job of loop-ing his end around the old stump in the center of the small pen.

"PULL! PULL HARD!" I yelled, trying to be heard over the routine objections and bellowing of the patient. Even though I had picked out a wimpy-looking six-hundred-pound first calf heifer to start with, she was giving a good account of herself. But she was no match for her muscular owner, who, in spite of his condition, had her pulled up securely to the stump in seconds. The venipuncture, ear tagging, and recording of information were easy, just as long as I avoided the flying kicks, slinging heads, and sashaying hind ends, and kept an eye peeled on the bull, who wasn't thrilled about one of his harem's being handled in such an impolite manner.

The most difficult part of my job was keeping the flying chunks, gobs, and specks of cow manure and other foreign matter off the official, white, brucellosis test sheets and trying to maintain all five copies and the four sheets of carbon paper in their correct positions. The official, government-approved, laboratory personnel in Auburn were right persnickety about those charts, and I continually received warning letters about the soiled condition of my test charts. One curt memo carried the initials "BNL," which signified Dr. B. N. Lauderdale, the head man in Montgomery. I didn't know much about him, but I had gathered that he was the Bear Bryant of blood testing and the mere mention of his name should cause veterinarians to tremble with fear.

I tried to be neat as I furiously scribbled numbers on the test chart. Suddenly, a chestnut-size spherule of green fecal material whistled past my right ear and splattered on the chart, completely obliterating Fowler's middle initial, his mailing address, and the identification numbers of the first two cows. I quickly flicked the smelly stuff off with the back of my hand, but that left a huge, unofficial light green stain that appeared to have been smeared there by the brush of some perverted artist.

With pursed lips and renewed resolution, I hurled the rope over the head of my next victim and tossed it over to Fowler. But Fowler was now on the ground and out like a light, his head resting comfortably against the gnarly stump. I observed a wry smile on his unconscious lips and then hastily retrieved the free end of the rope, which was by then wiggling crazily among the dead, thorny jimson-weeds of the corral.

In addition to leaving me without a helper, the drunk had collapsed up against my restraint stump. If I looped my rope around it now, the rope would also encircle Fowler, and the cow and I could rope-squeeze the very life out of his sorry carcass. The notion did appeal to me, but the possibility of a life sentence without parole in the Alabama State Penitentiary appealed to me a lot less. I figured the cow would be acquitted for being even stupider than me.

I scanned the posts on the periphery of the corral while trying to keep the cow off my downed client. Finally, I selected one of the biggest ones that seemed to be solidly tamped into the earth. It miraculously held the jumping cow, so I completed the procedure and then returned to see if I could find a way to awaken my comatose assistant. Calling his name was useless, and a couple of slaps to his jaws had no effect except to produce a pitiful moan. I jumped the fence and crossed the gravel road to the house. An elderly lady, whom I assumed to be the drunk's mother, met me at the door. I could hear strange piano music coming from a room on the right, which I assumed to be the parlor, and I smelled dinner cooking. I recognized the aromas of country cured ham frying and pinto beans boiling with a big chunk of sowbelly. My salivary glands began to work again.

"Ma'am, Mr. Fowler's kinda taken ill out in the corral, and I need some help to get him out of there. I'm afraid the cows are gonna step on him," I said. Of course, he wouldn't have been aware of it if they did.

The lady peered out over my shoulder and spied the man, some fifty yards away. She sighed and shook her head from side to side as if this had happened before.

"Thank you for telling me about poor little Bobby. Do you reckon you and the piano tuner in yonder could get him over here to his room?" That explained the horrendous sounds coming from the parlor.

Minutes later, the piano man and I were half dragging and half lifting little Bobby up onto the porch and then squeezing ourselves sideways through halls and doors until we finally flopped him down on his single bed. I coveted his expensive boots as I unlaced them, and the piano man made some complimentary remark about the quality of his down-filled vest. The lady, who admitted to being his mother, was also unbuttoning things and smoothing out his hair in between wringing her hands. Finally, she gave in to her frustration and cried out.

"I just don't know what's gotten into Bobby. That's already three times this week!" And it was only Wednesday!

With the help of the piano tuner. I finished the cows without any other major problems. The mailman stopped his delivery long enough to watch us catch three or four cows and take the samples, then asked the usual questions and made the usual astute observation.

"What are y'all doin'?"

"Don't them big needles hurt?"

"Them cows don't much like what y'all are doin' to 'em, do they?"

I answered his questions as best I could between grunts, groans, bellows, and yells. The soft hands and muscles of the piano man weren't much help, but he tried hard, and he was a sight better than my previous assistant. We had a nice conversation about the vast difference in our vocations and how little people know about the work that others do.

"Y'all boys come on in here and eat now," exclaimed Mrs. Fowler some time later. "I know it's barely eleven o'clock, but I've got plates ready for you, so come on and eat it before it gets cold." We found such a gesture hard to turn down, and after a rather long premeal prayer by the piano man, we were soon chowing down on good country food and sopping our plates with corn bread and biscuits. In typical country hostess fashion, the nice lady hovered over the set table, fiddling with the dishes and urging us to eat more, saying she hoped the food was fit to eat, such as it was. It was fittin', and it would have been fittin' even for royalty, perhaps even for Dr. B. N. Lauderdale, the King of the Blood Testers!

Unfortunately, I had more herds lined up for testing that morning, and I was about an hour behind. But the next farm was only a few miles away down the creek. When I arrived at the Horace Dunagin farm there were a couple of old trucks parked near an old but seemingly solid barn. I backed in among the other randomly parked vehicles. Three overall-clad men, two with canes, slowly walked out of the barn hall and exchanged pleasantries. The prospects for assistance with catching the cows there seemed rather bleak.

"I apologize for being late this morning. Took a little longer than I figured back up at the Fowlers' place," I said.

"Yes sir, the mailman said he'd seen you and the preacher up there working Bobby's cows," Mr. Horace replied. The piano tuner hadn't said anything about being a preacher, but after that agonizingly long blessing I should have guessed.

"Bobby under the weather again?" the oldest man asked.

"Yes sir, I don't think he felt very good today," I answered. The men glanced at each other knowingly.

"Well, we'd have been glad to help, but you never know what condition he's gonna be in, and it's kinda embarrassing to be around him when he's havin' one of them spells," said Mr. Horace. "He got bad messed up in Korea, you know." Well, I was glad to know there was a reason for his "spells."

"Where are the cows?" I was ready to get on with it.

"I got 'em all hemmed up in these stalls in the barn. About forty of 'em," he answered. "I thought maybe you had a chute contraption on wheels that we could back up the front door and run 'em through there."

"Yes sir, I do have one, but it's in the shop getting repaired. Some wild Brahmas over in Mississippi tore it up last week," I replied, looking over his shoulder and into a stall packed full of cattle. "I'll just wade in the stall amongst 'em here and you can hand me my stuff as I need it."

When one is young, strong, eager, and hungry, one does things that aren't considered safe by normal people. I had found that I could walk into a stall packed with a carpet of wall-to-wall cattle, grab one with a halter or nose tongs, get the blood sample from the jugular vein, then release her before a full-blown fracas developed. You just go with the flow, as if trapped in the midst of a huge crowd leaving the Auburn-Alabama football game. Still, there's the constant danger of getting your feet stomped, and the ground is usually muddy. And if you lost your footing and disappeared underneath the herd, you might never be seen again.

An hour and a half later the job was done. But when I emerged from the last stall, the men were amused by my appearance.

"Doc, you look like a janitor in a dung factory," declared one of them. Everybody had a nice laugh, including me. Fortunately, I had clean coveralls in the truck and Mr. Dunagin was on his way with a couple of buckets of water. I would be clean before I arrived at the next farm.

"I respect what you do for a livin', young man," the older man hoarsely whispered. "But I wouldn't have yo' job for no kind of money!"

Working with the brucellosis program in the 1950s and 1960s was hard and dirty work. I didn't realize it at the time, but it taught me valuable lessons about how to deal with people.

The most important thing is a well-developed sense of humor!

Fifteen

There are some people north of the Mason-Dixon line who think that the weather in the South is always just peachy, but it is very likely that those folks never had to vaccinate a drove of hogs against cholera in the middle of January.

It was ten degrees above zero the morning I was called to a large swine farm where several 150-pound hogs had been found dead that morning. When I arrived the wind was slicing out of the northwest at twenty to forty miles an hour and the humidity must have been at least 80 percent. I was staggered to see some fifty frozen swine carcasses littering the lots. There were at least another fifty that were visibly sick, standing still, and looking at the ground as if in deep concentration. When prodded, they were reluctant to move. They were in the "thinking phase" of cholera and were at death's door. The other two-hundred-plus head seemed healthy, but we all knew some of them were incubating the disease and would meet the same fate as their thinking associates.

My veterinary school professors and people who knew swine always said that hogs were not supposed to think, and when one was seen with his head down as if in deep thought, he had hog cholera for sure. On this cold day everything pointed to cholera as the problem, but I still had to perform a couple of postmortem exams to be sure. I dreaded that job on such a cold day and on a frozen carcass, but I knew it had to be done.

The owners, commonly referred to as the Pate brothers, were asking lots of questions and making comments about the problem as we moved to the first pig, a beautiful specimen of pork on the hoof worth a hundred dollars just hours ago, now fit only for the incinerator or deep burying with lots of lime.

"Why didn't we vaccinate them pigs, Jake?" complained his brother Luke. "We've lost our hind ends on this batch."

"I don't know why. Why didn't we, Doc?" asked Jake.

"I mentioned to y'all that cholera was around. Remember that day at the feed store when you were getting your buckshot and hunting licenses. You were going deer hunting when you should have been vaccinating for cholera," I said. I didn't want to say "I told you so," but it was important for them to understand how they could have prevented such a catastrophe. A dollar or so per hog is a lot cheaper than dead hogs everywhere. They just shook their heads in disbelief as I drew my necropsy knife back and forth over the whetstone.

My sharp knife and the threat of frostbite helped me make quick work of the first pig. Kneeling uncomfortably in the cloven-hoofed tracks in the frozen mud added to my speed. I sliced through the cartilaginous attachment where ribs meet sternum, then peeled the skin and muscles backward all the way to the pubic bone, then laid the viscera out of the abdominal cavity, looking for the classic lesions of cholera. Petechial hemorrhages of the kidney, commonly referred to as "turkey egg kidney," then petechia of the urinary bladder mucosa, and peripheral hemorrhages of the lymph nodes were all there, just like I had read about in *Textbook of Swine Diseases*. The one lesion that had been routinely burned in our student minds was that turkey egg kidney.

"The pathognomonic lesion of hog cholera is the turkey egg kidney," lectured all the large animal clinicians. It seemed to be one thing where they all agreed.

A second pig was likewise opened up, and it mirrored the lesions of the first. The findings were evidence enough to make a diagnosis of cholera.

"What we gone do now, Doc, just let 'em die?" one of the brothers asked, warming his hands over the old tire fire that he had made while I was doing the dirty work. The hot fire felt so good I could have stood there for an hour. But after five minutes of trying to avoid the irritating dense tire smoke that followed me wherever I moved, I decided it was time to tend to business.

"The only thing we can do is catch every last one of them and give an injection of anticholera serum. We'll save some, but you'll still have a good many deaths, depending on where they are in the incubation period. Since you have them in batches, that might be an advantage because some won't have picked up the virus yet."

After some discussion, including the cost and expected benefit, the decision was made to go forward with the vaccinations. It meant that every hog would need to be caught and injected at least twice, maybe more, depending upon its size. Since the dose of serum was proportional to the weight of the animal, several injection sites would be required. We would be injecting behind the ear, in the lower flank, and in the loose skin behind the armpit. Just catching the 150-pounders, more or less, and holding them for their shots was not going to be an easy task.

"I need to go back to the clinic and get the serum, so why don't one of you go by the feed store or poolroom and see if you can find us some strong hog holders who want to work," I suggested. Even with good help, treating two hundred head was going to take all morning and maybe into the middle of the afternoon. I'd have to cancel the calls already on the books, or get to them later than planned. It would be late when I got home that night.

An hour later we had four hog holders lined up and anxious to work. In addition to the owners, there were two strapping boys, Ben and Wilbert, who were in their late teens and were cut from the "can snatcher" mold. "Can snatchers" were those guys who rode the milk truck and snatched eighty-pound cans of milk off the side of the road onto the truck all day. Their upper arms, although covered with a mass of flannel shirts, were the size of Farmall tractor mufflers, thanks to their bulging biceps, and I was pretty sure that those arms were still bronzed from going shirtless in the hay fields during the past summer.

After a brief orientation as to how we would proceed, Ben spoke up.

"Wilbert," he slowly drawled, "ye got n' chewin' terbackey?"

"I got muh britches on, ain't I?" retorted Wilbert, in the identical drawl, as he tossed a pack toward his brother.

With great enthusiasm, Ben plunged five huge but stubby fingers into the store-bought bag of what looked like overheated barley silage. In short order, he had a large lump of the leafy stuff jammed into his mouth and situated between cheek and teeth. Now both brothers had the same lumpy-jawed appearance and were ready to commence the hog catching. Pants were hitched up, stocking caps reset, hands spat upon, and the proceedings begun.

Ben and Wilbert were experts at certain forms of farm work, such as haying, chopping cotton, and using a crosscut saw, but I noticed at once that catching hogs was not in their area of expertise. In spite of the fact that many of the hogs were walking zombies, they still possessed the uncanny talent for evading the groping paws of the boys. When disturbed, even some of the thinking pigs appeared to come alive and avoid a would-be tackler with a head fake, which would leave Wilbert skidding to an icy stop in the opposite direction. Then the porker would plunge into a mass of his colleagues, but not before looking back over his shoulder at his human pursuers and appearing to taunt them with a sneering grin. Once again I was reminded of the high intelligence of swine.

Eventually, though, the pigs would meet their Waterloo. One boy would grab a flopping pig ear and hold on tight, while his brother would seize a rear leg in his viselike paw, and they would easily turn the beast upside down for his turn with the serum needle. Problems arose quickly, however, because of the inclement weather. Hands, although covered with good-quality farm gloves, soon became painfully frostbitten. Expressions of excruciating pain began to show on the ruddy faces of all the participants.

"Hurry up, Doc!" Ben pleaded as he tried to hold on to a squirming spotted Poland China. "My holt is a'slippin' on this here shoat!"

I was trying to inject as fast as possible, but my hands were also hurting from the cold. In addition, the old worn-out syringe I was using leaked serum as I vaccinated and refilled, allowing the cold serum to ooze down my fingers onto the backs of both hands and freeze them into icicles, making my hands stiff as well as painful. At some defining moment that morning, I developed a healthy respect for all my colleagues in the frozen northland.

Somehow, a pig wiggled the wrong way just as I attempted the injection, and I vaccinated Wilbert by mistake. The half-inch, sixteen-gauge needle sank softly into his meaty thigh, right up to the hub. I was instantly aware of what I had done, since Wilbert's thigh had a much firmer feel through the syringe than the thin skin of a pig's flank.

"OW, OW, OW!" he screamed. "You've shot me in the laig, Doc!" He was hopping around on one leg, holding his vaccinated leg up in the air.

"I'm ruint!" he squalled, as he hopped into a group of scattering pigs. "My leg's gonna fall off from this here cholery!"

I felt terrible about the accident and tried to get close enough to see what I could do to help, but Wilbert kept as far away from me as possible. Finally, he went into the corncrib with Ben for an examination of the leg, warning me not to follow.

During the medical emergency we stoked up the tire fire and

began to defrost our frozen digits. As unpleasant as the black smoke was, it was good to get unthawed. There is nothing as welcome as a roaring fire on frostbitten fingers and toes. Minutes later, Ben and Wilbert returned with good news about the human vaccinatee. The needle had actually hit Wilbert at an angle, going through a small pinch of skin and coming out the side. I was relieved that the resistance I had felt was apparently the tip of the needle making contact with clothing.

But Wilbert kept away from me and was constantly mumbling and massaging the site of the vaccination accident on his massive leg. If I walked behind him, he turned all the way around, just to keep his eye on my every move.

"Do you feel like you're turnin' into a hog yet, Wilbert?" Ben teased, slapping his thighs with laughter. "Doc, are you gonna charge him for that vaccination?"

"Ben, you better shut up, fo' I bust you one! It may be funny to you, but you wouldn't be laughin' if it'd happened to you."

This brotherly exchange was greeted by more laughter from all the other participants, except for me. I had never before vaccinated a man against cholera, and I wasn't sure what would happen to that leg, but I was thankful it was just a shallow wound.

When I mentioned a trip to the hospital or the doctor's office, Wilbert adamantly refused to even consider the thought. "I ain't lettin' nobody ever touch me with a needle again!" he declared. Ben promised he would clean the wound and apply some hog salve.

According to Ben, Wilbert suffered no ill effects from the needle accident, except he seemed to be more hardheaded than ever. A month later I saw him headed my way on the sidewalk, going at a canter and showing no sign of lameness. But when he spied me, he stopped in his tracks, then quickly crossed the street, constantly looking warily backward in my direction. I sure was relieved that hog cholera hadn't taken him away.

The Pate brothers lost nearly a hundred head of hogs from the outbreak but were convinced that there would have been more had we not suffered through the vaccination process. They never forgot to vaccinate again, nor did any of the neighbors. But from then on, no vaccination program was ever complete without someone standing around a tire fire and reciting the tale of the vet vaccinating Wilbert in zero-degree weather.

Sixteen

Everybody has a "main man"; some even have several. Your main man is someone you trust with your life, enjoy being around, and regularly do unexpected things for, such as sharing fresh peaches or extra football game tickets, or leaving a sleeve of new golf balls on the seat of his pickup truck. The term simply indicates a high degree of friendship, respect, and admiration.

Claude was one of my main men. Like many of my clients, Claude responded above and beyond the call of duty when someone helped him out of a difficult situation. It might have been a late-night calf delivery, a prolapsed uterus deep in the woods where trucks couldn't go, a swine disease, or helping with a group of steers headed for a Kansas feedlot. Of course, there are always a few clients who are not the appreciative type, but they are in the minority.

Claude, however, would not only promptly pay his vet bill, he often wanted to give something extra.

Claude and his animals seemed especially accident-prone. We first became acquainted because of a pig problem. He and his neighbors were castrating pigs one day when the nicest pig herniated. They apparently hadn't noticed the unilateral swollen scrotum, and when the testicle was removed the intestines spilled to the outside. I'm sure the farmers were aghast at the unpleasant sight of a pig walking around dragging his intestines behind him, occasionally looking back, puzzled at the weird sight. But they had the foresight to respond quickly by grabbing up the porker and wrapping the viscera in someone's undershirt that had been dipped in the horses' water trough. Then they put pig and wrapped intestines into a "clean" burlap sack and came rocketing to town at breakneck speed in Claude's old Dodge pickup.

As he entered the town square, one of the passengers spied the veterinarian standing with a group of citizens in front of the courthouse. Claude immediately turned in at a diagonal parking place, ran both front wheels up onto the curb, and blew the horn while the crowd stood there gape-mouthed and post-legged.

"Doc, you better come over here as quick as you can," he announced before he was even completely out of the truck. Claude had a slight voice impediment, the result of some throat surgery done when he was much younger, and I didn't understand exactly what he was saying. But I did get his next two words.

"HURRY UP!" he yelled.

The group of disgruntled taxpayers followed me to the back of the truck, where we observed movement inside the burlap sack when one of Claude's brawny assistants began fiddling with the baler twine that was tied around the top. I knew the assistant well. It was Joe Bob (Sinkin') Jenkins, number one good ole boy, a willing assistant who always showed up to assist with area pig cuttings and bovine obstetrical work, and no doubt one of the state's most artistic collapsers at the sight of blood. If there had been a USA

Olympic fainting team, he would have been captain. Thankfully, he had been making progress in his quest to beat his fainting tendencies.

"What is it? What's that movin' around in there?" someone asked.

"Is it a snake?" Everybody jumped back. "They's a heap o' rattlesnakes down there on Claude's road."

"Maybe it's a mad dog." They jumped back farther.

"It's a plum mess, that's what it is," cried Claude. "Make haste with that string, Joe Bob! Let that tailgate down so Doc won't have to lean over so far." Finally, Joe Bob ran out of patience with the tight knot and simply snapped the twine with his meaty paws.

While Joe Bob stood by, hoping I would ask for his assistance, I rolled down the top of the burlap sack, then carefully peeked inside. Claude was right about it being a mess. The poor pig was lying in a nest of his own intestines, which were covered with leaves, dirt, hair, and chaff. All the stuff seemed to have been glued on.

"Whooo-weee!" I exclaimed. "I've never seen anything like this!" I saw Joe Bob grab for the side of the truck bed. That was an improvement. His previous falling-out spells involved an initial gagging noise and he would just collapse like a fallen tree, making no attempt to grab hold of the nearest object. Most fainters will at least try to grab on to something, their fingernails making horrible blackboard-scraping noises as they go for the ground.

"Joe Bob, don't look in that sack, look yonder way," Claude exclaimed, pointing toward the Confederate soldier statue in front of the courthouse. "Remember what that head doctor said?" he said. Joe Bob nodded his head affirmatively while looking away from the sack and in the direction Claude had suggested. I couldn't believe anybody in Choctaw County actually visited a psychiatrist, and certainly not Joe Bob Jenkins. That meant he had to go as far away as Meridian, Jackson, or maybe even Mobile. Obviously, the problem was more severe and dangerous than I had thought. But I was impressed with his efforts to correct the problem.

The bystanders were gasping. Women were slapping their bejeweled fingers to their mouths in shock. Embarrassed small children hid behind their parents' legs.

Only a couple of the men dared peek inside the opened sack. Even then they inched up and slowly peered into it. Just as the second observer got within viewing range, the pig jumped and grunted loudly, the way pigs do when they are alarmed or want to warn an unwanted intruder.

The two men jumped as if a bomb had exploded in their faces. They reeled backward, stepping on and kicking other observers' feet and shins, even as the helpful crowd tried to keep the startled men from falling. Purses were knocked loose from arms and cola cans boinked to the pavement, their contents now a slow-flowing mass of useless foam, even as other curiosity seekers were dangerously scurrying across the street and dodging the traffic in an effort to get to the scene of the excitement. This was one of the most exciting things to happen in the area since the Sweetwater State Bank was held up at gunpoint. And that had been some twenty miles away.

"Can you fix that shoat, Doc, or do you reckon I ought to just put 'im out of his misery?" asked Claude.

I hesitated, unsure if I could successfully place such a mass of mangled tissue back into such a small warm and breathing carcass. And I sure didn't want to do it on the town square. But before I could quit scratching my head and reply, a man in the crowd spontaneously testified on my behalf.

"Yes siree, that doctor can fix whatever it is that ails that dog!" exclaimed a rough-looking, leather-faced man.

"It's a hog, Ace," replied another bystander. Not everyone had heard the oinking porker or seen his snout when he scared the daylights out of the peeking observers.

"Don't matter. He can fix it up, I tell y'all. Shoulda seen my dog he fixed. That ole dog come runnin' out to meet me when I come home from crop dustin'. Just as I taxied up to the hangar the propeller caught 'im halfway between the eyes and mouth. Near 'bout cut that cur's nose off. This veteran here stuck a Dairy Queen straw up each nostril and sewed that nose back on there, pretty as you please. Why, that dog's normal as me or you, right this day."

I remembered the dog and I remembered Ace. It was said that he had been a terrific fighter pilot in the Pacific during World War II. I enjoyed watching his crop dusting skills and the uncanny way he maneuvered over fencerows, light poles, and trees. Several times I had stopped on a dirt road and watched as he did his thing, no more than ten feet off the soybean tops, heading directly toward my truck. He came so close I could even see his head leaning forward, the big grin on his lips and the devilment in his eyes. At the last possible moment I would buzz away from the spray, and he would climb almost straight up. When I turned my head and looked back, he'd be laughing like a little kid.

"Well, this pig is a lot different from a dog," I countered. "But let's take him up to the clinic and give it a try." Several of the watchers scattered, rushing to their cars in order to race to the clinic to secure good observation posts.

I have noticed that many people are fascinated by the mystery of surgery. It's probably because it's done in secret, behind closed doors, by masked people wearing funny outfits. Everyone is naturally curious about what happens the magical moment that scalpel meets flesh, and beyond. Since few individuals are allowed in the sterile hospital operating theater, except as paying patients, barnyard surgery satisfies their curiosity.

On the tailgate of the truck in my clinic backyard, we restrained the young pig and injected a sedative. After he was lightly sleeping, we gently washed the prolapsed viscera with warm water and saline solution. Luckily, once we got all the leaves and junk picked off the gut surface there wasn't much damage. Then we started the job of putting the intestines back through the opening from which they had come. However, replacing swollen gut loops into their original position almost defies logic. The intestines obviously had come from inside the unfortunate beast, but the body seems to reject all efforts to get them back into their rightful position.

Such was the case with Claude's pig. But after much grimacing, poking, and considerable conversation from the observers, I was blessed with success. No doubt the grimacing helped. Next, a few sutures were placed in the enlarged inguinal ring, drawn tight, and tied. With my fingertips, I checked carefully to be sure the edges came together nicely and closed the ring securely. A few sutures were put in the skin and the job was complete, except for the antibiotics.

"Now, Claude, he's gonna sleep for a few hours, so be sure and put him to himself somewhere in the cool. Don't let the others mess with him."

"Reckon he'll make it?" Claude asked.

"Of course he's gonna make it!" replied Ace before I could even open my mouth. "Doc'll even guarantee it, won't you, Doc?"

"No sir!" I declared. "That's a live hog, not a waffle iron."

"But what's the difference?" asked one of the watchers, now an expert on swine surgery.

"Let me answer it like this. Go over to the folks' hospital and get Dr. Paul or any one of the M.D.s over there to operate on you for a hernia. If he guarantees you'll live, then I'll guarantee a pig will live, providing he is in good health to start with."

Good-natured kidding about human surgery versus animal surgery ensued, with some claiming that surgery was surgery, while others said human surgery surely must be more difficult. I suggested that performing surgery on a human being had to be much easier.

"How come?" someone asked.

"Well, have you ever known a medical doctor who had to run a patient down, rope him, tie him up, and fight to get him anesthetized while doing everything by himself, sometimes by truck lights?"

"'At's right, Doc, you tell 'em," came the voice of one of my clients standing in the back.

"It's like apples and oranges," I declared. "I was just having a little fun, thinking about Dr. Paul running Joe Bob down the highway, trying to get a lariat around his neck so he could repair his hernia."

Folks were still laughing and debating the issue as they drove away from the clinic, probably heading for the barbershop, where they would continue the discussion, complete with an exaggerated version of the swine surgery that they had just witnessed.

Later that night Claude called.

"Doc, you remember that pig you fixed for me today? You said he'd sleep a pretty good while, didn't you?"

"Oh no," I said to myself, "that pig has died and now he wants a refund on that pittance I charged him."

"You mean he's still asleep?"

"Oh no, he was staggering around in the back of the truck before I got home. He's out there in his little pen right now with his nose in the feeder, looking for feed."

"Why, that's good, but I didn't expect him to be up and around this early. I guess everything's all right, then."

"Well, that's why I called," he answered sheepishly. "The pig actually belongs to my wife, and she wanted me to call and ask you something."

"Sure, what is it?"

"Uh, she wants to know if it'll be OK for him to have a small piece of watermelon tonight. I know you said not to feed him much." He was speaking in an apologetic tone.

"Oh, of course," I said, trying not to show my amusement. "Just don't put any salt on it and don't let him eat the rind. It might give him a sick tummyache and bust those stitches out."

"Right! No salt and no rind. Thanks, Doc."

Six months later Claude came by the clinic and left two packages of pork chops. They were fine but had an odd flavor. Jan said they tasted like her favorite fruit—watermelon.

~

Claude and I became great friends. He had lots of cows, but he never knew how many since they were so scattered out in the woods of his various properties. And he owned an abundance of property. He would buy a tract of prime timberland, then cut enough of the timber to pay off the cost of the land. People who know the woods and how to evaluate standing timber can make a lot of money in the pine belt.

There was always an ever-present group of sows around the barn at the home place or in the hog lot, some of which were claimed by his wife. Mostly the swine just went where they pleased because of the dilapidated fence. After the ruptured pig incident, Claude swore off all forms of swine surgery and insisted that I should visit the farm periodically and castrate and vaccinate the little pigs.

A few days before castration day, he would begin feeding all the pigs in the only escape-proof stall in the barn so they would be accustomed to the new arrangement. When I arrived early on C-day, usually somewhere between thirty and sixty head of twenty-pound boars and gilts would be stalled and waiting. All the pigs knew something was up since their rations had been skimpy that morning, but I doubt if they realized the seriousness of the situation. When I peeked over the stall wall at their staring faces and twitching noses, several of the more intelligent ones knew they wanted no part of what the stranger had to offer and began searching for an out. They tried to nose under the bottom board and even scramble up the wall, but their efforts were fruitless because the stall was like a big wooden box with no top.

Our procedure followed a set routine. Personnel allowed inside the stall was limited to a grabber, a sexer, a cutter, and a fly repellant swabber. The grabber would reach down into the mass of squirming pigs and grab one; the sexer would loudly yell whether it was a boar or gilt. I would then vaccinate each pig, and if it was a gilt it would be handed over the wall to a catcher who would release the pig back into the hall of the barn. If it was a male, he would be held upside down by his hind legs, his belly facing my direction, and I would perform the surgery, which took only five seconds or so. Next, fly repellant would be swabbed on the incision site. Claude would have none of my fancy drug company sprays, but instead demanded the use of diesel fuel.

"I'm not putting diesel fuel on those pigs, Claude," I declared one day. "It'll irritate their skin."

"Then I will!" he said. "I been doin' it all my life. Besides, I don't trust that stuff you got in that spray can. It don't smell bad enough to keep flies off that cut."

From then on Claude set himself up as the designated fly repellant swabber. He would go to the tractor shed, find an empty motor oil can, and pump it half full of diesel fuel. Then he would find a sturdy stick about twelve inches long and an inch in diameter, and wrap an old rag or throwaway sock around the end of it. That was his swab stick, and he was the only one allowed access to that difficult chore.

The observers were mostly critics and braggers. Fifty percent of their time on the wall was spent yelling at each other and criticizing the catching, vaccinating, and castrating procedures, and the other half bragging on how much better their own pigs were than Claude's and why they were better veterinarians than the one down in the stall. If Joe Bob (Sinkin') Jenkins happened to be present that day, someone was the designated Sinkin' watcher. His job was to watch Sinkin' very closely, and if he started to collapse, to try to push him away from the pitchfork, the manure spreader, and other sharp-edged machinery lying around the barn.

Some may think all this sounds like a lot of fun, and it often is, except for one irritating feature—the noise. If a pig is touched by anything besides another pig, he or she feels duty bound to squeal and to squeal as loudly as possible. Conversation is near impossible in the immediate vicinity of a squealing hog. You can see lips moving, and you might be good at reading them, but that is unreliable because of the involuntary eye blinking caused by the noise. Of course, a hog man usually knows what the other is liable to be saying anyway, especially when a pig is squealing. Other loud grunting and snorting racket comes from the pigs' mothers, who have gathered at the front door of the barn to voice their displeasure at what is happening to their offspring.

The family dog is always there on C-day, too, adding even more decibels, sticking his nose into small wall cracks and constantly biting at the stall door, desperately wanting to get into the fray. Claude spent countless minutes on those days yelling at Duke, whom he called "Nuke" because of his speech impediment.

"Go t'house, Nuke!" he yelled constantly—into my right ear, since his swabbing duties required that position. I believe squealing pigs and Claude's yelling are the main reasons for the hearing loss in my right ear today.

Mrs. Claude wasn't part of the pig-castration team. She stayed in the house brewing tea, which she brought out to the tailgate of the truck under the chinaberry tree when the project was completed. She could tell when it was over because of the blessed quiet. We always enjoyed her strong iced tea, even though our ears were roaring, and when someone spoke, he sounded farther away than he appeared.

Few veterinarians do this kind of work anymore. Farmers cut their own pigs, or have their employees do it as part of their job description. They probably even replace the hernias and suture the inguinal rings, and get to wear earplugs while doing it all. But somehow it just doesn't seem quite as much fun as my C-days at Claude's.

Seventeen

The trips to Claude's farms became more frequent, as did his telephone calls. He might call and get my opinion about the cattle market and whether I thought he should sell a load of calves sooner or later. He often called about a calf that didn't look just right and have me decide whether or not I should make a farm call. And he continued his quiet, generous ways. It was a rare visit to his barns when I didn't find some thoughtful gift placed on the seat of my truck, usually some fresh garden produce, meat from the freezer, or fresh sausage.

"Ain't you cold, Noc?" he asked one bitter-cold Sunday night. I had taken off my shirt and was lying on the ground, attempting to deliver a calf from a middle-aged half–Santa Gertrudis cow. Our only light was from truck headlights and a couple of weak flashlights. Naturally, the patient had run off to the most distant point in the pasture to have her baby, and we were there only because of Claude's persistence and knowledge of the terrain.

"Yeah, a little, but it's gotta be done." I grunted, pushing and sorting out spindly and slippery calf limbs.

"I don't see how you can do it. I'm freezing just watching you," he said. "I couldn't do yo' job." I could count four collars around his neck, and since his slim 150-pound figure had ballooned so that he looked as if he weighed at least 200 pounds, I assumed he was also wearing several pairs of pants. He'd topped that off with a pair of white coveralls, which gave him the appearance of a snowman.

"Must be all that rat poison you're taking to keep from having a stroke," I said. "That's why you feel so weak all the time." It was hard for me to guess his age, but I thought he was in his late sixties.

After getting the head and front legs rerouted, I easily extracted the smallish fetus. When I checked the uterus, there was a second one, which also came out easily because of its small size. Claude had his back to me as he was briskly rubbing the first baby with his ever-present burlap sack, and so he had not seen the birth of the second baby. He was shocked when he turned and saw another calf. Other cows had presented him with twins before, but it was still unusual and unexpected.

"Well, shuckins!" he exclaimed. "I never expected this."

"Both red heifers, too!" I said, checking the identifying anatomy.

"But won't they be sterile? Somebody told me that for a fact the other day down at the feed store."

"Nope, that's just when a bull and heifer are born twins," I reassured him. "The heifer will be sterile about seventy-five percent of the time, because her reproductive tract doesn't develop normally."

Moments later, we moved the new babies around to the front of their mother, who had sat up and seemed no worse for the wear, and then we moved away to observe them bonding. At the scent of first one calf and then the other, the older cow came alive, half snorting, half grunting, and smelling her new additions from top line to cannon bone. She arose and commenced a vigorous cleaning with her rasplike tongue, taking turns licking one, then the other. The rough lingual massage stimulated the calves, now shaking their heads and snorting mucus from their nostrils. It was a lesson direct from nature's big instruction manual, and I knew Claude's thinking paralleled mine.

"How do they know? And they can't even read!" Each time I assisted in a birthing experience with animals, I found my head shaking in awe. Of course, there was the occasional crazy heifer that gave birth and immediately fled, but that only happened because of human interference or hormonal confusion.

Because of the cold weather and the small size of the calves, we decided to put them on the downed tailgate of Claude's truck and haul them to a lean-to shelter, which was about two hundred yards away. While I slowly angled across the terraces of the hilly pasture, Claude made little guttural calf noises while sitting on the tailgate with one calf in his lap and another at his side, which apparently encouraged the cow into following the slow-moving truck. Walking as close to the moving truck as possible, she never let her anxious eyes leave her newborns.

When the three were finally safe and wobbling unsteadily in the straw bedding away from the icy northwest wind, Claude made a strange pronouncement.

"Noc, I want to give you a calf," he said seriously. I wasn't sure what he meant, but I assumed he was offering me a calf in payment for the bill.

"Uh, well, I don't have a place to keep her, living in town and all, so I reckon I'd just as soon have the money. They're nice calves, too, but I'm gone so much, doctoring everybody else's stock, I wouldn't have the time to take care of her."

"Naw, I'm gonna pay the bill like I always do! I want to give you a calf so you can start your own herd. I'll keep it here for you, feed it and everything, breed it, and in a few years when you retire, you'll have your own herd. You're always coming out here and helping me on Sundays and nights, and I just wanted to do something for you."

I was flabbergasted, but did take him up on his offer. I picked out the first twin born, even though later neither of us could tell the difference between the two. As they grew, mine became slightly bigger and had a small white spot just behind her navel. We visited the herd frequently, not only for professional reasons but to socialize, too. Over the next few years, Claude presented me with several other calves, and I was excited when they matured and started having their own calves.

Early one Saturday morning, Claude called and we had a pleasant conversation about random subjects. Finally, in his calmest demeanor, he got around to telling me about the crowd of sick cows he had just seen over at the Price place, a property that he was renting.

"Noc, you better come on down here as soon as you can," he said without any excitement in his voice.

"What's going on?"

"That bunch of cows over there got out last night and broke into that corncrib full of ear corn. They ate a bait of that corn, I reckon, 'cause there's four dead 'uns and several more down and in a bad way." In the South, a "bait" of something is a batch, or a bunch, or a considerable amount. "Junior ate a bait of barbecue for dinner," for example.

"Four dead! More sick!" I yelled. "Hang up the phone and look for a cloud of dust! I'll be right there." I get excited when there's more than one dead animal at a time, even if the owner doesn't.

On the way to the farm, I reviewed the various treatments for rumen overload acidosis. I could pass a stomach tube and pump in laxatives, or evacuate the rumen contents by doing a rumenotomy. The treatment, one author had recently written, was to pass a very large stomach tube, then use a garden hose to force a large quantity of cold water into the rumen. Then the offending material was siphoned out. The trouble with the garden hose method is that the rumen overload cases I saw were invariably in the woods and there was no hose available. It was obvious the author of that article didn't treat any cows that had broken into corncribs in the woods. Like so many things in a veterinarian's day, it helps to be creative, because there is often no workable textbook solution.

"I found two more dead in the woods," Claude announced when I drove through the wire gap. "That's six so far, and two of 'em are your heifers." Now I was more excited. These were my cows!

"Get in and let's drive out and look at the sick ones," I suggested. "Come on, let's go!" But Claude never got in a hurry; he even went back to his truck and picked his morning newspaper off the dash.

We spied one of his cows standing by the edge of the pond and went bumping over the terraces too fast. My instruments and medicine in the back were being thrown around, and Claude was holding on to the passenger door handle with both hands.

"Slow down!" he cried. "You ain't goin' to a fire!"

The poor cow was deathly sick. She was standing still as a statue, with her head straight out and her legs propped in a sawhorse stance. Her eyes were sunken and she was severely bloated on both sides.

When we were within roping range, I stopped, grabbed my lariat, stepped out of the truck, and let the loop fly. She started to fight when the rope began to tighten around her neck, then suddenly her eyes began blinking erratically. Even though the rope wasn't tight enough for her to choke down, I slacked off just as she fell over sideways, her legs stiff as cedar posts.

I started cow CPR by jumping up and down on the chest of the motionless beast with both knees, but as expected she couldn't be revived. When I looked back at Claude, he was still sitting in the pickup, reading the comic page.

"Don't hurt your knees, Noc, 'cause I think she just passed through the Pearly Gate," he replied nonchalantly. He looked up briefly, then went back to the comics.

I reluctantly stopped the resuscitation effort, took one last look, and hopped into the truck.

"What happened?" asked Claude.

"Heart trouble," I answered, pointing the truck in the direction of another identically affected cow standing on the next terrace over.

Again I hopped from the truck, roped the second cow, and looped my end of the rope around my front bumper. When she felt the lasso, this cow was livelier than the first, weaving drunkenly and bellowing with tongue lolled out, trying desperately to escape the restraining rope around her neck. I was finally able to make a temporary halter out of the rope, which calmed her down enough for treatment.

A few minutes later, I was easing the large-bore stomach tube down her throat. Everything seemed to be proceeding nicely until her body began the jerking syndrome that signals eminent collapse and probable death. Her eyes were flipping around, and as I watched in horror, she also keeled over in the same stiff-legged manner as her late colleague.

This time I was too shocked to do anything other than step to the side and gape. It was a terrible feeling, seeing a half ton of beef lying motionless at my feet because of my treatment failure. At that moment, I felt guilty, incompetent, and unworthy of being called a veterinarian, in spite of the cow's grave condition before treatment. When I looked back at Claude, now standing on the opposite side of the deceased, his gaze was fixed on the cow's head. He uttered the most profound statement I ever heard in my cow-doctoring career.

"Noc, we ain't makin' no progress! I think we'd save time and money if I just got my deer rifle and just shot 'em." Then he returned to the truck and buried his head in the sports page. I thought I had detected a hint of sarcasm in his voice, but if he had any feelings of ill-will toward me he didn't show them.

He was right! Even before I started veterinary school, Dr. Berry, our hometown vet, had emphasized the importance of not making matters worse when treating an animal.

"If they're sick, don't make 'em any sicker. Whatever you do, don't be responsible for their demise," he had preached.

We treated no more cows that day. Although two more died, they did it on their own, without human interference.

One of the things I was learning was that some of my patients were not going to survive, regardless of my heroic treatments or hopeful prayers. And there are times when no treatment is the best treatment, especially if it requires forceful handling that causes too much stress on gravely ill patients. Claude's two cows reinforced that lesson for me.

I lost two members of my herd that day, but I accumulated a nice group over a period of several years. However, one summer we experienced a severe drought and were forced to sell all the cows on Claude's farm. It was a sad, depressing day when Claude and I stood silently side by side at the corral gate and watched the last trailer load of cattle disappear over the hill, heading for the sale barn. Not long after that, my friend Claude passed away, and I've had no enthusiasm to raise my own cattle since.

Eighteen

H ello, Doctuh, is that you theah?" the lady caller yelled loudly, but properly, over the phone. It was Miss Ruby McCord, proprietress of McCord's Gen. Sto. & Ser. Sta., according to the sign above her door.

"Yes, ma'am, I can hear you. Go ahead," I replied. Miss Ruby always shouted over the phone. She was a good seven miles east of town, after all, and like many of my clients, she still wasn't quite comfortable speaking into that relatively new telephone contraption. Still, for some of her poor neighbors, her phone was the only line of communication to the outside world, and she was the one who usually made the call for them. Since they couldn't see the party on the other end, they had no confidence talking into the strange device.

"Doctuh, this is Ruby McCord," she continued, but now hollering. "I need for you to stop by the stoah the next passing and make an examination of one of my dogs. He's become weak in his hind quawters and has difficulty rising." She was always so proper in her conversation. I wondered if she had colleged at one of those schools for women over in Mississippi or just had a knack for good, old-timey, Southern English. I loved hearing her pronounce words such as "doctuh," "quawter," "befoah," and "heah."

"Yes, ma'am, Miss Ruby, I understand," I answered just as loudly, wanting to make sure she would understand over the staticky line. "I'll try to stop there on my way back from Mr. Kent's place tomorrow. Probably be around noontime."

Miss Ruby's store was an oasis of gustatory delight located between the tiny towns of Lisman and Cromwell, and it was my favorite snack stop in the county. She always had cold milk in the refrigerator, sodas in the ice water drink box, Moon Pies, Vienna sausages, Possum-brand sardines, and soda crackers on the shelves. But best of all, she always had a big round of hoop cheese on the counter, sitting on an old cutting device. To get a portion of the cheddar, you just raised the cleaverlike knife and turned the cheese around to the amount you wanted, then pulled down on the handle, and the cleaver would do the rest. Of course, proper cheese-cutting etiquette required the laying down of a small piece of white wrapping paper close to the face of the cheese so that the cut portion flopped onto the paper. I knew that I was a very privileged guest in Miss Ruby's store because I was the only person she allowed to cut his or her own allotment.

In addition to the superb cuisine, there were fringe benefits. Six or eight cats, depending on the present kitten crop and strays, were allowed free run of the store. There were always three or four gray tabbies, at least three tricolors, and an old yellow tom, there not only to catch the occasional mouse who was dumb enough to drop in but also for Miss Ruby's companionship and the entertainment of the store guests. I always whacked off a little extra cheese to share with the cats.

It was amusing, as well as relaxing, to sit on a nail keg in front of the potbellied stove and toss the cats a few small chunks of cheddar. To make it more challenging for them, I would toss the choice morsels in between and behind the sacks of livestock feed and blocks of salt that were propped up in front of the counter. All the cats would dive into the crack simultaneously, each one with one greedy paw extended. The triumphant cat would then sprint away, a low warning growl issuing from his throat as he retreated behind a pile of horse collars to enjoy his prize alone. The less fortunate would return to their posts at my feet, gazing intently as my hand moved from lap to mouth, occasionally licking the drool from their lips, and never taking their eyes off my snack.

Another benefit of relaxing at Miss Ruby's was the store sitters. It was common to find one or more visitors there, including the most prominent store sitter, Carney Sam Jenkins, who was a great philosopher, gifted seer, taxidermist, and jackleg or "homemade" veterinarian. Then there were several other regulars, including Hoosier Turner, Bighead Turner, Cappy Lou Akins, and Joe Frank Ford, who was called Roy for some unknown reason. The sole purpose for the sitters to be there was to insult incoming customers by making fun of their pickup trucks, low-rating their hunting dogs, and joking about how many weeds were in their cotton patches. A stranger wasn't messed with much, unless the foreigner said something disrespectful about the bad condition of the local roads or how backward everybody around there seemed. Then he was fair game, especially if he owned up to being from Memphis or Birmingham. Most outsiders who smarted off would be overwhelmed and have to escape out the door and scratch off in their cars, the echoes of the sitters' guffaws ringing in their ears. What they wouldn't understand was it was just a group of friends having fun, and if they had just laughed along they might have enjoyed themselves. Actually, once the sitters got to know you, it was a bad sign it they didn't throw at least one good-natured insult your way.

The day after Miss Ruby's phone call, I arrived at the store a little before one P.M. and found more cars and trucks circled around the store than usual. I even wondered if something was amiss. Somehow the place looked different and brighter, but I couldn't decide why—until I looked up above the store. A bright and shiny new TV antenna stood at the highest point of the roof, reaching for the sky. Some of the surrounding tree limbs had been cut back, and there were four guy wires angling down to tree trunks or roof corners.

"Glory be! Miss Ruby's gone and put a TV in the store!" I said out loud. "Things won't ever be the same again."

Upon entering the front door, I was greeted by rare silence, except for the blare of the TV. And it was even in color! Every eye was beamed right to the screen, hypnotized by the trashy soap opera actors hugging and kissing right there in broad daylight. I was stunned that Miss Ruby would allow such shenanigans to take place in her store.

"Hey, what y'all doin'?" I said.

"Hi, Doc," Joe Frank said, glancing up at me for a split second before turning back to the screen. Five others peered intently at the program, not even bothering to look up and say hi. The show wasn't coming in very well, and the color wasn't right either. Everything was too blue.

"Miss Ruby get a new—"

"Shhh, shhh!" Carney Sam rebuked, his hand waving me down from behind, his eyes never leaving the screen. Not another soul uttered a word. I noticed the cats sprawled atop the feed sacks, their eyes tightly shut and in deep sleep, apparently undisturbed by the new noise.

"Now, isn't this something," I thought. "All these tough, independent, no-frills, so-called farmers in here watching TV. This has got to be the end of the world as I have known it!"

Finally, there was a break in the action and a commercial about deodorant replaced the sob sisters.

"What you doin' up here, Doc? Tryin' to run over some dogs?" one said.

"Yeah, somebody down there in town told me that Miz Doc had a dog raker on the front of that big station wagon," declared a second.

"Naw, he's goin' around the county sowin' blackleg germs and sprayin' the air with hog cholery virus," declared Carney Sam.

Now, that was more like it! I felt a lot better now that the commercial had returned their sanity. Several others offered amateur attempts at insult humor, recalling dogs that had been mysteriously run down, then wondering aloud if Doc and Miz Doc had had a hand in the trauma.

"Doctuh, can you wait just a few minutes until this program is ovuh? This is my favorite show," Miss Ruby asked from her post behind the counter. I wondered how well she could see the screen with five heads in her line of view. "Then we'll go up to the house and see about Rex."

"Whatsamatter wi' Rex, Ruby?" asked Carney Sam.

"Down and can't hardly get up. Drags himself around."

"Uh huh, it's them kidneys. I call it kidneyitis. The kidneys drop down out of position and git chilled. It's on account of him jumpin' up on that fence and barkin' all the time." He was on a roll now, and I knew the only thing that would stop him was the end of the TV commercial. He loved delivering lectures on animal health, and when I was in the audience, he would always end his long-winded remarks by saying "Ain't t'at right, Doc?"

"Why, that's right," Miss Ruby said, stunned. "He does jump on that fence a right smart."

"Shh! Shh!" warned one of the sitters. The soap was coming back on, with another earthshaking crisis guaranteed. I tore myself away, went to the truck, and started cleaning up my little drug department in the back, shaking my head in amazement.

A few minutes later Miss Ruby came hopping down the steps with purse in hand, and we were off to her house, a half mile away.

"How do you like my new TV, Doctuh?"

"Oh, it's very nice, and I'm sure it's a lot of company for you."

"Yes, and it's one of the only coluh ones in the area. I've had a steady crowd of customuhs ever since the Sears and Roebuck man brought it ovuh last week."

Rex was an old weimaraner that Miss Ruby kept in her yard as a "guard dog," she told me. But when we found him bedded down among the rosebushes near the front porch, I knew he was at the shank end of his guarding days. He offered no resistance when I eased him out onto the grass for an examination. His front teeth were just nubs, and some of the molars were in a rotten condition. His breath smelled of kidney failure.

"How old is he, Miss Ruby?"

"He's about twenty, I reckon," she stated after a few moments of thought. "Is it his kidneys? Carney said his kidneys were dropped."

"Well, not exactly, but his kidneys are failing. And look at these bad teeth here," I said, pulling back the lips for her examination. But she didn't tarry when she got a whiff of poor Rex's breath. "He's just old and all his parts are worn out. I can give him an injection of vitamins and some 'old folks' hormone and leave you some pills, but I'm afraid his time is about up. Have you been giving him anything?"

"Yes, I've been seeing all those wonduh drugs on TV, so I've tried Bufferins, Bayuh aspirins, Dristans, and then I rubbed Ben-Gay on his back. Then last night I drenched him with a big dose of Hadacol," she replied. She even seemed to be proud of it.

"Why, you know that stuff is mostly alcohol. It isn't fit for a dog!" I exclaimed.

"On the TV they claimed that their medicine would cure almost anything, so I decided to give it a try on old Rex here."

"Do you think it helped?"

"No sir, but that was befoah I knew about his kidneyitis. Have you got a shot for that?"

"I'm afraid not," I said softly. "I think we should put him to sleep."

"Will he be better when he wakes up?" she asked.

"Oh, I apologize. What I was suggesting was to put him to sleep for good, to get him out of his misery. I don't think he'll ever get well," I said.

"Why don't you give him the shot and leave me those pills you mentioned. I don't think I'm ready to do away with him. You never know what new cure might get reported on the news any day."

We treated Rex and left the pills, but they didn't help any more than the Hadacol. A few days later when I stopped in at the store I heard the sad news that Rex had been found dead in the rosebushes the night before. I helped bury him in the corner of the yard.

As I drove away from the store, I thought about the TV and Carney Sam and poor old Rex. I'm sure none of the medications Rex was given had any effect on his living or dying, but I smiled when I thought about how Carney and TV conjured up more ailments than the latest textbooks. I suppose they both helped me to make a living in a strange sort of way.

Nineteen

W hat would you do without your hired hand buddies?" Jan asked me one night after I'd related the day's activities, telling her how hard some of the cowboys had worked penning the cattle, separating the cows from the calves, putting them through the chute, and catching their heads.

"I don't know." That night I vowed to thank this hardworking group of people each time I was on the farm.

The hired hands are the ones who look after the livestock down on the nitty-gritty level. They feed the hogs, hay the beef cows, milk the dairy cows two or three times a day, and muck out the horse stalls. They see the little things that the owners sometimes miss— things like "cow 74's milk was down about twenty pounds this morning" or "a couple of ewes were lagging behind the rest of the flock last night." Such observations are important and are signals that a health problem might be about to surface.

Most of these hired people are real characters with real character names. Buck, Mule, Benny Lee, Little Junior (L.J.), Bubbahead, Tennessee, Cat, Hustler, and Yank are just a few I have worked with. They seem to have a somewhat more jovial and carefree outlook on life than the rest of the population. Maybe it's because they, unlike the owners, are not worried about making a big payment on the farm in a few days. If one's brain is not overloaded with thoughts of financial statements, cash flow estimates, quarterly reports, and past-due feed bills, one can concentrate more on the little things, such as always having a new joke for the vet or playing tricks on the milk truck driver.

Two of my favorite workers were a middle-aged man called "Pool Do" and his younger associate, J.B. They were Joe Frank's hired men. For a couple of years I thought Pool Do was nicknamed after that little duck-looking animal with a chicken beak that some call a Pouldoo. Finally one day I asked him why someone stuck him with a name like "Pool Do."

"Well, me an' J.B. was loadin' paperwood on a truck," he replied. "I'se on one side an' B.J. on the other. All of a sudden J.B. tho'ed a ten-inch-thick stick of paperwood up on the truck so hard it came all the way over on my side and bonked me upside the head. It knocked me out cold as a wedge."

He paused for a few seconds, pulled off his old greasy felt hat, leaned his head over into my face, and fingered an old scar right in the middle of his cranium.

"Yeah, I feel it. Left a bad scar, didn't it," I answered. "But where'd the name come from?"

"Well, J.B. claimed that when that stick of wood whopped me upside the head, it sounded like it had landed on concrete. Said it went 'POOOOL-DOOOO.'"

When he made the high-pitched "POOOOL-DOOOO" sound with his mouth, I could just imagine how the sound would echo if you dropped a locust post straight down onto an inside concrete floor. I was sure the nickname was very appropriate. Pool Do sounded good to me and seemed to fit him just right.

J.B. and Pool Do helped me vaccinate, deworm, and dehorn newly arrived cattle at Joe Frank's large feedlot. Joe Frank was usually absent when we worked cattle, playing a lot of golf, going to field trials with his fine beagle dogs, or just generally handling important farm or recreational matters somewhere else. But the farm operation ran smoother when Joe Frank was away, because the two hired men knew more about the everyday workings than he did.

J.B. and Pool Do had no equals when it came to the proper handling, working, and restraining of cattle. The squeeze chute was always operated by the muscular J.B., while the shy Pool Do worked in the back, keeping the chute and alleyway full of cattle. They were two tough men—the type you would want to have in your foxhole during a war.

As tough as they were, each had his own little sensitivity. Pool Do, for instance, absolutely could not stand it when I had to treat a steer's eye for pinkeye.

"Look at this, Pool Do!" I'd say just before injecting medication around an infected eye.

"Aw, Doc," he'd complain, grimacing, while turning his head away and closing his eyes. "How can you do that? I couldn't do that even if the high sheriff held a gun to my head!"

J.B. had a very weak stomach, too, on certain occasions. Watching and assisting with dewormings and castrations caused him no problem, but observing obstetrical procedures made him downright queasy. His biggest problem came, however, when we had to treat a neglected or infected wound on an unfortunate horse. This caused J.B. gastrointestinal distress of great magnitude, because the odor was offensive and he was downwind.

His reaction was always the same, and the signs became familiar. After standing by briefly and holding on to the horse's head while I worked, he would suddenly drop the lead shank and step away.

"Doc, I gotta step over to the barn for a minute," he'd mumble softly.

When I looked at him, his brow would be wrinkled, his eyes half closed, and he would be drooling like a mad dog. As he neared the corner of the barn, J.B. would put out his left hand and support himself with it while he stood with his head bent over. After a minute or so of this, he would slowly slide down the side of the barn and sit there until I had finished with the horse. Occasionally, he would raise his head and look my way, but he was down for the count and useless working with livestock that day.

Even though they were best friends, Pool Do showed J.B. no mercy during his nausea attacks. While J.B. was moaning in misery over by the barn, Pool Do was laughing and making jokes.

"Good thing Doc's here," he'd say with a laugh. "Spec' he ought to give you a doest of that mule medicine he's got over there in his satchel!" Then he would guffaw and slap his thighs. I would try to keep a straight face, but I too was soon unable to control my snickering.

One day while Pool Do was loudly guffawing, J.B. became so infuriated that he picked up a smooth, flat river rock and hurled it at Pool Do, catching him right in the back of the head. Now I had two distractions, both of them down on the ground, knee walking and moaning.

The wound on Pool Do's head was bleeding profusely, so I rushed to the truck for gauze and tape. When I whizzed by J.B. at the corner of the barn, he was making terrible retching sounds punctuated by coughs and snorts.

While Pool Do was calling J.B. terrible names, I bandaged his wound, wrapping horse leg tape all around his head. He looked like a wounded soldier.

Meanwhile, J.B. had pulled off his shirt, dipped it into the water trough, and was mopping his head and chest with it. He finished up by wrapping the shirt around his head, turbanlike. He looked like a zombie.

Suddenly, Joe Frank's sedan came speeding into the barnyard and slid to a gravel-spraying stop near the tractor. When he jumped from the car and slammed the door, I knew he was hot about something. Since he was wearing his baby blue golf outfit, white shoes, and sun visor, I assumed that he had been playing golf and had lost several bets.

He had stomped about six steps toward the barn when he spied J.B. kneeling by the horse trough, his hands over in the water and a coiled-up shirt over his head. Then he saw Pool Do sitting up against the corral fence with his head swathed in horse leg wrappings.

"What's goin' on here?" he blurted. He was jerking his shoulder profusely, a nervous habit of his which increased in frequency as his temper rose. "What's wrong with you, Pool Do?"

"J.B., he busted me upside the head with one of them big rocks over there," he said, motioning toward a pile of rocks.

"I never done it!" yelled a suddenly rejuvenated J.B. "It was just a little old gravel. He didn't have no call to make fun of me just 'cause I'se sick. He's all time onto me 'cause I got a weak stomach."

Joe Frank was furious. He shoulder was in almost constant jerking motion, and now he was rapidly spitting, another nervous habit of his.

"Y'all just git out!" he exploded. "Just leave. I'm sick and tired of all y'all's mess!" Then he stomped back to his car without so much as throwing a howdy in my direction, got in, and tore out, his tires slinging gravel, grass, and dirt skyward.

The two men slowly got to their feet while I finished with the horse, and busied themselves opening and closing gates as if nothing had happened. When I unbridled the horse, J.B. groggily put him in the right pen and made sure he had hay and water.

"Well, what are y'all gonna do now?" I asked. My two favorite farmhands had just lost their jobs!

"We got to fix fences over on the back side," Pool Do said. "Then we got to work on that silage unloader."

"But I thought he just fired y'all!" I exclaimed.

"Aw, Doc, he fires us at least once a week," allowed J.B. "He don't mean nothin' by that. I been livin' on this place all my life. I worked for his daddy. Pool Do's been here longer than I have. We may be hired hands but this place is our home, too!"

"Yeah, we could quit and leave here, I reckon," said Pool Do. "But I wouldn't know where to go. Besides, Mr. Joe Frank couldn't run this place without us! He wouldn't know where to find nothin'! If we left he'd be huntin' for us before dark!"

Hired men like Pool Do and J.B. don't get the credit they deserve for all the hard work they do. I know they make my job easier, except when they're fooling around with each other.

Twenty

Some of our new clients expressed surprise when they observed my diplomas and other official-looking certificates on the walls of the waiting, examination, and surgery rooms of the clinic.

"With all that many years of school, why didn't you just become a real doctor?" some asked. At first I would feel insulted, but as time passed, I just made a joke of it, sometimes remarking, "Because I hate people." I tried to remember that the ones who asked that question had probably never used a veterinarian before and had no knowledge of the education required to become a D.V.M.

I find that our work with animals benefits human life in many ways. Once in a while, even a country vet is directly responsible for the saving of a human life. Back in the 1960s, I'm sure I actually saved the life of a hunting acquaintance, Bill Jack Smith. B.J.'s life was ruled by two strong forces: hunting and his tough-as-nails wife, Lorene. He was fanatic about hunting raccoons with his pack of hounds, primarily in order to get away from Lorene and her constant nagging and never-ending list of "honey do" directives. B.J. was a runty little fellow, while Lorene was a good six inches taller and at least a hundred pounds heavier. I never understood the attraction. She frequently beat up on poor old B.J., and on several occasions he had shown up for work at the paper mill wearing bruises, black eyes, and scrapes at strange locations on his person.

One Sunday afternoon, on the spur of the moment and unbeknownst to Lorene, B.J. drove his pickup truck over to Meridian, Mississippi, and paid a thousand dollars for what was supposed to be a fine young female hunting dog. According to the information he was given by the seller, the young bluetick hound was the result of a carefully planned mating of two special canines with world-bragging qualities. Even so, the local coon-hunting elite questioned her coon-treeing ability and suspected that B.J. had been taken to the cleaners. A thousand dollars was a lot of money to pay for a hunting dog in those days, although I knew others had paid even more for quality dogs. Nevertheless, B.J. was very proud of his purchase and named her C.K., short for "Coon Killer."

As dogs go, C.K. was a "looker." About a year old, she was long and lean, and just a little higher in the rear than the front, which B.J. thought would give her the advantage of speed in the woods. Glossy white hair occasionally speckled with small blue ticking covered some 60 percent of her body, while the remainder was covered with several large navy blue splotches. Her beautiful coat indicated she had been fed well, dewormed properly, and defleaed regularly. Her upright tail wagged and her doggy face gave the hint of a smile at the sight of a human. The only flaw I saw was her drooping lower eyelids, which made her seem sad. But B.J. said that was the way blueticks were supposed to look.

If Lorene had been informed in advance about C.K.'s arrival, she would have instantly vetoed the project and then punched out B.J.'s lights for even thinking about such a foolish and expensive notion. But when her husband arrived home with the dog, he also wisely arrived with a pound of chocolate-covered peanuts and a case of Falstaff beer, Lorene's favorite afternoon snacks. In an uncharacteristically weak moment, she not only allowed him to keep C.K., she even refrained from knocking him senseless.

Things began to go awry very soon, however. The first evening, the dog escaped from her new private pen and chewed her way into Lorene's henhouse and killed all five of her beloved egg-laying Dominecker hens. B.J. and Lorene were blissfully unaware of the commotion, thanks to the racket made by their secondhand window air conditioner. The carnage was not discovered until midnight, when B.J. shuffled out the back door and met C.K., sporting several downy feathers on her nose and head and emanating the unmistakable aroma of deceased poultry. To make matters worse, she didn't even have the decency to consume her kill. B.J. was again spared from violence, this time because Lorene, having consumed half the beer and almost all the chocolates, had slipped into a semicoma, which made her only semiviolent. Instead of resorting to fisticuffs, she ordered her man to defeather and dress the hens, which she made into chicken salad. B.J. ate chicken salad twice a day for a month.

Two nights later, C.K. escaped again and was on the lam for twenty-four hours. The following afternoon she came staggering up to the house, her belly swollen and her breath reeking of rotten meat. When B.J. came home from the day shift at 3:15 P.M., his prize hound was down, paralyzed, and unable even to crawl. Within minutes B.J. and C.K. arrived at the clinic, he in a frenzy and she nearly dead. It was obvious that he feared more for his own life than that of his dog. He knew if the thousand-dollar dog died, his life would be in grave danger.

"Doc, please don't let this dog die," he pleaded, wringing his hands and pacing the exam room floor. "Lorene'll kill me, Doc!"

C.K. was suffering from an obscure ailment called "coon dog paralysis," also known as "pseudobotulism." It is apparently caused by the consumption of spoiled meat, since it frequently occurs when dogs are let out of their pens and they find and eat decomposing carcasses out in the woods. Once the toxins get into the dog's system and the dog becomes paralyzed, there is no cure. Good nursing care, force feeding, and intravenous fluids are the usual treatments. It was a commonly seen condition in Choctaw County hunting dogs, especially at the start of deer-hunting season.

Somehow, B.J. had convinced Lorene that some dog hater had released the dog from her pen and had intentionally fed her some deadly poison. Instead of harassing him, she went around harassing the neighbors, trying to find the culprit.

I didn't think the patient had a chance for survival, but I had to try—not only for her sake, but also for the well-being of her master. So, I kept her at the clinic, and with Jan's, Sue's and Tim's help, did my best to treat her. We used lots of vitamins, antibiotics, IV fluids, cow calcium, and a host of other drugs. At least twice a day we passed a tube down her esophagus and pumped gruels of all sorts into her stomach. We were careful to keep her on soft pads or blankets, and keep her rotated and as comfortable as possible. At least twice a day either B.J. or Lorene or one of their kids called to get an update on C.K.'s condition and someone from their neighborhood paid her a visit. For two weeks there was no change in her condition. The fact that she was still hanging on was motivation enough for most of us, including the owners, to keep trying. I was the one who was the least encouraged and was about ready to throw in the towel, because I could see the mounting cost of the treatments. I wondered if we were going to be stuck with the bill. But early on the morning of her seventeenth day of hospitalization, C.K. wagged her tail ever so slightly as I approached her cage for her first feeding of the day. From then on, she made steady progress, and on the thirty-first day, Lorene and the children came and picked her up. It was a happy time for all of us. Lorene especially was in high spirits, smiling and thanking everybody who had had a part in saving C.K. She was her usual loud and boisterous self, but cheerful for a change.

"Why are you so happy?" I asked. "I thought you hated that dog."

"Oh, it's not so much the dog that I'm thrilled about," she declared. "It's B.J. Doc, if that dog had died, I'd have killed him! Don't you see? You not only saved that no-account coon dog, but you also saved that no-account man. He ain't good for much, but he's mine."

With that, she gave me a bear hug that momentarily rendered me helpless. If I had never before been concerned for B.J.'s safety, I certainly was at that instant. I really do believe she would have caused great bodily harm to that poor man.

All the local coon hound critics were right about C.K.'s hunting ability. On her first hunt, some months after her stay at the clinic, B.J. reported that she stayed glued to his side the entire evening. When she heard the other dogs baying and finally treeing the coon, she looked up at her master in wide-eyed wonder as if to say, "What are those fool dogs doin'?"

Whether her hunting ability was affected by her severe illness—or by the fact that Lorene and the kids made a car-riding, sweater-wearing, house-dwelling lapdog out of her—I don't know. I just figured any so-called hunting dog that refuses to ride in the back of a pickup truck probably doesn't possess the proper coon-hunting genes.

I was happy because I had not given up on her. I have often wondered what would have happened between B.J. and Lorene if I had failed to save her. I'm delighted I didn't have to find out and have to carry that guilt around for the rest of my life.

Twenty-one

I had seen the old barn many times in passing and had some-times spied a few shorthorn-looking cows and yearlings in the barn lot or standing under the added-on lean-to out of the rain. In the late afternoon a passerby could see through the spaces between the boards and notice there were people inside milking the few cows by hand and probably hoping that the barn wouldn't fall over before they finished their chores. I presumed there just weren't enough cows to justify the expense of a mechanical milker. Also, a milking machine needed electricity, and from the looks of the fresh dirt around the new roadside light poles, that was a relatively new luxury for them. I had never been invited there until now, except for the time we blood-tested all the cattle for brucellosis, and govern-ment business didn't count as an invitation.

The dilapidated barn was right next to the gravel road and set at an odd angle so the rear corner of the lean-to was less than three feet from the fence that guarded the road. The eave actually hung out over the edge of the ditch, and the whole thing was leaning badly, but away from the road.

A milk can always sat just outside the doorway—the door had fallen off its hinges. At milking time there was a strainer in the top of the can with cheesecloth or a clean fertilizer sack stretched over it so the milk would be debris-free when it hit the bottom of the can. Compared to the hand-extracted, nonpasteurized product of that age, today's milk is practically sterile.

That morning the grandmother and owner of the cow, Mrs. Turner, had called the office requesting assistance.

"Mr. McCormack," she said seriously, "we've got a cow that's done gone plum crazy. I believe that a mad dog musta bit 'er."

"How's she acting, Mrs. Turner?" I asked.

"Oh, she's acting real nervous. Lickin' the side of the barn continuously, all gaunted up in the belly, and her breath smells funny. She's been that way pert' near all mornin'. Reckon she's got the hydrophobie?" I reckoned to myself that most cows have funny-smelling breath.

"Well, she could have. We do see rabies here once in a while. And we're always seeing rabid coons, you know. Tell me, when did she have her last calf?" Many health problems in cows are directly related to calving and the commencing of the milk flow.

"She came in about a month ago and was giving a Borden bucket full of milk twice a day till this happened. Now from the looks of her udder she won't give a teacup full, I imagine. I want you to come out here and look at her for me this morning. We won't be here today, but the cow will be under the shed or around the barn when you get here. I'll call back later on this afternoon and see what you think's wrong with her. If she's been bit by a mad dog, I don't want a thing more to do with her."

I have always liked treating cows with nervous acetonemia, also called ketosis, because they respond so quickly to intravenous glucose injections. I was quite sure this cow was suffering from that seemingly mysterious malady.

Pulling up to the barnyard gate, I spied the old black Jersey cow standing under the lean-to, rhythmically licking the side of the corncrib as if she had a natural craving for oak boards.

As I drew closer to the barn, I began to detect the unmistakable odor of ketotic cow's breath. Just as I had suspected, she was suffering from the nervous form of acetonemia.

Physiologists have a field day when lecturing on bovine acetonemia. These brainy experts go into great and boring detail when trying to explain the complex metabolic pathways involved in something called Kreb's cycle, which veterinary students must memorize and quote back to those egghead physiology professors or stern state board examiners, many of whom have never had the "pleasurable" task of restraining and treating a cow suffering from this condition.

Simply put, cows with ketosis do not get enough energy, so they convert too much of their body fat into glucose. A side effect of this is the accumulation of the potentially toxic ketone bodies, which causes some cows to go loco. Some cows even turn violent, giving their owners good reason to suspect rabies.

The patient paid no attention to me until I moved to catch her with my rope. The instant my rope made contact with her neck, chaos commenced. She hurled herself into the barn, crashed into the side of the crib, bellowed wildly, and started bucking and leaping around under the shed like a vicious, stiff-legged rodeo bull.

I was shocked and unprepared for this sudden and violent surge. As the berserk cow banged and ricocheted against the fragile barn walls, artistically creating long and deep scars in the soft dirt floor with her hooves, I scanned the cramped premises for a suitable hitching post. There was none. But since there was a wild, half-ton, deranged cow cavorting on the end of my rope, I knew I needed to find a strong, well-implanted post, and as soon as possible. After a second scan of the area, I selected a post that seemed only semirotten and made a fast loop around it with the free end of the lariat.

That was a mistake, as I realized some five seconds later, when the irritated cow continued her onslaught on the shabby structure. She bellowed, with tongue lolling out, her head sideways, as her breathing became raspy and loud. I knew the way she was fighting the support beam she was on the verge of choking down. Suddenly, the post buckled in the middle and the building started to creak and groan. The next thing I knew there was a popping crash and I was left holding a tightly drawn lariat with an insane cow on the other end. In the middle was an old cedar post twirling around the rope like a majorette's baton. Beams began to pop and gnarly sheets of tin began to rain down. The noise of falling lumber was deafening for what seemed to be a couple of minutes but, in reality was about three seconds. I found myself lying on my back with boards, tin, and flakes of hay stacked randomly on top of me. Dust was billowing everywhere.

The rope had been jerked from my hand, and the cow was nowhere to be seen, but in the sudden quiet of the collapse, I detected a strange licking or scraping sound coming from the vicinity of the tractor a few yards away. My patient had escaped the predicament that had befallen me and was now trying to chew and lick the flywheel off the old John Deere tractor.

"Why do I keep getting myself in these messes?" I recall mumbling to myself. It seemed I just attracted trouble.

As I laid there gazing in awe at the rubble around me and hearing the sounds of the cow chowing down on the farm implements, I wondered if I was dreaming. If not, then what was I doing just lying there? I began thrashing around, knocking and kicking sheets of tin and splintered planks aside with my number-eleven, four-buckle overshoes. Eventually, I was able to move rafters and enough of the debris over to one side so that I could crawl to safety.

I was trying to brush the dirt off my pants when Goat, the mailman, stopped at the Turner mailbox and peered out his car window at the destruction.

"D-D-Doc, did y-you do that?" he stammered, peering at the colossal pile of kindling.

"Go on, Goat," I yelled, frustration getting the better of me. "Just deliver your letters. Can't you see I'm up to my neck in problems?" He drove off in a huff.

The patient still had my rope around her neck, and she was trying to bite chunks out of the cleats on the tractor's right rear tire. I slipped up to the long end of the rope lying motionless on the ground and quickly looped it around the tractor's drawbar.

"Let's just see if you can pull the tractor off," I snorted to her.

As expected, she went into a flipping and twisting midair fit, which resulted in a peculiar body slam that shook the bare earth when she landed. But the tractor hardly flinched. I had dextrose ready for IV infusion in short order, and while dodging flying hooves and a wildly switching tail, eventually got most of the medication into the correct place. When I released the rope, she seemed to be a different cow, walking calmly to the water trough and, after quenching her considerable thirst, headed for the hayrack. She was eating with gusto when I realized that a strong wind was blowing out of the southwest. Dust was being kicked up, stray pieces of tin were rattling, and drops of rain were coming down at a forty-five degree angle, hitting my bare skin with piercing force.

On my way to the next farm call I tried to come up with a diplomatic way of telling Mrs. Turner that her cow and I had accidentally razed her barn. I sure hoped she didn't call on one of Choctaw County's fine lawyers to start lawsuit proceedings. Of course, since the cow had made such a dramatic recovery, maybe she wouldn't go that far.

The storm was getting worse, and small hail began to fall. I was glad that I had finished with the Turner cow catastrophe before the bad weather arrived. As I passed a farmhouse along my way back home, I saw an aproned housewife making a beeline toward her loaded clothesline, while her neighbor a quarter mile down the road was snatching her morning wash from a yard fence, both throwing quick but concerned glaces toward the southwest skies. Both, as busy as they were, still had the courtesy and time to throw up their hands at the passerby. A friendly wave is a small gesture, but it is one of the big perks of small-town and country living.

The next few hours were filled with a series of large animal calls and routine country veterinary work. Blood samples were drawn from a few show cattle, several horses were presented for dental work, and then there was the usual stopping in the middle of the road to discuss the prospects for hunting season with friends. Between the two-way radio's crackling and a number of farm stops, I didn't have much time to reflect on the Turner cow. But late that afternoon, Jan called me on the radio.

"Mrs. Turner was just on the phone, and she was pretty excited," Jan said.

"Well, uh, uh, what did she say?"

"Oh, she said that the cow you treated this morning was completely well."

"Well, good," I replied. "I guess she realizes that rabies wasn't the problem. What else did she say?"

"Well, she thinks you are a pretty good doctor, she's appreciative, and she will be in Saturday to pay the bill."

"Is that all?"

"Oh, yes, you won't believe the excitement they had out there," she continued. "Seems they must've had a tornado touch down there during that bad cloud today, and it tore her barn down. She said it was a miracle that the cow wasn't killed, since she stayed under that shed most of the time. Wasn't that luck?"

"Yep," I muttered. "We were all very, very lucky today."

"She said they had been planning on tearing the old barn down anyway because it was so rickety, but they were waiting for Junior to come home on leave from the army so he could help."

If Goat, the mailman, ever realized that he saw the barn collapsed before the tornado, he never did say so. . . .

Twenty-two

It never failed to amaze me how many odd conditions I saw that weren't described or even mentioned in the veterinary textbooks and other literature: foreign bodies that jabbed their way into strange anatomical sites on farm animals; dogs that swallowed corncobs, fishing lures, needles, and even large rocks; not to mention some very weird skin conditions.

One of my most unforgettable oddball cases was that of Waldo and Kathy King's "piano pigs." Kathy called on an April evening with the word that Bulldog, one of their three sows, had produced a fine litter of eleven pigs and all the dozen swine were doing just fine. Ten of the piglets were white or otherwise light colored, and only one was red. He was a runt, the red one, but a scrappy little booger, according to Kathy. Bulldog, the daughter of Bertha, was of spotted Poland China ancestry and had inherited some of her momma's hot temper genes. A few months before, Bertha had been my first porcine cosmetic surgery patient, since then commonly referred to as "that face-lift hawg" by all the neighbors on King Road. Even though I had been kind enough to remove a large, unsightly growth from her upper lip and had moved some cheek skin around to enhance her appearance, she and I had not been on speaking terms since the surgery, nor had her sutures been removed. In my last and only attempt to do so, she angrily ran me up to the top of a self-feeder in her private lot. I regretted not taking before and after photos of Bertha's face, like those big-city plastic surgeons do, so that I could advertise my skill in *Swine Beautiful* magazine. The Kings were certainly impressed with the results, as were all the neighbors. The proud father of Bulldog's new piglets was a burnt-orange-color, half-Duroc boar who answered to the name of Tennessee, obviously because he was the color of a University of Tennessee football jersey. With his blunt and twisted nose, and tusks curving upward and outward from his always-slobbering lips, he was not a pleasant sight, but as I kept trying to explain to Kathy, a boar is supposed to be ugly and stinky, and therefore doesn't need a veterinary face-lift. I was sure that giving him a new look and removing the scent gland from its very sensitive location would make him less attractive to his piggy girlfriends. Kathy was raised up in downtown Mobile and didn't know much about the well-being of swine. But she was trying to become well-versed in animal agriculture, reading all sorts of livestock production books and pamphlets and calling her favorite veterinarian every few minutes.

"Are you gonna name all these pigs?" I asked when I dropped by to pay my respects to the new arrivals a few days later. She customarily named everything on the farm, which I thought was a nice touch. Some of the local cattlemen scoffed at such a notion, however, and thought a numbered ear tag would be more appropriate. "What's she gonna do when she runs out of names?" one snorted. "Besides, I don't want to know their first names, I just want to know what they weigh and how much a pound I'm gonna git."

I could understand how names might be a problem if there were five hundred head out there and they were all the exact size and color, but I still thought naming animals was a nice touch for Choctaw County animal owners, since most of them had fewer than a hundred head. "I'm gonna name the dark runt Fred, but the others are all identical, so I may just sell them before they get older enough to display their individual personalities," she stated with authority. "I'll keep Fred, maybe as a pet, 'cause he's so little and feisty."

"Why the name Fred?"

"I don't know, it just came to me."

About two or three weeks later, a nighttime phone call came in from Kathy.

"How're you doin', Doc?"

"I'm doin' fine, but it's hot for April, isn't it? I really worked up a sweat today. And the man says it's gonna continue to be in the eighties for several more days. How are the babies?"

"I'm not sure. Something seems to be wrong. I know this sounds crazy, but some of 'em seem to be dipping down in the rear end when they are walking, and sometimes they act a little jumpy."

"Huh, that doesn't sound familiar. Are they still in the barn stall?"

"Well, yeah, at night they are. But every morning I let them out in the lot between the barn and the house so they can get some exercise."

"Why don't I run by there in the morning and we'll take a look," I suggested. "It's probably nothing, but let's check it out."

I thought about the things that caused jumpy pigs. Perhaps it was a new disease and I would go down in history as the first animal health worker to describe it in the literature. I laughed to myself just thinking about "Jittery John Swine Syndrome" and how I might be asked to present a big paper on it at the World Pork Congress in Poland or somewhere way off. A picture of me in my white loafing lab coat, while sternly peering down into one of those two-headed microscopes, would appear in the *Hog World* magazine.

Seriously, though, I thought about pseudo-rabies, or maybe a weird form of hypoglycemia, or possibly poisoning from some of the hemlock plants growing in the lot that I had warned Kathy about. I had seen salt poisoning in older pigs, but not in pigs getting all their nutrition from their momma. Nothing rang a bell.

Twelve hours later, I was staring at the eleven little pigs, all like peas in a pod, except for Fred, who was much smaller than his littermates, but just as active and seemingly perfect. When we moved them out into the outside lot with Bulldog they lined up side by side, as if trained, and were momentarily motionless, until Bertha realized that was exactly what we wanted. No self-respecting sow is going to do what a human being wants her to do. The sun was shining brightly in the cloudless sky as the family of twelve eased across the lot, the quiet and serenity of the farm punctuated by the cackling of a hen and the signaling of Bulldog's contentment and presence by her repetitive grunting bulletins. I was still at a loss for a possible diagnosis because I had seen nothing amiss.

"I don't see it, Kathy. They seem just right to me," I opined.

"Uh huh, I guess so, but something's not right. I just can't put my finger on it," she declared. "But they're not doing this morning what they were doing last night."

"I'm gonna head on, 'cause I got a lot to do today. You know, it's gonna be nearly ninety degrees today?"

It was six P.M. when I again set foot in the King barnyard. Both Kathy and Waldo were sitting under the roof of a lean-to on the house side of the barn. When she heard my tires crunch gravel, Kathy sprang from her seat and raced to my truck. I knew something was up.

"They're doin' it again! 'Cept this time it's a lot worse. Come on and look at this."

Waldo never left his seat, just quietly and rhythmically raised his huge glass of iced tea from lap to mouth, then lowered it back to his overalled leg. "This beats all I ever saw," he declared. "I've been around hogs all my life, and this is the weirdest thing I ever saw," he uttered, shaking his head from side to side. "I wonder if we ought to get a veterinarian out here." Good old Waldo, always acting the smart aleck that he was apparently born to be.

The pigs were all lined up, just as before, but this time they were alternately dipping down, in quick, weird, curtsy fashion, then standing back up again for a few seconds. The scene reminded me for all the world like the way the ivories moved up and down on a player piano as it belted out a tune. As I watched, Kathy kept pushing me for an instant diagnosis.

"Well, what is it? What is it? What can you do for 'em? I told you they were sick!" she said, pacing back and forth while doing the hand-ringing thing.

"Wait a minute! Just let me think!" I pleaded.

"Boy, it was hot today," declared Waldo, mopping his brow. "That sun was hotter than a north Alabama cookstove!"

When he said the words "hot sun," it hit me upside the head. I looked closer at the little white pigs while Bulldog was enjoying a shelled corn snack. They appeared unusually pink, and they felt hot to the touch, all except Fred, the runt. And he wasn't showing any signs of the modified curtsy movement either. The pigs were sunburned! It made sense when I saw the white skins now pink, and remembered the history of the pigs' being escorted out into the hot, sun-kissed field in the daytime, then back to shelter for the evening. That's why the symptoms were worse late in the evening. By the following morning the dipping syndrome had improved but going into the sunlight again the next day started the cycle all over again.

A few years earlier in veterinary school, a pink piglet had been brought into the clinic with the same strange symptoms, plus the additional sign of nystagmus, an involuntary sideways jerking of the eyes. The little patient was surrounded by a raft of bright students and several Ph.D.-type professors who were discussing diagnoses. Just as I had done on the phone, they too were listing all the possible central nervous system diseases and going into detail about which lab tests were appropriate in order to make an accurate diagnosis. When the elderly janitor eased by the stall, sweeping up the bits of hay we had kicked around, he peeked his head down at the patient and simply said, 'little feller's done got hissef sunburned, hadn't 'e?" Then he swept on by, humming to himself. Without a word, the learned professors looked at each other, then turned and stomped back into their offices, no doubt to secretly pore over their old school notes and the latest textbooks. We wanted to ask the janitor how to treat the pig, but were afraid the instructors would find out and sabotage our graduation plans. We used some cool compresses, a darkened stall, and a small amount of steroid injection. He improved rapidly, probably due to the cool and dark aspects of our therapy.

"I know what's wrong with these pigs, and it's so simple that even someone from downtown Mobile should have been able to figure it out," I announced, staring right at Kathy. She reached down to the ground, scooped up two corncobs, and faked a throw at my head.

"Well . . ."

"Well, what?" I answered.

"WHAT'S WRONG WITH MY DADBURNED PIGS?"

"Now you got it, they're burned!" I said, taking Waldo's place as smart aleck of the moment.

Another fake cob throw, but I ducked just to be sure.

"They've got solar poisoning," I said. There was instant quiet; even the tinkle of ice in Waldo's glass tinkled no more. Bulldog even turned a floppy ear in my direction.

"What in the Sam Hill is solar poisoning?" exclaimed Waldo.

"Well, up north they'd call it sun poisoning," I answered. "Or where I was raised they'd call it sunburn, but it looks better on the record as solar poisoning."

"Yeah, on the statement, too!" declared Waldo. "A fancy diagnosis like that adds another ten dollars to the bill." Kathy stared first at me and then at Waldo, as if disgusted with both of us.

"All kidding aside, now, this really is sunburn. Just think about what has happened and the fact that little Fred isn't affected, and it really does make sense. Just put them in the shade and keep them there until this clears up, which it will in a few days. You can spray cool water over 'em if you'd like. Now, if you want to get fancy, we can give them all anti–solar poisoning injections, which are quite expensive. Because I do know that you want the best for your babies." I almost suggested slathering them with suntan lotion, but I thought she might actually do it.

Kathy dropped her corncob weapons and was almost speechless. Waldo started to laugh first, then she giggled a few times. She took her animal health matters a little more seriously than he did. "No, I don't want 'em needled, that'll hurt."

The pigs survived and had no lasting effects from the sun. But their story again reinforced why a veterinarian should always use horse sense when dealing with animals. It also gave all the neighbors on King Road something to talk about for years and years.

Bulldog's pigs recovered nicely from their bout with the sun and were growing like weeds. All except Fred. Kathy was having a difficult time accepting the fact that no matter how much she fed him, he wasn't going to catch up with the others. I tried to explain that he'd been born a runt and would remain a runt for the rest of his life—unless some high-tech university scientist came up quickly with a dramatic cure for that dreaded affliction, porcine runtism. She wanted to know the names of the land grant college swine researchers so she could contact them and ask them personally had they done research on runtism. I explained that I didn't know who they were and I was positive that no Ph.D. professor in his right mind would be caught doing runt studies.

"In those big hog operations they put runts to sleep or give them away to folks on the edge of town for pets," I stated. "A runt pig is a liability."

She was not impressed with my answers and tried hard to prove me wrong. She supplemented his momma's milk diet with pig starter and placed it before him in clean receptacles twice a day in the privacy of his own cubicle. His drinking water was cool, clean, and pure, having been hand-pulleyed from a deep well and certified by an up-north, educated man who worked for the county health department. Fred did his part by consuming his victuals with hearty zeal and oinking for more. Still, he couldn't catch his contemporaries in weight and stature, but he surpassed them in the amount of personal attention and love he commanded.

A few weeks after the famous sunburn episode, Fred suffered a spell of physical and emotional trauma. Bulldog, in a moment of rage, not only tossed him from the nest with her smelly snout but also stomped on him with one of her large cloven hooves. The wiry little porker probably avoided passing through the Pearly Gates by playing dead in the deep straw for several hours. When Kathy found him, his outer claw on his left front foot was smashed and bleeding badly. She attempted emergency first aid by wrapping the wound tightly to prevent further blood loss.

"Doc, Fred's been hurt real bad," yelled Waldo over the phone. "Old Bulldog just stomped the little feller nearly to death! I need ye!"

It wasn't long before I was at Fred's side. His toe was hanging by a small strand of skin, and it was obvious that a quick snip with the scissors and a tight wrap was in order. "This won't take but a second," I announced, reaching for a sharp instrument.

"Wait, don't cut!" screamed Kathy. "Can't you go to the slaughterhouse, get another toe, and graft it on, kind of like they do with fruit trees?"

I stared at her, speechless, and there was dead silence for a few moments while I pondered the unusual request. All I could do was blink my eyes and try to figure out how I was going to get this animal lover to listen to reason.

"Look, Kathy, you know I don't have the technical know-how to perform transplant surgery, and I don't believe we can get a hold of anybody who will do it on a pig. Besides, it would be prohibitively expensive."

"I don't care what it costs, dadgummit!" she retorted. "It just doesn't seem right to make my little Freddie go through the rest of his life with only one toe on that side."

Have mercy! What could I say? I knew she was wondering why no one was doing research on toe problems as well as runtism.

"I understand your thinking, but I can assure you this little piggy will be able to live the good life without that toe. He'll still hunt for acorns and root around in the dirt just like a normal hog, after a short period of convalescence, of course." I never thought I'd become a "piggyatrician."

"What's this period of convalescence?" she asked.

"Well, you'll need to keep him up here in this private stall, away from his mother, of course, and continue your attention and tender loving care. Then you'll need to change his bandage every few days. That will mean extra work for you, but I know how much you love all your animals."

"I won't mind that, and you can depend on me to take care of my pigs. But you'll have to do your part, too, by dropping by here on your rounds and checking on him. So go ahead and do your surgery, but you better not hurt him, you hear?"

"Yes'm, I hear you," I said sheepishly.

With Kathy holding the squirming and squealing creature, I injected the claw with a small amount of local anesthetic, scrubbed with antiseptic soap, and snipped the toe off. Next, I wrapped the remaining digit snugly from dewclaws down to the tip of the toe and gave Fred an injection of penicillin. He was a wiggling but docile patient the entire time. That would soon change.

When I returned several days later, Fred looked fine as he peered at me through the cracks in the stall door while snacking on his food. He'd stare, take a few slurps of his gruel, then pause briefly in his lip smacking and stare at me intently.

When I opened the door and stepped into the stall, the rascal charged at me like a rodeo bull! He went for my right ankle, his sharp needle teeth flashing. In shock, I hightailed it out of the stall.

I had been attacked by sows, dogs, cows, bulls, parakeets, sneaky rams, horses, and farmers, but never before by a baby pig.

"What's happenin', Doc?" asked Kathy as she strolled into the barn hall.

"I'll tell you what's happening," I said. "Your little Fred just attacked me. Just look at these slobber marks on my coveralls." I pointed to the cuff of my right pant leg.

She glanced quickly at the alleged attack site, and then she laughed. Now, I often laugh at myself and usually join in the guffawing when I make a dumb mistake. But I don't like to be made fun of by an animal owner when one of her pets or livestock has attacked me.

"Why don't you go in there and try him," I suggested.

"Of course I will," she offered, "seeing as how you are scared of such a sweet little feller."

"Wonderful," I mumbled, then just bit my lip.

Kathy hopped over the sill into the stall and started making the appropriate pig noises with her mouth, sort of a "tsk, tsk" sound. Even though Kathy still had a bit of big-city twang to her livestock-calling repertoire, she had made tremendous progress in the few years I had known her.

To a nonpig person, this description must be amusing and confusing, but it is important to converse in "pig talk" or "cow talk" or whatever when dealing with the various animal species. When calling adult swine in from junky lots, a completely different jargon is necessary—something that sounds sort of akin to "Whooo-eepiiggg!" yelled with hands cupped around the mouth. In actuality, it means "Suey pig!" but after years of hollering, "Whoo-eeee" is less strenuous on the noisemaking parts of the throat and lips. But as Waldo once lectured, "It don't much matter to a hog what you holler out, just as long as it's the same every day. After all, they call hogs in China, too, and anybody knows a hog don't understand Chinese." Waldo's natural wit would have made him a multimillionaire if we could have ever gotten him to New York City, but he wouldn't even hear of making the trip. "I ain't about to ride no Trailways bus to New Yawk!" he'd squawk.

This day Fred had backed himself into a corner, trying to hide, and was paying no attention to Kathy's "tsk, tsks" and sweet-talking pleas. So when he saw the second human leg invade his territory in less than five minutes, he sank his teeth into it with equal little-pig vigor. I tried hard to conceal my mirth, but some of the giggles escaped from around my hands covering my mouth. It was neat for the vet not to be the one being laughed at for a change.

"You little three-legged, runty sapsucker!" Kathy yelled as she jumped from the stall. "I oughta get me a broom and work on yo' head!" It was the first time I had seen her get seething mad with one of her pets.

"I tell you what, let me get a piece of plywood from the junk pile and we'll hem him up in the corner," I said after I could speak without giggling. "Is your leg OK? Want me to look at it?" She glared at me, but refused to even rub the ankle.

In minutes we had him cornered, picked up, mouth wrapped securely shut with twine, and again tightly held in a red-faced Kathy's grip. The bandage was changed in short order.

This routine was repeated several more times, and each time the conflict resulted in flared tempers on both sides, and I would be disgusted with Fred's unnecessary rude behavior. But he did recover nicely and walked without a limp.

However, Fred continued to be a terror on the farm, tormenting his associates, both large and small. He came about it honestly, though, because his maternal grandmother, Bertha, obviously handed all her mean genes down to him. Eventually, Kathy and Waldo tired of his shenanigans and sold him to a neighbor on King Road.

They reported later that Runt's sausage was too tough to eat.

Twenty-three

I was hopelessly lost on the ribbon of backwoods blacktop as my faithful truck and I sped up and down the small hills of either Mississippi or Alabama, I wasn't sure which. I was not only confused about my present county location, I was equally befuddled about which state I was in. There had been miles and miles of tall pines, the taller ones almost brushing the ceiling of cloudy overcast of the February day, but no matter how hard I looked, there had been no signs advising me of my whereabouts and only few signs of human habitation other than an occasional rutty and muddy side road wobbling off the main road, seemingly to disappear into endless rows of evergreen and standing pine bark. I thought surely the word *infinity* was first coined by a surveyor as he peered down a straight but narrow logging road that disappeared into the horizon of a million pines.

Asking for directions is against my principles, and I only ask when absolutely necessary. It's just not manly to admit being lost and to risk being considered a wimp by pleading for directions. Of course, there are exceptions, and this was one of those times. Besides, Jan wasn't along and she would never know that I had admitted to being lost. Now I just needed to find someone, anyone, to send me in the direction of the John Tom Tew dairy farm! I was certain that I had made several wrong turns.

I was wishing that I had never agreed to visit a new farm client some fifty miles or so from home, but Mr. Tew had seemed so desperate for veterinary service that I couldn't say no. Now I was already late for the first appointment and still had no earthly idea of where I was going or when I was going to get back to my calls in Choctaw County.

While motoring aimlessly I thought about the directions that he gave to me over the phone. They were sketchy at best, and I realized he was like many of my clients back home. They knew where they lived, but couldn't tell a stranger how to get there. Typical directions to a farm might be as follows.

"OK, we're about a half a mile past the old Smith place."

"Well, I'm kinda new here, you know, and I'm not familiar with that farm," I'd apologize. Of course, that statement would label me a moron in their eyes. "Could you tell me what direction you are from Butler?"

"Toward Silas."

"All right, that's real helpful. That'd be south."

Once we'd establish the direction from my office or house, then I'd try to plot out the location on a large county map that Mr. Sexton, the county agent, had given me.

An occasional client would call in and ask Jan, Sue, Timmy, or Dick to send me to their place. When asked for directions, they'd say, "Oh, Doc's been here before, he knows the way." In spite of a good memory, I would sometimes fail to recognize the name of the person or farm. But nighttime calls were the worst.

"Come to the third dirt road to the left past the old Toxey school-house. Then come to the big oak tree across from the campground. Turn right. Come about, say, four miles. You'll see a green car parked in front of a brown house trailer. The horse is in a pen behind the trailer."

What they failed to say was that the old schoolhouse had been torn down years ago and the dirt road was hidden by kudzu vines. There was a white oak, a red oak, and a water oak across from where the campground used to be, and there are three dirt roads in the immediate vicinity. And how can a color-blind vet tell the color of a car and a trailer in pitch-black dark? Truck headlights at night can't always tell me anything except the car is a dark one. But it is a challenge, and would probably be a barrel of fun, if time wasn't money.

A good piece of advice to new veterinary school graduates is to try to avoid asking directions at honky-tonks. On an earlier wild-goose chase in the middle of the night, somewhere near the state line, I wheeled into the parking lot of a place the sign identified as "The First Chance." I knew I had come in from the dry Alabama side, since on the Mississippi side it declared "The Last Chance." There were two Harleys, several trucks, mostly four-wheel drives, all parked up close to the building, while others had attempted to pull off the road and parallel park, but in their haste had left the edges of their bumpers protruding into a traffic lane. No doubt their drivers couldn't wait to blow the foam off a few. A familiar voice in my head told me it was risky for a stranger to enter those swinging doors so late at night, but when the twangy country voice of Hank Williams came wafting through the open window, my heart was lulled into a false sense of security. Why would anybody be incited to violence when such a gifted singer was crooning such thought-provoking tunes?

But when I approached the door, I realized it was one of those places I had heard about, where they check you for a knife or gun when you walk in. If you don't have one, they issue you one. I managed a weak smile over such a weak little joke. Then I tried to put on a strong face as I walked through the door, kicking sawdust and peanut hulls out of my way.

The rednecks and roughnecks around the bar and tables numbered about a dozen, and their appearance was enough to chill the spine of the toughest hockey player in snow country. I quit kicking things on the floor.

"What'll it be, Big Red?" the bartender bellowed. He looked linebacker tough and nose guard ugly, and was wearing a T-shirt that'd had its arms cut out—probably with a switchblade knife, from the looks of them. From the way he moved behind the bar, it was plain to see he loved his job. Maybe he just loved helping people, or more likely, he was simply anticipating his nightly ritual of throwing toughs out into the gravel of the parking lot.

"I just need to get directions to a Junior Smith's horse farm," I said. I had always wished my name was Junior, or Buck, or maybe something with initials, such as J.B., M.D., or my all-time favorite initials name, Y.C.

"Any y'all know where Junior Smith's horse farm is?" he yelled on my behalf. The question quieted the drinkers down a few decibels, but Hank kept right on moanin' the blues, now going on about being in the doghouse. He must have had tough luck with his women.

"Who wants to know?" asked a bearded outlaw roughly as he turned and pointed his cantilevered belly in my general direction. His quaffing associate, a taller but less-bellied version, finished his beer and with one hand slammed the metal can down on the table, crushing it into a watch fob–size mass. He grinned a toothless grin, then adjusted the red bandana that was tied around his balding head just above his bushy eyebrows. He had much more hair below the bandana than above it, counting a full beard and ponytail. I figured he and Big Belly were the Harley riders.

The entire crowd then turned to stare at the uninvited stranger.

"I'm the vet, and one of Junior's horses is bad sick. He asked me to come over here, but I can't seem to find the cutoff road that he said to take," I said, trying to be polite but not real polite. I thought maybe it was a good idea to tell them I was a doctor. Surely nobody wants to fight a doctor out trying to save a life, whether human or horse.

"Are you the same vet that killed Fred's cow?" bristled a runt-sized guy at the end of the bar. While I pondered an answer, he took a long and deep five-second draw from a cigarette. He used both hands to fiddle with his pack of Picayune brand cigarettes, flipping the pack over and over. A friend once bragged to me that only real men smoke Picayunes, but I found out later that his first drag from one put him on the ground. I wondered if Runt might just be the toughest guy there, as dense smoke belched from both nostrils into a dense, carcinogenic cloud so thick his face was almost obscured. Even though I was some six feet away, I had an urge to cough.

"Naw sir, it wasn't me. Must have been Dr. McDaniel over at Red Hill," I said apologetically. I didn't know which Fred he was talking about.

One of the more sober of the group was trying to be helpful, so he came over and tried to explain how to get to my destination.

"Go back down the blacktop towards the creek. Just past the creek is a gravel road to the left. Go down that road till you come to a crossroads, then—"

"Naw, that ain't right, Buck," slurred another drinker. I cut my eyes over toward Runt, and he was still eyeing me and taking more long drags off that Picayune, never taking it from his lips. He had not used the ashtray since he lit up, and the ashes were long and drooping, just seconds away from breaking off and causing a problem. Sure enough, as my direction givers were arguing, the ashy mass broke off and scattered down Runt's shirt and into his lap. Like a monkey on springs, he leapt from the bar stool, slapping and slashing at the mess on his shirt and pants, but never removing the butt from his lips. When I was satisfied that Runt wasn't going to be fried to a crisp, I turned my attention back to the direction argument, which seemed to be getting me nowhere.

"It'd be better if he'd go back the other way and come in by the rock quarry," continued the man who disagreed with Buck.

"Both o' y'all are wrong," growled the bartender. "That bridge is out over by the Moss plantation, so he'd better come by that loggin' road on the land that the Rudder Hill crowd leased." If the bartender knew how to get there, I wondered why he hadn't told me earlier and avoided all the brouhaha.

"Look," said a fourth guy. "You just can't get there from here. He'll have to go back to Butler and start from there." Whoever this guy was, he seemed to get everybody at the bar riled up. I knew it was time for me to say my thanks for all the help and vamoose.

"Thanks!" I allowed, and fled out the door. As I made my way over the rough gravel, broken bottles, and empty cans, I could hear the argument getting louder about how to get to Junior's place. It sounded as if bar stools were sliding across the floor, and there was the sound of a beer bottle hitting the side of the building. When I backed out and pulled onto the blacktop road, two scuffling bodies came hurtling out of the barroom door amid flailing arms and flying cowboy hats. I realized that none of the cowboy hats had even been in the direction-giving argument two minutes earlier. All I had asked for were simple directions to a horse farm, but I had innocently instigated a war.

I did find Junior's horse farm. I knew that the on-duty Alabama state trooper would come as far as the state line on his nightly rounds, make a U-turn, and head back into Choctaw County. So I waited for him about a hundred yards inside the Alabama line.

It wasn't long before he came along, turned around, and pulled in behind me, then turned on his flashing lights.

"Can I see your driver's license, please. . . . Doc, is that you?" he asked.

"Yep, it's me, and I need your help."

"OK, what's the problem? Now, Doc, you haven't been drinking, have you? I sure do get the aroma of alcohol."

I told him about stopping at the First Chance for directions, the fracas that had ensued, and why I needed him to call in to head-quarters and find out where Junior's place was. It only took about one minute, since one of the night people at the state patrol office was Junior's first cousin. I was on my way, but only after a short lecture.

"Doc, don't you ever go in that beer place again! They've got a motorcycle gang that frequents that place, and they just love to pick fights with college boys and folks from Butler. You're lucky you got out of that place without getting cut up. You understand me?"

He didn't need to tell me twice. That's a real good reason to get your directions elsewhere.

⌒

I was sure that John Tom Tew's farm must be somewhere nearby. If only I could find a house or country store—anything but a honky-tonk. Suddenly, a sign appeared on the roadside a hundred yards ahead that proclaimed "Buford's Gas and Groc. 2 mile ahead."

The little country store was not unlike Miss Ruby McCord's Groc and Ser. Sta. I enjoy the abbreviating that so many small stores use. I'm sure it's done that way to save the cost of a bigger sign.

Today, Buford's store would be a classic. It wasn't much more than a shack covered with signs of all kinds advertising various foods, medicines, and farm supplies. There was "Drink Dr Pepper, ten, two, and four," "Dr. LeGear's Lice Killer," "Absorbine Jr. Liniment," "Mother's Friend," and "Cardui," just to name a few. There was hog and chicken mash, mineral blocks, and a kerosene tank on the front porch, but nothing advertising cold beverages, all reminiscent of Miss Ruby's place. I felt elated to have found such a safe, deep woods oasis, and the trucks parked out front promised people of goodwill inside. All vehicles wore Mississippi license plates, so I felt relieved at finally knowing where I was.

Once inside, I exchanged pleasantries with the group of store sitters, being careful not to immediately blurt out the question about directions. I bought a pint of milk and a box of animal crackers, since I was apparently too far away from Chattanooga to get a Moon Pie. The small amount of conversation and the fact that no one seemed to recognize me were enough to convince them that I was a stranger to those parts for sure.

"You ain't from aroun' hyeah, are ye, boy?" questioned the head sitter. He was sitting on an empty Nehi cola case turned up on its end.

"No sir, I'm not," I replied. "I missed a turn somewhere and I'm a little bit lost. Do any of y'all know where John Tom Tew's place is?" The question was met with blank stares and negative head shakes.

"Who?" asked sitter number one. He squinted his eyes and looked hard in my direction. In a flat three seconds, he had examined my boots, coveralls, cap, hair color, glasses, and everything in between. I'm sure he learned enough about me in those three seconds to present an hour seminar on my clothing sizes, health status, and how many times my nose had been broken.

"John Tom Tew. He runs a dairy around here somewhere."

"A milk dairy?" queried sitter number two. He looked confused. Like number one, he also sat on an upended soft drink case, but it was a Pepsi-Cola brand instead of a Nehi. He was attired in Tuf-Nut brand overalls and had each pant leg turned up in a good ten-inch cuff. Probably bought them extra long so his wife could cut off the extra and use it for patching older overalls that developed holes in their knees. Lots of people picked cotton on their knees so they wouldn't have to bend over so much.

"Yes sir, a milk dairy," I answered, trying not to laugh or even give any evidence of any humor. I've often wondered what other kind of dairy there could be, other than a "milk dairy." I suppose that must be like saying "widow woman" or "tooth dentist."

"Don't nobody live 'round here by that name," number two replied.

All heads again shook in the negative, even those belonging to the silent standers who weren't yet allowed a seat. As the heads shook from side to side, it was amusing to observe the way their eyes were riveted to my head. It was as if the naysaying routine was a long practiced ritual. But I knew they were only trying to protect their neighbor. They didn't know who I was or what I did, so they just assumed I was from some branch of the "govmint," and they had no reason to help me find my victim.

"Well, I can't figure out where I missed my turn," I allowed, looking at the makeshift map I had drawn from John Tom's telephone instructions. "He asked me to come over from Choctaw County and consult with him about some sick cows. He's gonna be real peeved when I don't show up."

"Oh, you mean *that* John Tom Tew!" exclaimed number one. "Look yonder through that window. See them blue silos across the woods, where the power line goes? That's John Tom's place."

"You some kind of a cow doctor or somethin'?" asked number two.

"Yes sir, I'm a veterinarian," I replied. "Y'all must not have a veterinarian around here, do you?"

"Oh yeah, we got lots of vetrans around here who fool with stock," he said emphatically. "Matter of fact, Doc Kirkland lives right up the road here."

"Dr. Kirkland? I don't recall that name," I answered, perplexed at my poor memory. "Do you know where he went to vet school?"

"Well, I don't reckon he went to no kind of school. He just takened it up 'cause they was a need for it in the community," number two replied. Presently, a friendly debate broke out over who was the best vet in the area. Several names were mentioned and their strengths and weaknesses were discussed. Since none of the names were familiar, I assumed they were individuals who "took up" the practice of veterinary medicine without the benefit of licensing or state board approval. Finally, one of the young apprentice store sitters broke his silence and revealed his choice for best vet.

"I heard tell of a vetnerry somewhere over yonder in Alabama," he testified, "and he operated on some fancy black Angus bull that was owned by a rich rancher. He cut that bull open, then reached way down in his innards and pulled out a six-inch piece of balin' warr with a crook on the end of it."

"Naw!" replied the shocked listeners, almost in unison.

"That's amazin'!" exclaimed number two.

"Naw, what's amazin' is that he told 'em beforehand exactly what that piece of warr was gonna look like and exactly where it was gonna be located in that bull's entrails," said the young man, gesturing excitedly with his hands. "He even told 'em it'd have that crook on the end!"

"Well, I know who—" I said, puffing up with pride. However, I was quickly interrupted by the storekeeper, who was leaning over the counter, chewing on the stub of a cigar. I would tell them later that I knew that vet very well.

"Wonder if that was the same vet who killed Fred Turner's black Jersey cow," he queried, looking suspiciously in my direction. "I heard it was a vet out of Alabama." I shrugged my shoulders and shook my head rapidly from side to side.

"Yeah, his old Jersey cow had just found a calf and she was bad off, down, bloated, and couldn't get up. Clyde sent for this jackleg vet, and while he was givin' that cow a jug of calcium, her eyes walled back in her head and she flopped over, graveyard dead."

"What did he say?"

"Aw, he claimed it wasn't the medicine that killed her, said it was 'cause her heart was so weak she couldn't take it and something about she had gotten some feed down her windpipe," answered the storekeeper.

"That's amazin'," allowed one of the sitters, just as before.

"Naw, what's amazin' is that he had the gall to charge ole Fred thirty dollars even after he'd killed that pore old cow. Y'all know Fred, he's just barely gittin' by on that railroad pension check every month, and you know how much good, rich milk a black Jersey like that gives. Well sir, that cow gave enough milk that his wife churned butter to make a few extra dollars every week. Y'all know we even sold that butter right here in the store. I believe it was the sweetest butter I ever tasted." All heads sadly nodded in the affirmative, and a couple of them appeared almost teary-eyed.

"You know anything about that, mister? You know anything about that greedy, no—account vet?" asked number one. "Somebody ought to whup his hin' end!"

Every head immediately turned and stared in my direction, stared daggers into both my eyes. There was a brief silence while I shuffled my feet.

"Uh, well, uh," I stammered, "there's several of my colleagues around who work occasionally in this area. But I'm not sure who the vets are that you are talking about." I was getting nervous and beginning to sweat, so I looked at my watch, then looked up to be sure my escape route was open.

"My goodness, look at the time!" I exclaimed. "I didn't realize it was so late. John Tom will have turned all those cows out if I don't get on right now!"

I hit the door, waving, grinning, and looking back at the unsmiling crew of sitters. It really wasn't all that late, but I wanted to get out of there before I confessed to being the vet responsible for the demise of Fred Turner's cow. All that good work done removing a wire from the sick bull wouldn't be enough to counteract a dead family milk cow. I was concerned they would gang up on me and demand a thirty-dollar rebate.

As I sped away, I took one last look at the store, and I saw a piece of cardboard nailed to one of the front porch support posts. Scribbled on it was a short, sad message:

NO BUTER

COW DEAD

Twenty-four

Veterinarians are injury-prone. And it is no wonder, since our patients are seldom cooperative and are never enthusiastic about what we are trying to do to them. I have visited with countless veterinary groups when they entertained themselves between educational sessions by comparing and identifying dog bite scars.

"See that one right there," an older practitioner would say, pointing to an inch-long scar on his left middle finger. "That's a Chow bite. And this one on my left thumb is—"

"Don't tell me. It's a black cocker spaniel, 'cause I got one just like it, right here on the side of my hand," would boast a colleague. "And this one on my little finger is a Chihuahua rip-out." Each veterinarian present would take the obligatory fleeting glance at their blemishes and immediately present his own battle scars, some even rolling up their sleeves to exhibit wrist and forearm disfigurements, each one claiming to have been attacked by a more vicious animal. I have seen bad monkey bite scars on clients' hands, who wished that they had left the primate in the jungle, where it belonged. Back in the sixties, there were no restrictions in Choctaw County about keeping monkeys as pets.

One beautiful spring Sunday morning a portly, blue-haired lady came into the clinic while I was treating the in-house patients. She was tugging on the end of a taut, well-used plow line, the other end fastened to a reluctant, red-eyed, half-Chow boy dog with his black tongue lolling out the side of his mouth, occasionally chewing on the rope. I noticed that he was standing in a stiff, "bowed up" position. As he slung his slobbery jowls, I could see that the points of some of his teeth were blunted, probably from biting on slow yard intruders and retrieving rocks thrown by his master.

"Oh, I just know it's that awful prostrate gland again, Doctor," she sobbed, wringing her hands and breathing in short, raspy bursts. "That little trashy cur down the street is in season again, and I just can't keep him away from her. Somebody needs to do something about her." I didn't understand what she had in mind, since I didn't know what she wanted "somebody" to do about the normal canine reproductive process. But I noticed that she used the word *prostrate*, and just in the interest of science, I did correct that for her.

"Prostate," I said.

"What?"

"It's prostate, not prostrate. Prostrate means he's down and won't get up."

"Oh, yes, he's that, too!" She seemed pleased that she owned a black-tongued, red-eyed, ill-prostated, prostrate canine.

People might not be aware that male dogs have prostate glands, nor do they even care, unless their dog has a problem with his. How the gland is examined will not be covered here, except to say that it is done the same way in human males.

"What's his name?" I asked the lady as I made a superficial examination.

"We call him 'Scruffy.' It was easy to see why. He needed a good bath, a comb out, his nails clipped, and his teeth cleaned.

"Does he bite?" I asked.

"Oh no, the grandkids wallow all over him, and he doesn't offer to snap at them or anything like that," she reported.

"Maybe I should put a muzzle on him, just in case," I suggested.

"Oh no, that would be so cruel. I can hold him, I promise," she pleaded.

Knowing better, I agreed to do it her way. Presently, I prepared to do what medical personnel do when examining the prostate gland. Prostate exams on animals have shown me that boy dogs experience just as much minor "discomfort" with the procedure as do their masters. The big difference, I am certain, is that dogs don't worry and fret about it for days ahead of the dreaded appointment with the urologist.

"Hold his head real tight, please, ma'am," I requested. That was in the days before malpractice insurance guidelines strongly suggested against allowing owners to restrain their animals being examined in the veterinary clinic.

The nice lady was kissing Scruffy's old scarred-up head as I gloved up and circled around to the end of the exam table. I noticed his eyes followed my every move. I slowly raised his tail and had just made contact with the gland in question when he went off like dynamite in a lard can.

In the space of two long seconds, Scruffy growl-barked, quickly escaped the weak grip of his panicked owner, reversed himself on the table, and sunk all four of his dull canines through the middle of my right hand. Actually, the owner had screamed and released Scruffy at first growl, and threw her arms toward the ceiling. Then, as I grabbed my wrist in agony, he jumped off the table, used the bottom half of the north wall as if it were a bathroom fixture, then looked up at me with a satisfied smirk on his clownlike face.

"What an idiot I was to let her hold that dog," was my first thought, as I dripped blood on the floor heading for the sink. "And why didn't I go ahead and muzzle him? I knew better!"

My second thought was of the 1:10 P.M. tee time at the golf course. All week long I had been looking forward to the rematch that my pharmacist buddy, Loren Caudle, and I had arranged with Billy Davis and Jim (Titanic) Thompson. A recent match had been interrupted because a horse owner called the golf course with an emergency. I wondered if it would be possible to even lightly grip a club with my mangled right hand. It continued to bleed and then swell right before my eyes.

Loren was not going to be pleased about this latest injury. The previous week, I had suffered from spasms in my lower back as a result of a strain caused when an Arabian mare fell on me while I was suturing a cut on her right hock. Before that, a ram had crashed into my chest and I had nicked my left forefinger while descenting a skunk.

Meanwhile, the lady had removed Scruffy to the waiting room and was giving him a short lecture on why it was impolite to bite people, but there was never any mention of why he shouldn't bite Dr. John. I assumed her thinking was that it didn't matter if I was getting paid to take the chance. That seemed to be the client rationale in some of the previous bites and kicks that I had suffered.

After a short discussion with the owner, we both decided that trying to give Scruffy an injection at that time would be dangerous, so we decided to medicate his feed with an antibiotic since his appetite had not been affected by his assumed infection. I dispensed a bottle of a new wonder drug developed for turkeys, which I thought was the appropriate medication for Scruffy, and smilingly escorted the two to their car, then broke, wild-eyed, for the ice cubes.

But the ice pack made the pain worse. It felt like there were four great corkscrews poking and twisting inside the bones and tendons of the hand. A close examination of the injury indicated that the wounds weren't as deep as I had first thought, thanks to the blunted canines, and the damage was primarily a large bruise. I toughed out the ice pack long enough for the hand to become numb, blotted it dry, and smeared it with a mixture of turkeymycin and bullcillin, then wrapped it carefully, using my left hand and my front teeth. Then I took two aspirin tablets.

I refused to attend church that day since there would have to be complete explanations and dozens of bone-crushing handshakes. I didn't mind the handshakes, I could do that with my left hand, but the discussions of dog bite wounds would get quite tiresome and gory, since each person would want to share a home remedy and relate a story of someone they knew who died or had their hand fall off because of a bite just exactly like mine.

When I arrived at the golf course a few minutes before our tee time, the pain had subsided. Remarkably, the hand didn't hurt except when I attempted normal finger movement. It was heavy, though, with all the fluid accumulation.

"What's wrong today, vetran?" asked Loren when he noticed me discreetly holding the affected hand atop my head. It throbbed less in that position.

"Nothing, farmist, it's just a scratch," I lied.

"Naw, you been dog bit again, ain't you?" he fumed. "Have you ever given any thought to getting a regular job?"

I neglected to tell him that the same thought had been running through my mind recently. Instead, I stepped over to the practice tee and started to experiment with the various grips of my golf clubs while the remainder of the foursome discussed my present affliction and how it would likely impact the day's match.

"I spec' y'all better give us two strokes a side," I heard Loren plead. "Got dog-bit again." I waited for the usual painful expression of shock, followed by the certain rejection of such an "outrageous and asinine idea" by our adversaries.

"Two strokes a side! Y'all been eatin' locoweed?" Billy and Ti screamed in unison.

"I wouldn't give my grandma two strokes a side!" one of them whined.

"I know it," replied the other. "McCormack comes out here every other week with that old dog bite stuff, just tryin' to get strokes and sympathy. Well, I been bit and burnt the last time."

Finally, though, after serious, almost tearful pleading and then allowing them to examine the actual wounds, I observed the telltale sympathy in their eyes. When they viewed my trembling hand and saw the dangerous streaks networking their way up near the wrist, we reached a compromise. They would give me a stroke on number four, a par five hole, and I would be allowed to hit from the ladies' tee on number seven, another par five. Further negotiations would resume upon completion of the outgoing nine holes.

My drive off the first tee hooked severely and disappeared over the left-side tree line, finally landing in Cliff Dansby's prize kudzu thicket some 250 yards away. Billy and Ti exploded into side-cracking guffawing, while Loren and I both stared in open-mouthed disbelief. It was the first time I had ever pulled the ball to the left in the presence of live golfers.

As the others hit their usual middle-busting shots, I retired to the back of the tee and re-examined my grip. I discovered that on the previous shot I'd applied too much pressure with my injured right hand at the moment of impact. Apparently, the pain caused by the pressure of the hand caused me to flinch, which was responsible for the disastrous mislick.

"Don't let that right hand do anything but go along for the ride, kinda like a roller coaster," advised Loren. "I been tryin' to tell you all along to keep your right hand out of the shot. That's why you're always slicing it over to the right."

"What I need is some tape," I mumbled, rummaging through the side pockets of my golf bag. I discovered a roll of wide horse tape and encircled the wounded hand with several layers of the stuff. The end result was a bound-up hand that was incapable of even minor bending and grasping. The hand couldn't do anything except rest lifelessly on the grip in sort of a half-closed, weak position.

"Hit, McCormack, if you're able!" bellowed Ti.

Several practice swings revealed there was little pain involved as a result of my new hand wrap and modified grip. Therefore, with renewed vigor and some degree of irritation with our opponents, I briskly marched forward, teed up the ball, and drove it far down the fairway, twenty yards ahead of the other drives.

There was silence on the tee, except for the snorting of Loren and the impolite mumblings of the other side.

"We've been had again, Ti," declared Billy. My ball was still hopping down the arid fairway, finally rolling to a stop within wedge distance of the green.

Ti said nothing, but instead stomped off down the far side of the fairway, snatching and jerking along his old, worn-out, squeaking cart. It was clear he wanted nothing further to do with me.

I had only a sixty-yard pitch to the green, so I extracted a wedge from my bag and loosely swung at the ball. Unfortunately, I skulled the thing, and instead of the high arching shot that I had envisioned, it took off in clothesline fashion, right at belt buckle level, accompanied by the Billy-Ti giggling chorus. But their merriment ceased abruptly when the ball made solid contact with the flagstick, then miraculously dropped straight down, two inches short of the hole. The flagstick, now bending to the right because of the powerful punch to its middle, ceased its rattling just as Ti and Billy launched into their second tirade of the day.

It was just plain embarrassing! Not because I had made a bogie five on the hole, but because I'd done it after Loren and I had weaseled strokes out of them on account of my allegedly injured hand. My credibility was seriously and possibly fatally injured. Never again would Billy and Ti believe anything I had to say.

The remaining seventeen holes were played in even par, which gave me an eighteen-hole, once-in-a-lifetime score of seventy-three. Each shot was an amateur's dream, and each putt was stroked in total concentration and confidence. Loren reminded me of our earlier match, when I had been called away on the eleventh hole to treat a horse. Even though we were ahead that day, the match had been declared void. I even pinched myself to be sure I wasn't dreaming. I should have been ecstatic, but because of the adjustments we were forced to make after nine holes, the match ended in a tie.

However, there was another problem. Golfers who routinely have scores in the mid-eighties are not supposed to shoot in the low sev-

enties, especially if they are given the advantage over their opponents. Billy and Ti had said little after the fiasco on the first hole,
and even Loren quit speaking to me after my long putt found the
hole on number five green. There were no compliments on good
shots, no one would walk with me down the fairways, nor did they
thank me when I found their errant shots in the deep rough.

It was my one moment of golfing glory in a lifetime of shanks,
chili dips, rainbow slices, worm burners, and jerked putts, but there
was no joy in it. And if you can't talk about a great round with
friends, what's the use of even playing it?

A couple of days after the golf match, Scruffy's owner called to say
that he was no better and she thought he needed a shot. "I'll bring
James, my yard man, and let him hold Scruffy while you give him
some wonderful drug," she said. "And by the way, I heard that
Scruffy brought you good luck by helping you to play better golf last
Sunday."

"How did you hear that?" I replied. Of course, I wasn't puzzled
about hearing the news in such a small town where everybody knew
everything about everybody else. But I was curious about where
she'd heard the news.

"Well, my husband went by Loren's drugstore to pick up a pre-
scription for me, and Loren told him all about it. Also, some of the
ladies at Lucille's beauty shop were also playing out there Sunday
and heard Mr. Idrain talking about it." Things are never boring in a
small town—if you like up-to-date local news and rumors.

A few hours later, Scruffy was on the exam table, vised in James's
huge arms, with his mouth tightly taped shut. Then, using my left
hand, the exam was completed, and my suspicions were confirmed.
His prostate was enlarged and infected, which required several days
of injections. James faithfully accompanied Scruffy to the clinic for
a week and kept me from being further mutilated.

After three weeks of estrangement and rest, my right hand
decreased in size enough that I could get it back into the golf shot
in the usual incorrect manner. Mercifully, my scores again ascended

into the eighties and I was cautiously welcomed back into the brotherhood of local golfers. It was great to again be pulling and pushing wood shots, hitting iron shots off line, and three putting from ten feet.

Every now and then I get the urge to play better golf. I've even had the silly notion of going by Scruffy's place and sticking my hand in his mouth, but I have decided the friendship of my golfing buddies is more important than scoring in the seventies.

Twenty-five

As I became more experienced in restraining dogs and cats, the number of bites and scratches decreased. But I seemed to be more prone to on-the-farm injuries, probably because the years slowed down the reflexes. My eyes still saw the kicks coming and the mind sensed the horse getting ready to strike, but the legs were slower about getting the body out of the way. Smarter thinking probably helped some, because I don't jump fences with a black bag anymore, nor do I try to overpower yearling calves or shetland ponies, like in the past.

Dogs, cats, and cows aside, the hog lot is one of the worst places to get hurt. And to make things worse, there's the embarrassment of walking into the doctor's office or hospital smelling like a pig sty. The general public does not enjoy the smell of hog excrement, nor do they take kindly to human beings who emit the same aroma.

Right out of veterinary school in the early sixties, I was employed as an associate veterinarian by Dr. Max Foreman in his busy practice in Baldwin County, Alabama. It is the longest county, from north to south, east of the Mississippi River, and at the time was one of the most productive agricultural counties in the nation. The practice treated all species of animals and covered a large territory, so our farm calls were coordinated by two-way radio and what we called "flag down."

"I need the vet right now!" a frantic animal owner might declare over the phone.

"OK, run out to the road and flag him down. He's coming your way right now. Hurry!" would be the reply from the clinic.

Occasionally, a message would come over the radio that someone needed service just as I happened to be right at their driveway. I'd wheel the truck in and stop at the back door of the farmhouse. Presently, the owner would open the door and see the vet truck sitting there idling, just waiting for directions from the farmer.

"How'd you get here so fast? I just hung up the phone!" the shocked person would stammer.

"We try to give good service," I'd tell him. "Plus, I drove fast."

"Well, you better slow down, or you'll be goin' as fast as Dr. Foreman. He goes by here sometimes doin' at least a hundred!" Dr. Max Foreman was well-known for his heavy foot.

"John, go to the Black brothers hog farm; they've got a sow with an off-feed and milk let-down problem," Dr. Foreman yelled over the two-way one afternoon. "She's the white one." That wasn't much help, since all fifty of them were all white. Max was a great veterinarian, but his directions to farms and his identifications of the patients were almost worthless. His favorite directions included "you can't miss it."

"By the way, she's in the third crate on the left," he suddenly blasted over the radio.

"Ten-four, base, I'll whip by there right now. I'm in the vicinity," I replied. We were always "whipping by" a farm somewhere.

There was no one at the farrowing house upon my arrival, so I gathered black bag and bucket, then broke into a run and hurdled the three-foot board fence. Unfortunately, I came down hard on my right ankle, and it buckled under the load. There was a sickening sound of ligaments and tarsal bones being ripped asunder as I staggered and fell into a huge puddle of gummy mud and hog manure. The increasing intensity of white-hot pain indicated that this was not the usual sprain that would go away in a few days. Writhing and wallowing in pain, I wondered for a brief instant why I hadn't decided to enter a small animal practice in Memphis. Surely no dog bite could be worse than this predicament.

After several minutes of grimacing and ankle-holding, it became apparent that I would not be able to seek out the sick sow and treat her. Then I remembered there were other calls to be made. I tried to reassure myself. Surely a few minutes' rest would make things better, and perhaps I could then get on with the work that was awaiting.

But the former slim and supple ankle was getting tighter inside my Justin boot. It was a struggle to remove the boot, accompanied by considerable misery, but it finally slipped off, giving some blessed relief from the throbbing pain. Before my very eyes, I could see the swelling increasing.

"Gotta get up, gettin' sick at my stomach," I mumbled. Maybe it was the pain shooting up my leg, or perhaps it was the offensive odor of the hog lot.

Hobbling to the truck with the aid of a two-by-four scantling I found in the junk pile, I called into the office on the two-way.

"Mobile three to base, mobile three to base," I called in a weak and pitifully shaky voice. Moments later the soothing voice of Mrs. Cornelia broke the silence.

"Go ahead, Dr. John," she answered.

"Mrs. Cornelia, I've broken my ankle! It's swollen up real bad, and I can't put any weight on it, and it hurts real bad every time I try to step on it."

"Oh no!" she cried. "Hold tight for a minute, you poor dear."

I eased down on the seat of the truck with my leg elevated on a box of calcium, the thought of help arriving soon secure in my mind. The pain seemed to have diminished some, or perhaps the thought that my friends would soon be on the way consoled me.

I closed my eyes in a semifaint and envisioned my volunteer firemen buddies scurrying about, leaving their offices and homes in four-wheel-drive Jeeps and pickup trucks, kicking up sand and leaving great clouds of dust as they spun out into the main road. I could picture them as they sped through the red light in town, their horns blaring and arms waving. Surely the town's one ambulance would be following close behind, its siren wide open, the tiny red light blinking in the windshield. Without a doubt the sheriff and town constable would come running when they found out that good ol' Doc had really boogered up his leg.

"Ah, it is great to have friends like this," I thought to myself. "Who needs a safe, white-smocked small animal practice in Memphis anyway." I felt guilty about even thinking about living anywhere else. Give me a small town anytime!

The crackle of the radio brought me out of my lethargy.

"Dr. John, are you there?"

I groaned into the microphone.

"Dr. John, Dr. Foreman said to tell you since it is already four-thirty, you go ahead and take the rest of the day off. He'll take the rest of your farm calls for you," she recited in an apologetic tone.

"What? You mean nobody's coming out here to get me?" I said in disbelief. "I'm dyin'!"

"Well, everybody here is tied up, Dr. John. Whitney is clipping those poodles in the back right now, Dr. Foreman is in the north end of the county, and Woody is breeding cows at Silver Valley Dairy. I called down at the donut shop and none of the volunteer fire guys were there, and I heard earlier today that the ambulance is down, having a new transmission installed," she said. "Maybe you can put some Bag Balm on that ankle and that will take the swelling out and make it all better."

"What? Bag Balm?" I ranted to myself. "I'm out here all by myself, dyin' in a stinkin' hog sty and she tells me to smear Bag Balm on this ankle that is just five minutes from fallin' off! A lesser man probably would've been dead by now."

The sound of truck tires on crushed stone interrupted my tirade. It was Mr. Black, owner of the swine farm, who'd decided to breeze by and see what I had done about the sow.

"I'm very sorry, sir," I began. "As you can see by the size of the leg over yonder on that box, I will be unable to perform an examination and treat your sow. My leg is severely and probably permanently disabled. I was hoping for an ambulance."

"Does that mean you won't be charging me for a call?" he asked happily. Then without as much as a "Can I hep ye?" he turned and went into the hog lot via the gate provided for that purpose. Apparently, he wasn't a fence jumper.

As adrenaline surged through my boiling circulatory system, my previous feelings of affection and brotherhood disappeared. Looking back, I'm sure the pain made me delirious.

With teeth clenched and eyelids narrowed, I decided to show them all that I didn't need their help. I would drive myself to the hospital, walk in the front door dragging the injured leg, and tell 'em to get me some help right now! And furthermore, I'd just double dog dare any one of 'em to say one word about my being covered in stinking hog manure.

The ten-mile drive into town can best be described as an ordeal. Since the truck had a manual transmission, it was difficult to manipulate clutch, brake, and accelerator with my sound left foot. I found that by using the trash pile two-by-four scantling as an accelerator-mashing device, I could propel the vehicle. There was a lot of jumping and jerking, sudden stops, and veering off the road.

But that type of driving is not considered abnormal at all for large animal veterinarians in that area of Alabama, maybe even in Wisconsin. So when I met the locals on the road, they would give a wide berth to the vet's truck, as usual, and not even realize that the weaving and jerking truck and the panic-stricken look on the driver's face were not normal operating procedure.

My arrival at the hospital clinic was uneventful, except for a lot of nose holding and astonished frowns that were directed toward the smelly vet. That problem was corrected quickly by issuing the patient a regulation blue gown with the entire back part missing. The odoriferous clothes were taken out of the emergency area on a long broom handle and incinerated, while forms were filled out and questions were asked about insurance. Then a very young doctor looked at the leg and ordered radiographs.

An angel of mercy appeared and stabbed my arm with a sedative, and the next thing I vaguely remember was talk about casting materials and healing times. Then I heard loud talk by a different nurse.

"That sure is a big and heavy cast, isn't it," she literally shouted to her colleague, who was just inches away.

"Yep, sure is!" screamed nurse number two. "I'll bet he'll be staying inside the vet clinic for a long time working on scratchy poodles and coughing Chihuahuas."

"Why do you say that?" I asked groggily.

"I was raised on a dairy farm," she yelled, "and I know that a vet can't get around a muddy lot and cow barn wearing a big cast like that."

"Well, what do you think we should have done?" asked the young doctor sarcastically as he arrived on the scene.

"Since it was such a minor break, I'd have just smeared another layer of that Bag Balm on there and sent him out the door," she countered.

I flopped my head back onto the pillow and went to sleep. In spite of the bulky cast I was able to get around at half speed, but dealing with the crutches was a hassle. In order to eliminate that minor problem, Dr. Foreman and Whitney decided to create a walking pad on the bottom of the cast.

"We do it for calves all the time, so why can't we do it for the calf doctor?" he said, going to work with an aluminum rod, a piece of tire recapping, and a roll of three-inch horse tape. When they were finished, I could walk pain-free, but running was a little more difficult. He even taped a small extension board onto the accelerator for easier driving.

I don't recall taking any days off, though.

⌒

The ankle didn't heal well, probably because we removed the cast too early or I was more active than I should have been. It was weak and it was always getting twisted, which caused a lot of swelling and moderate discomfort. I found that wearing an ankle brace and high-top work brogans laced all the way to the top provided the necessary support against the constant threat of sprains.

Thirty years later, the same ankle was re-broken thanks to the antics of a wild Tennessee Charolais heifer. While being checked for pregnancy, she suddenly became rambunctious, jumping and bellowing, and unfortunately stomping the ankle with her left hind food. This time I heard the muffled *crack,* which was accompanied by the searing heat and pain. And to make matters worse, it was early November, which was always a very busy month for the practice. I was also several counties away from home and the family orthopedic surgeon, who in the 1990s would probably insist on something more bone-healing friendly than a 1960s taped-up walking cast.

The owner of the cow did not see the accident because he was in the back of the corral sorting out the remainder of the cows to check. But he knew something was wrong when he returned and saw the vet standing on one leg.

"What's wrong? You didn't step on a nail, did you? I thought I got all of those nails up," he said.

"No, no nail, just broke my leg again," I replied. It didn't seem to be as painful as before, perhaps because of all the scar tissue or because the foot nerves had deteriorated with age. I kept trying to touch the ground with it, but it wouldn't support my weight.

"B-b-b-broke? Are you sure? Uh, uh, how?" His face was ashen and he appeared ready to perform a "Sinkin'" Jenkins routine.

"You better sit down," I cautioned, looking around for a seat. But our trucks were parked on the other side of the barn, and there was nothing on the working side but mud and a large mound of bovine fertilizer mixed with straw.

"I'll be awright, just let me lean up against the fence here for a minute," he replied, blindly grabbing for the side of the corral.

"Do you want to go to the truck? You don't need to be fallin' out here in this mud," I advised. There was no way a one-legged vet could get him out of the mud and drag him to safety.

He was OK in a minute or so, and began to apologize profusely for his cow and offered to help. "Can I take you to the hospital?"

"How many more cows are back there to check?" I asked.

"I think there's eight, but you can't do that, can you?"

"If you'll put a cow in the chute and catch her head, I'll get the work done on the rear end. I've come too far to not get it done. Just get me a two-by-four to use as a crutch."

Thirty minutes later my truck and I were pulling out of the driveway over the protests of the client, who wanted a nurse acquaintance to take a quick look at the leg. But I was getting relief from the extra-strength BC powders that I was taking, and the truck had an automatic transmission, which made one-foot driving possible. I wanted to go home.

My truck tires crunched the gravel of the driveway of home late that evening, but I wasn't drowsy in the least. The caffeine and aspirin in the BC had done their job efficiently enough that the trip had been tolerable, except for the one rest stop. The ankle balked still when I tried to use it for walking.

"Got something to tell you," I told Jan when we arose later that morning.

"OK, how bad is it this time?" she said, bolting upright in the bed.

"How do you know it's something bad?"

"I just know. Do you need to go to the doctor?"

"Naw, the hospital. It's Sunday, isn't it?" That brought her springing from the bed, examining the huge black-and-blue ankle, constantly peppering her profuse remarks with such expressions as "Oh, my word," "You are so cavalier about your health," and "You are just trying to get yourself killed or maimed for life." There was even the predictable question of why I hadn't gone to the hospital immediately. Hours later at the hospital, after much paperwork, X rays, and numerous questions about how the injury occurred, the phone rang in our emergency cubicle. It was the orthopedic surgeon with the verdict.

"This is Dr. Maye, and I just looked at your radiographs. You have a fracture of the medial malleolus of the tibia and we need to put a couple of screws in there. I'm in surgery across town today, so I'll get 'em to put you in a room there and we'll fix that leg tomorrow."

"How about today? I've got herd work to do tomorrow."

"Listen to me very carefully, Dr. McCormack. You won't be doing anything involving cows except drinking milk for at least six weeks, maybe longer," he declared firmly. "If you have cow veterinary work scheduled, cancel it."

"But—"

"But I will come over there and get that little job done today after I get a bite to eat. Let me speak to the nurse," he said. "Have you had anything to eat?"

"Yes, just had a Moon Pie and pint of milk."

"Then we better give you a spinal instead of general. That OK?"

"It's fine with me, just want to get it over with."

In a few minutes, things began to happen. Chest was X rayed, blood was drawn, more papers signed, and then the sedative injection. Then I was wheelchaired down to the presurgical area, where the spinal anesthetic was injected. The anesthetist was shocked when he found out that veterinarians routinely use epidural injections on cows and that we used many of the same drugs.

I remember snoozing lightly when someone nudged my arm and called my name.

"Excuse me, Dr. McCormack, can you sign this?" As my eyelids slowly blinked open to the brightness of the prep room ceiling, a long-haired head appeared in the glow of the fluorescent lights. A clearer focus revealed a luxuriance of light brown hair that was meticulously combed and perfectly framed an obviously masculine face as it cascaded downward, curling outward ever so slightly when it made contact with the broad shoulders. My first thought was that I had passed on, since the figure in my vision greatly resembled the painting of Jesus Christ that many of my clients kept over the fireplace mantels in their homes. But the thought was fleeting, thanks to my good nose. Heaven probably doesn't smell like stray anesthetic agents and staphylococcus-eradicating concoctions, nor would I be numb from the waist down if this were Heaven.

"Huh, what now?" I spoke groggily.

"I'm Dr. Maye, and I need you to sign one more form," the male voice said. I thought to myself that Christ probably didn't speak with a south Alabama accent, either.

After scribbling my name at the bottom of the page and hearing some reassuring words from the doctor, I was left to my own thoughts.

Some hours later, with several titanium screws joining the fractured fragments back together, Dr. Maye was at my bedside, his hair now in a ponytail, explaining it all to me, lecturing on aftercare and all the things I shouldn't do for at least six weeks. Then two short-haired guys dressed in all-white outfits showed up with a set of crutches and made a big to-do out of instructing me on their use. I wondered why it took two crutch instructors, but I understood later when the bill came.

The leg healed well, and I have not had any more problems with weakness and sprains, probably because everything was screwed back together in fine fashion. The ankle deal taught me two things.

First, I should be more concerned about my health, and I should take fewer chances doing dangerous things.

Second, I shouldn't judge the competence of people by the length of their hair. Dr. Maye has helped members of my family and dozens of my friends and clients with their orthopedic problems. He is not only a great doctor but a great friend. And he still hasn't cut his hair. . . .

Twenty-six

"Doc, this old red bull of mine has a big knot on his side," the early-morning caller declared.

Actually, it was real early. I was awake but had not yet crawled out of bed that Monday morning. My mind was reviewing the schedule for the day, wondering how many additional calls were going to come in and whether or not I was going to make the cattlemen's meeting that night. Mondays were usually busy days, since some folks tried to hold their minor, nonemergency problems until the weekend was over. Saturdays and Sundays were already busy enough with weekend warriors who didn't pay much attention to their stock during weekdays but scrutinized them carefully on Sunday after church, a big dinner, and a two-hour nap.

"Well, that's an oddball thing," I replied sarcastically. "They taught me over at the university that knots were on trees but bulls and cows had swellings, cysts, abscesses, and tumors. 'Course around here some refer to 'em as winds, pones and thingamajigs. Maybe we ought to call the newspaper and get a picture of this knot on a bull."

I am not in the habit of talking such trash with just anyone who calls for my advice. But this was one of my best friends and a good neighbor, Mr. Woodson, and it was important that I get my licks in fairly early. He owned several hundred head of cattle and was one of the best farmers in the county, having won several awards for his farm program. I had been an invited guest there for an assortment of veterinary problems, from all-day herd workings to checking a scrawny kitten. But most conversations with him and his associates were spiced with good-natured needling, verbal barbs, and humorous references to almost any subject that was brought up.

As expected, he was ready for me. "Boy, you're sharp this morning," he said. "You have razor bran for breakfast? Think you're sharp enough to cure this swelling I'm trying to tell you about, or have I got to find a real veterinarian?"

A few months earlier, he and his working associates, Shelnutt and Choice, had gotten on my case about my ineptness with a lariat because of a little difficulty I had trying to rope a three-legged-lame calf. Ordinarily, I was about average with a rope, but when there were gigglers and criticizers lining the fence, I sometimes let myself get flustered by their constant mouthing. After about six pursed-lipped and wide-of-the-mark throws, I finally caught the beast by the front leg, and as any bystander could have predicted, a frenzy of bovine bellowing and human guffawing erupted. All were too busy cracking their sides to help with the bucking steer, and even if they had offered, I wanted to prove that I could do it by myself. Since that sorry exhibition of roping skills, no farm call was complete without some sarcastic reference to the calf-roping episode.

Another item that seldom escaped discussion was the encounter I'd had with a rather small but very quick calf. The two-hundred-pound bull looked gentle and friendly, but when I tried to flank him to the ground to check a swollen navel, he exploded into a kicking frenzy. As expected, no help was forthcoming because of their laughter. Meanwhile, the bottoms of the poor beast's little hooves were being tattooed repeatedly by my arms, shoulders, and the side of my head.

"Here's one about your speed, Doc," Shelnutt allowed one day, pointing to a wobbly, twenty-four-hour-old sixty-pound Angus. "Reckon you can get the best of him?"

All I could do was smile and laugh along with them. I am the first to concede that hardworking farmers need a lot to smile about. They work so hard and get so little in return for their product, I am happy to be able to supply a few minutes of humor.

I arrived at Mr. Woodson's right after lunch to examine and treat the bull with the "knot" on his side. No one was around, and all was quiet except for the faint sound of my patient's mouth as he chewed his cud with enjoyment while slobbery saliva gradually accumulated at the corners of his mouth. Every few seconds, a string of the slimy, bubbly stuff formed and began to drop from the mass, lazily point downward, until the bottom part finally made contact on the ground of the catch pen. At the moment of touchdown, however, the string would suddenly snap in half, resulting in the top half's springing back up to the safety of the bull's mouth, where the entire process began again. He eyed me curiously but never missed a chew. Suddenly, he stopped chewing, swallowed the entire wad that had been masticated to his satisfaction, paused for a few seconds, then belched up another cud. I could clearly see its roundish outline as reverse peristalsis sped it back up the esophagus and into his big mouth. He started chewing again as expertly as Mr. Wrigley chewed his Spearmint gum.

I doubt if the general public has ever given this cud-chewing phenomenon any great thought. But sometimes when I have spare time I just sit or stand quietly and watch cows chew their cuds, and marvel at these amazing creatures. Their ability to graze and grow, even produce milk, from grasses, forages and other sometimes almost useless products from land that is unsuitable for anything else is a physiological miracle. The resulting meat and milk are highly prized by man. Maybe even more valuable are the by-products of cattle, such as leather, pharmaceutical preparations, gelatin, and dozens of other products that we never realize come from cows. I even found out in veterinary school that the saliva swallowed while chewing the cud several hours each day acts as a buffer for the cow's first stomach, sort of like taking a double handful of Alka-Seltzers.

"How many times you reckon a cow chews her cud before she swallows it?" my dad asked me many years ago.

Since then I have frequently counted the chews. Woodson's red bull chewed one cud fifty-two times before he sent it back down the gullet and retrieved another.

Getting back to business, I saw the swelling on the left side of the patient. It was the size of a cantaloupe and was located at the level of the elbow, but back a few inches on the ninth rib, not a rare place for a swelling, but a little unusual for an abscess.

The bull went into the chute real nice, and I put a locust post behind him before catching his head. As I palpated the mass, Woodson came slowly walking from the house, and from the looks of his eyes, it was obvious he had been taking an after-dinner nap.

"Oh, I'm sorry, did I disturb your beauty sleep? Next time I'll try to make less racket. I took a nap once when I was little, and I know how cranky you can get when you first wake up," I said. "But you didn't need to get up and come way out here just to help little ole me!"

He sneered, yawned, and sat down on an upside-down bucket. I could tell my insults had been for naught, because he wasn't reacting in normal fashion. Too bad I had wasted one of my best verbal efforts with no one there to hear it.

"What is it?" he said.

"A big abscess, I think," I replied.

"How come?"

"Don't know. Probably stuck something in it, or got kicked by a cow."

"Whatcha gonna do?"

"Lance it."

"Right now?"

"Yeah, right now, after I do a test puncture with this needle."

"Will it heal up?"

"Yep."

With the conversation out of the way, I scrubbed and shaved a small area where the swelling was the softest, then quickly stuck it with a needle to be sure it was what I thought it was. Sure enough, thick and dirty yellow pus oozed from the test puncture.

"Now I've got to lance it," I stated

"Why not just drain it with that needle?" Woodson asked.

"Because I've got to make a pretty good sized hole so it will drain better, then I'll have to flush it clean, and then put some iodine-saturated gauze up in there to cauterize the lining."

After injecting a little novocaine over the intended site of injection, I donned a pair of rubber gloves and quickly made a stab incision over the soft spot with a scalpel, and then enlarged it with a controlled slash. The old bull was pretty stoic, but the sting of the wider incision extended beyond the line of anesthesia, and I'm sure he felt obligated to make a halfhearted kick with his right rear foot toward the vicinity of my hand. About a gallon of pus and other gunk slowly flowed out.

"Man, that's nasty," said Choice, who had just sauntered up. He'd been napping, too.

"I coulda done that," declared Woodson, "and saved gettin' another ridiculous bill in a few days. All I would have needed is that fancy knife, a nickel's worth of that iodine-looking stuff, and a pair of those rubber gloves."

"Well, why didn't you?" I replied while packing the abscess with a roll of iodined gauze. "I sure got plenty else to do."

"I figured you needed the practice."

"Naw, but I do need the money. And I do like coming to these wealthy turkey and cow farmers 'cause I know they've got plenty of it."

"Shoot, I'm so broke I can't even pay attention!" he exclaimed. "And by the way, have you ever seen one of these things before?"

"Sure, lots of times. These things are real common in *Bos taurus.*" I said. Folks frequently asked me that question. They obviously didn't want an amateur experimenting on an unknown disease or condition with their animal.

"What's that boss thing you just said?"

"*Bos taurus.* You know, that's the big word for a short-eared cow. *Bos indicus* is the word for those long-eared Brahma cows your neighbor owns. It's an old Indian word meaning 'corral-destroying fool.' " I giggled at my own attempt at humor, but wondered what the Brahma-owning neighbor would have said had he heard my description of his herd. Each time I visited the Brahma farm it was war, and when we finished our herd work, the corral was in a shambles.

"Using those big words is what makes your bill so high, Woodson," declared Choice. "Every time he drops one of 'em in conversation the bill goes up five dollars. It's enough to stagger a feller when he opens up that envelope with the picture window on the front."

"Uh huh, I know about all his tricks. That's why I don't open it up unless I'm holding on to a post. Usually, I get Becky to do that, 'cause I can't stand the shock."

"I don't understand y'all," I said. "If you go over to the folks' hospital with a sore knee, you think it's pretty sophisticated if the doctor puts a big name on your problem, like "ruptured medial meniscus," instead of just saying "a boogered-up knee." Then you come back to the café bragging about the big diagnosis and how smart that doctor must be because he's charging so much. I'm just trying to get with the program."

They rolled their eyes and muttered, but I was making rattling noises washing up buckets and slamming truck doors. I was enjoying jawing with my friends, but it was time to move on to the next call.

Two or three weeks later Woodson called and left word that the sweet corn was ready and I should come by and pick some. While I was filling my sack, I heard his truck pull up behind mine. Presently, we met in between the corn rows.

"What you doin' in my corn patch, boy?" he yelled.

"Just checking for disease in these nubbins," I allowed. "Got to confiscate a few dozen ears, take them back to my home laboratory for a free-of-charge examination. Looks like they may have worms."

"That's right thoughtful of you. I assume you'll get back to me with a full report," he answered sarcastically. "But, Doc, about the red bull. I just looked at him, and that thing on his side is bigger than ever. We need to check that out as soon as you've got the time."

"Uh oh, why don't we do it right now."

Recurring abscesses frequently mean that a foreign body is present somewhere in the mass. That's what I told Woodson after the second examination.

"OK, here's what I think has happened. You know how cows sometimes pick up nails and pieces of wire and other metal as they graze or eat baled hay? Now, when I open this abscess this time, we're gonna find a piece of baling wire four or five inches long with a crook on the other end. It's trying to work its way to the outside."

The usual doubts and second-guessing followed my pronouncement, along with the expected chatter about why I hadn't extracted the alleged wire on the initial call. I too wondered if I had checked out the interior of the mass like I should have.

Minutes later, after repeating the drainage and flushing procedure, my gloved finger felt the tip of something sharp imbedded between the ribs. After exploring and some manipulation with a pair of long-handled forceps, I gently eased out a four-inch piece of corroded baling wire. Just as I had predicted, there was a crook on the end I held in my forceps. It is always a shock to remove large foreign objects from odd places in animals. I knew the onlookers would be impressed with my ability to get the thing out, as well as being able to predict its exact appearance.

As I held it high for good viewing, Woodson, Choice, and Shellnut came near for close inspection of the object. I thought sure a pat on the back or a word or two of appreciation for my great knowledge of the bovine species would be forthcoming. I should have known better.

"What do you think of that?" I asked proudly. Surely they would say something about my skill as a bull surgeon.

"It took two expensive trips out here to find a piece of wire? You must think we've got Blue Cross on this bull!" someone said.

"You're not so smart, Doc," declared Shellnut. "You said that crook was gonna be on the other end of that wire!"

Well, at least they had a new mistake to remind me of. Maybe that would give my inaccurate rope-throwing technique a rest.

Sometimes it is difficult for a stranger to understand how good friends cultivate and maintain their friendships in such an odd manner, but perhaps we'd all be better off if we laughed more and growled less.

Twenty-seven

J ohn Harlow, my stockbroker cow-owning client, took great pride in his purebred Angus herd. I was a visitor on the farm most every week, sometimes just to observe and offer opinions, and frequently "just to look" at an animal that he didn't think was "just right." Vaccinations and routine exams were planned months ahead, and nothing short of a hurricane or a family crisis would interfere with the scheduled date, although there was one hundred-degree August day that resulted in our calling off work because the first few cows that came through the chute were panting and in obvious distress. James and Bubbahead, the head herdsman and assistant herdsman, respectively, had said from daybreak that it wasn't "fittin' to be foolin' with cows" on such a hot and humid day. At first I disagreed, because I figured that Bubbahead just said so because he had a hankering to get into the beverage cooler in the back of the pickup. But when cow tongues began to loll and respiratory rates started to skyrocket, I knew they were right. Work was terminated, and the herd was moved to the shade of the nearby grove of pine trees and cool water.

In a very short time John had learned about the cattle business from scratch by reading everything he could find about raising cattle, calling experts all over the country for their opinions, and then putting those ideas to work on his own farm. He dialed my number often, sometimes more than once a day, just to ask my opinion about something he had heard at a cattlemen's meeting or read in the latest issue of *Drover's Journal.* So it wasn't surprising when he called about a new bull calf that had just been born on the farm. It was a birth that we all had awaited with much anticipation.

"Doc, supercalf is on the ground, and it's a bull. Weighed seventy-eight and a half pounds," he reported breathlessly. "He's still wobbly, but he's sucking to beat the band. You better come on down right away and give him the once-over." I remember wondering if I could make a living as a bovine neonatologist/pediatrician. Maybe it was possible in Wisconsin or one of the big cow states, but not in the timber country of southwest Alabama.

Still, I pretended to be that famous bovine baby specialist as I examined John's prize animal. Heart, lungs, mouth, palate, ears, navel, and everything else attached was scrutinized. I even looked at his retinas with my dog ophthalmoscope. Anything that I missed, John and momma cow were right over my shoulder with a quick reminder. I could find no defects except for one ear that flopped a little, probably from the way he had been lying inside the womb. John questioned me about surgical correction of the ear, but I tried to convince him to give it some time to straighten out. We named him Ebony. Later, John amended that, calling him King Ebony, or K.E. for short.

As Ebony grew, John became increasingly proud of the magnificent animal. He would rather talk about him than his grandchildren and would whip out his billfold in an instant to show his photos to any people he met, whether they expressed any interest or not. His snapshots were arranged so that K.E.'s were on top of the stack, with the grandchildren relegated to the bottom. It got to the point that it was embarrassing to carry on a conversation with John, since it was just a nonstop testimony to the most splendid beast of the pasture.

And what a beautiful bull King Ebony turned out to be. As a two-year-old, he weighed over a ton, possessed straight and curvy lines in all their respective proper places, and seemed to have all the physical attributes expected from the planned mating. Never had I seen a more beautiful animal. Even his flopped ear was now proud and straight, and he could swivel it around for improved hearing just as the Master had planned.

Animal scientists, bull lovers, and sire analysts came from near and far to view King Ebony and to pass judgment on his impeccable conformation. All tried to find some fault or minor blemish, but most went away shaking their heads in awe, secretly wishing the bull were grazing in their pasture instead of John's. Most grudgingly agreed that he was the finest bovine specimen ever grown in the county. He must have been magnificent, because cow folks don't allow compliments on other folks' cattle to pass their lips easily.

Several bull stud farms expressed an interest in purchasing K.E., and after several weeks of discussions, pedigree evaluations, and negotiations, John called one night with the exciting news that a sale had been made, subject to K.E.'s passing all the stringent health requirements. In addition to passing the health regulations of the state of destination, he had to meet the much higher regulations of the famous artificial insemination center. After all, if it worked out as planned, K.E.'s semen would be collected, frozen in liquid nitrogen, and shipped all over the world. Foreign countries are real picky about frozen bull semen, so we made an appointment to commence the necessary examinations and blood testing.

It was my first experience carrying out such detailed examinations, and I had no idea there were so many tests necessary. But I vowed to do everything by the book—or, more specifically, by the letter that was mailed to me from the stud farm. On my first trip, I drew blood to send to the diagnostic laboratory to test for brucellosis, bluetongue, and leukosis, as well as other diseases. Then I began the physical exam by doing the same things I had done on the day he was born. In addition, I palpated his lymph glands, stethoscoped both sides of his abdominal cavity, performed the "scooch test" for hardware disease, checked his ear tattoos for proper identification, and checked tongue, teeth, and throat. I found that one ear tattoo had been put in at an angle. Bulls despise having their throats checked, whether by long arm or mouth gag and flashlight. I again ophthalmoscoped his eyes, peering back into his beautifully colored retinas for scars and flaws. Then, because John didn't have a weighing device, I taped his chest for an approximate weight. Lastly, since it was the test that involved a probe, a long arm, and some short-lived discomfort, I assessed his reproductive function. K.E. resented this even more than the throat test.

"I can't find anything wrong with this bull. He is in excellent health!" I finally announced.

"Doc, you're a one-man Mayo Clinic," John allowed as I rested in a feed bunker. "I wish I could get a checkup that thorough."

"Maybe you could, if you were as good a specimen as this bull," I replied. "But if you'll get in line, you can be next. Just don't be stomping and bellowing when I put you in this squeeze chute."

A couple of weeks later, all the test results were available, and the news was good. As expected, King Ebony had passed all the tests. I returned to the farm armed with a stack of completed documents and a pad of health certificates. Another complete exam revealed that nothing had changed. All systems were go. When I wrote out the health certificates, I did so using my most careful handwriting.

Nothing was heard from John for the next several days, and I assumed that the patient had left the county for his new home up north. I didn't know there was one final checkup.

"Doc," said John a few nights later, "the bull limousine is leaving up north tomorrow morning coming south. It will be here to pick up K.E. in forty-eight hours, probably about five in the afternoon. The bull-buying coordinator wants you to come out the day of the pickup for a last inspection."

Two mornings later, I was again on the farm redoing the physical exam, peering into the bull's every inspectable function. As on the previous appointments, no abnormality was found, except for the crooked tattoo. I wrote that down on my report and on the health certificate.

"He's got to be the healthiest bull in the state," I told John.

Once again, I reviewed the health papers that we had hand carried to the state veterinarian's office for prior approval, and put them all in a fancy carrying envelope bearing the clinic name and address. Later that afternoon, the limousine chauffeur called the clinic from a rest stop to see if the bull was ready to be picked up.

"Yes sir, he's in the corral, his hair curled and toenails painted, ready for a new home," I stated.

"Is he healthy?" the chauffeur asked. I just said yes, and assumed that was the last time I would ever lay eyes on King Ebony. But at five minutes past six, the phone rang. It even sounded frantic.

"HE'S DEAD, DOC. HE'S GRAVEYARD DEAD!" The excited heavy-breathing voice screamed.

At times like this, without any identification from the caller, my first thoughts are that one of my jokester classmates or silly friends is making a crank call. But I could hear no tinkling of cocktail glasses or tear-jerking jukebox melodies in the background. Nothing but heavy breathing.

"Who's this?" I cried. I hate it when I cannot figure out the identity of a caller, but I have learned that some callers are so upset about the condition of their animal they don't think about such a minor thing. Nearly everyone has some unique voice trait that eventually gives them away, even when they're trying to fool the callee. Even "Big 'Un" Patrick, the master of voice disguises, cannot trick me if he stays on the line long enough for me to get his South Carolina accent.

"It's John, Doc! You know. The bull's dead, I'm tellin' you! Come down here, and please *hurrrry!*"

I have never understood why owners of dead stock want the vet to hurry. If the poor animal has passed, what's the use of risking getting a traffic ticket or crashing the truck? Nevertheless, I wasted no time because I knew John needed some support. Turning in at the corral gate, I saw a crowd assembled corral-side.

Some were already seated atop the corral fence, while others were milling about, kicking at weeds, clods, dried cow patties, and anything else that needed kicking. When I exited the truck, I could hear opinions being offered from 100 percent of the crowd. Farmers love to congregate when there has been an animal death, they just don't bring along a casserole. Mostly they are there to give their opinion of the cause of death.

"Blackleg."

"Lightning."

"Pneumonia."

"Nitrate poisoning."

"Heart attack."

"Arsenic poisoning."

I had heard it all before, and each diagnosis had merit. One had to consider the diseases and conditions the farmers mentioned, especially lightning strike and poisoning.

It seems the limousine driver had backed to the corral gate, then detrucked before noticing the bull lying there. King Ebony was in the middle of the corral, and it appeared that he had just gone to sleep and had never waked up. There was no sign of a struggle, no evidence of trauma, nor any sign of poisonous plants or suspicious paint buckets anywhere in the corral. I knew the chances were slim that I was going to tell the crowd what they wanted to hear, but I knew I had to do a complete necropsy exam on the spot. An hour later I had examined every organ owned by the bull without observing anything that could have caused death.

"Everything looks OK to me. I'll have to send the samples to the lab," I said. "It's gonna take a couple of weeks."

As expected, John and the crowd exhibited their displeasure by throwing the sticks they were chewing and whittling down to the ground. Others kicked at more stuff in the grass. John kept repeating the very words I had uttered.

"He was the healthiest bull in the county! That's what you said, Doc."

But I had no answer for him. I'd just have to wait on the report from the lab.

A week later the lab called with a report. There were numerous cysts of the *Sarcocystis* parasite imbedded in the heart muscle. That was the only abnormal finding. The pathologist and I theorized that the heavy parasite load had interfered with the conductivity of the heart muscle, resulting in heart failure. There was no way that I could have known!

Death is inevitable for every living thing. Yet it is difficult for every living thing to accept, especially medical specialists who fight death day and night, and those who have just pronounced a living thing "the healthiest in the county."

As expected, the death of King Ebony hurt John to the core. He never had the same enthusiasm for breeding livestock again, and I'm sure he had the same thoughts I did.

We might have overinspected that bull!

Twenty-eight

I remember it clearly. My veterinary school classmates and I were in an afternoon laboratory, learning about how to properly restrain our big patients. I was practicing a tail tie on one of the clinic animals, a middle-aged steer named Leroy. Leroy had a grand lifestyle, being a kept steer, only having to serve as a veterinary school guinea pig for the pokes, peeks, and palpations of the rookie animal doctors.

The purpose of a tail tie is to immobilize the tail so that examination and treatment of the cow can be done easier and more safely. Depending on the area of the patient being examined, I can usually expect the tail to be constantly flung in the direction of my face and ears. Some cows have such good aim and timing they can actually flick a stethoscope from the ears of an unsuspecting veterinarian. I understand that the cow resents being poked and jabbed in the side by some stranger, being harassed by flying insects, and being sniffed at by curious associates, but it is very difficult for me to use a stethoscope and concentrate on bowel and lung sounds while being assaulted by a skillfully used tail switch.

"Don't ever tie a bull's tail to anything but himself," the tough, marinelike instructor had announced to the class. I heard his words, but apparently I wasn't paying close enough attention or didn't get the exact meaning of his pronouncement at the time.

I also remember that the devilish horn flies were out in full force that southern September day, and they were making life miserable for both Leroy and me. He kept trying to snatch his tail away while I was practicing my tail-tying technique. Occasionally, he would yank the tail out of my hands and quickly whack me in the face with the cocklebur-infested switch.

Finally, my rope and I made the perfect tail tie, and then, to celebrate my accomplishment, I looped the free end of the rope around the nearby fence post and tied it in a proper slipknot. As I stood admiring my newly acquired rope-tying skills, a late-season horsefly the size of a hummingbird swooped down and alit right on top of Leroy's tenderloin. It was well known by all the upperclassmen that Leroy didn't like to have his back messed with. But more than one unsuspecting first-year vet student had tried to make friends with Leroy by rubbing his back, only to be rewarded with a lifelong leg scar from a kick-bruise to the thigh or shin with his lightning-fast hooves.

Before the fly had even settled, Leroy began fidgeting, sashaying around and tugging mightily on his tightly tied tail. It never dawned on me that a minor tragedy and a major embarrassment were imminent.

Suddenly, Leroy made a great lunge to his left, stomping the top of one daydreaming student's foot and sending another one backward into the lap of the ill-tempered professor, who was demonstrating the proper method of picking up the rear foot of a neighboring cow.

Now the entire class had suspended its assignments, and each member was gazing with much interest at the disruption by the fence. At the very instant when the gaze of every eye was riveted to the scene, a loud noise, greatly resembling the sound of corduroy pants being ripped, echoed throughout the barnyard. Momentarily, there was slack-jawed silence, except for the rapid wind-whistling waggings of poor Leroy's tail, which was a foot or two shorter than it had been only seconds before. A quick glance toward the fence revealed the amputated switch still dangling, but firmly knotted, at the end of my rope.

"Well, I'm good as dead," I thought sadly and ineptly. "But at least my rope didn't come loose."

Returning my vision to the victim, I observed that blood was dripping from the hideous stub of his tail at an alarming rate, except when he made rapid slinging movements with the remnant. In seconds, the only students not spattered with flecks of blood were those bright enough to hide behind the front-row gawkers.

Finally, I slowly turned and forced myself to face the professor. As expected, he had come up snarling from his foot-trimming position. His face was contorted into several different frowns as he expressed his displeasure over the unfortunate event. At that moment, I assumed that I would be expelled from veterinary school, prosecuted by the National Humane Society, and forced to pay for some kind of a tail transplant or switch toupee.

"What idiot is responsible for this?" he barked as he grabbed Leroy's tail in mid-swing and used his closed fist as a tourniquet. "Speak up! Who? Who did it?" Even in my panic-sticken condition I noticed classmates frantically using handerkerchiefs and pant legs to wipe blood from spectacles, the covers of new textbooks, notebooks, even fancy lariats that some of the cowboy types had recently purchased from the serum company in Montgomery. Unfortunately, they were doing nothing more than smearing the blood all around, making a bigger mess. Their collective frowns told me what they were thinking. I tried to confess to my sins, but when I opened my mouth nothing came forth except a pitiful squeak.

Chills were jumping up and down my spine like tiny racing yo-yos as I contemplated how I would explain my sudden return home to my parents after being in a faraway school for only a week or so.

Then a strange thing happened. The professor suddenly mellowed as if touched by a magic wand.

"It doesn't matter who did it," he said softly. "Somebody grab that bag over there, and let's get this bleeding tail stump cleaned up and wrapped."

With my heart throbbing in my throat, I darted for the black bag, handed it to him, and then tried to swallow. It was difficult getting my throat muscles to work since they were constricted so tightly around my heart.

"What we'll do, troops, is to apply a little of this yellow antibiotic ointment on the wound, like this," he calmly declared. "Then we'll place a few of these four-by-fours over that. Then we'll wrap it up good and tight with this wide adhesive tape."

It didn't look half bad. When the tail was released, old Leroy switched it several times as if trying out a new baseball bat.

"All right, people," gently repeated the professor, "let this be a good lesson. Remember, never tie a bull's tail to anything but himself!"

I escaped that episode without being expelled or flunking animal restraint, but was subjected to considerable ridicule from my associates. I vowed never to be responsible for an improper tail tie again.

In spite of my tail-preserving vow, it happened again at a vet school, some twenty years later when I was a new professor at the University of Georgia. A colleague had referred a lame Angus bull to our clinic for diagnosis and treatment. He was a high-powered, high-bred, high-priced, 2,500-pound wonder. He also had a high-class name, something like Black Cat of Hall Plantation. He arrived at the clinic in style, riding comfortably in a massive trailer similar to a Trailways bus, pulled by the latest and biggest crew cab Chevrolet available. The trailer also contained comfortable sleeping quarters for the bull's touring and showing entourage. Even the most indifferent critic of the cattle industry couldn't help but be impressed.

The unloading ceremony onto our puny grass lot was equally impressive. After placing the trailer at the most level site, the chauffeur swung open the doors, and Black Cat slowly sauntered down the exit ramp, accompanied by two attendants. The attendants were cowboys, or actors attired in the usual cowboy garb. Judging from the way they were moving, their spotless jeans, shirts, and possibly undies contained at least a quart of additional starch. It was obvious they had been standing for the entire fifty-mile journey because the only creases present in their pants and shirts were the ones that were required to be there by the cowboy dress code. In addition, their Stetson hats were big and white, and almost as wide as their handlebar mustaches, which were perfectly twirled into wax-enhanced points. In reality, I had never seen such cowboy outfits in real life, but according to some pictures I had seen from an event in Nevada where cowboys congregated to recite their poems, I was pretty sure that was how they were supposed to look when they were dressed up. I found myself wondering how they could possibly deliver a calf in such getup, not to mention perform surgery while squatting down behind a bull calf in a narrow and soiled squeeze chute.

When our properly shampooed and combed-out patient touched earth, his first move was to reach down in one great swoop and grab a swath of fescue with his massive mouth. Instantly the head cowboy, the one with the widest mustache, retrieved the forage grass treat from the bull's mouth and quickly gave it an inspection, then shook and picked away a couple of small clods of dirt and debris from it before offering it back to the bull's mouth. I noticed the assistant cowboy flick a couple of specks of dirt from the left cuff of his shirt.

By then the event had drawn a crowd. Other clients who had dropped by with their animals, staff, and even passersby had stopped their vehicles and were peering at the commotion going on in the clinic yard. Several eager veterinary students were there to observe and help, hoping to convert their book learning into practical, in-the-trenches veterinary medicine.

While the attendants led the patient to the back of the clinic, all eyes were trained on Black Cat's gait. It was obvious to nearly every observer, even to Roy, the ever-present feebleminded town clown, that the animal was quite lame. Unfortunately, figuring out which of the four legs was causing the lameness problem is sometimes challenging, and this caused poor Roy to make an erroneous diagnosis.

"It's his left front laig," declared Roy. "I spec' it's broke, or he boogered up his knee." He was never bashful about telling the world, and especially veterinary students, what he thought was wrong with an animal. He was also frequently giving me advice about how to proceed with outdoor large animal surgical procedures, most of which he had never even seen or heard of before.

"I don't think so, Roy," I said. "Just watch from the rear and you'll see he's not putting much weight on that right rear leg." Each time the bull touched ground with the foot, he flinched, his head popping up as the lame member attempted to carry weight.

"What do you doctors think?" I asked the vet students. They were ready with an answer.

"Right rear limb. Probably in the foot, since ninety percent of lameness in the bovine is in the foot. Examine foot first, then go proximal. If it's not foot it will probably be stifle, perhaps a ruptured meniscus and anterior cruciate. But we didn't hear any crepitus, and his anterior stride isn't shortened, as described in Blood and Henderson's textbook."

I stopped and smiled at the students, and wondered who had taught them so well. Obviously, it was someone who had been there and done that. Sometimes those who write textbook chapters get their information from another textbook or an article that wasn't exactly correct the first time. In my opinion they were right on with their diagnosis, even though some of it had come from a textbook. Then I asked them how to proceed.

"Got to pick up that foot and check for a foreign object, then use the hoof testers all around the hard tissue," recited the student who had apparently been selected as the spokesperson.

"How are you gonna pick up that big ole foot?" I queried.

"That, I don't know," the spokesvet confessed.

"We're gonna do it the easy way, in the chute," I announced.

Minutes later we had the cooperative patient in a squeeze chute, his leg lifted with the aid of a strong rope, while a half dozen people knelt, trying to be the first to spot the roofing nail or other foreign body suspected to be imbedded in the hoof tissue. Nothing could be found, but when the outside claw was lightly pinched with the hoof tester, he jerked his foot away in obvious pain.

"Must be a subsolar abscess, don't you think?" I said. A majority of heads nodded agreement. "OK, then, I think we'll put him on the table and anesthetize that foot, open and drain the abscess, and then glue a wooden block on his good claw. That will give him relief from pain and allow the sore foot to heal much quicker."

While we were making preparations, I heard the value of Black Cat placed at $80,000, then a few minutes later one of the attendants allowed that the value was more like $125,000. Later, I heard even higher figures. I have always thought it was strange that the more serious the ailment the higher the value of the animal.

Our haltered patient was led up the chute to the Shanks table that now stood in vertical position. His head and the down foreleg were secured at the proper positions, two large belly bands wrapped around the front and rear of his abdomen, then the table was lowered to the horizontal position. Black Cat, not having much choice about the matter, let the table take him over with little more than a few grunts and a couple of halfhearted squirms. The two cowboys were at his head, gently rubbing his brow and mumbling soothing messages in his ear. In my opinion, the tilt table for large animals ranks very high on the list of handiest devices ever invented. Of course, not all bulls accept the table as easily as Black Cat, but a sedative injection sometimes make matters easier.

A minute later, all four legs were secured with ropes and we had a more convenient view of the sore foot. A tourniquet was placed around the leg and local anesthetic was injected below the tourniquet. But the bull kept switching his mighty tail, which was frequently landing blows to my head.

"Will somebody hang on to that tail?" I requested, never looking up from the foot.

Presently, things were going my way. No more tail swishing, and no more pain for the bull. I went to work paring hoof tissue away over the area where the pain had been exhibited. Soon, smelly pus spewed from the opening I had made, causing an evacuation of several of the queasiest spectators. More paring through the sole resulted in a hole almost an inch in diameter. It was important to create a large opening for proper drainage of the abscess.

After the opening was pared to my satisfaction and treated with iodine, we glued a one-inch wooden block to the healthy claw of the same foot in order to keep the sore digit off the ground, used a hair dryer to help the acrylic glue to set up, then lightly wrapped the foot with roll gauze and three-inch tape. The tourniquet was slowly removed and an antibiotic injection was given.

The straps and ropes were loosened, the table tilted upright, and soon Black Cat was led away, walking a little stiltedly because of his first experience with a single high-heeled shoe. On his third tentative step, I heard the same loud ripping noise I had heard some twenty years before, an "Uh oh!" from a member of the crowd, and a second later felt several drops of blood as they were slung onto my face and glasses. I knew what had happened without looking. Someone had tied Black Cat's beautiful tail switch to the table and had forgotten all about it when detabling time came.

"What idiot tied this fine bull's tail to the table?" I heard myself rant, no doubt red-faced as a beet. "Who? Who did it?"

As it was years before, silence prevailed, except for the open-mouthed gasps of the grand entourage and the rapid swishing of the suddenly shortened tail. Also, my heart was in my throat, as before, and I'm sure it could be heard for a considerable distance.

"Well, I've done it again!" I thought to myself. "But I didn't even touch his tail this time."

When I finally decided to peek at the "detailed" bovine, I discovered that he had ripped off about two thirds of the switch. There was still a small tuft of short hairs left for fly-fighting purposes. I reckoned that I had to make some sort of statement to the team of attendants that encircled the patient.

"What can I say, folks?" I said slowly. "We made a mistake and tied the tail to the table."

Much to my surprise, there was no hollering and screaming from the cowboys; no knives or pistols were drawn and coldly placed next to the erring vet's head. I wondered if they realized the switch wouldn't grow back. Finally, the head groom spoke.

"Aw, don't worry about it, Doc." He shrugged. "What's done is done. We keep plenty of fly dope around, so he won't really need his tail that much anyway. Besides, there's kind of a move on nowadays to make the switch shorter on show animals."

I was surprised by this remark and wondered if he were speaking on behalf of the absentee owner. Perhaps he was so concerned about the severe lameness that he considered the shortened tail a minor problem. But as the trailer pulled out onto the highway, I had a feeling that I had not heard the last from Black Cat.

Sure enough, that night I received a call from my colleague who had referred the case.

"What happened down there today, John?" he queried. "This crowd of cowboys came by here on their way home and blessed everybody out, then went down to the county agent's office and lit into everybody down there. What's going on?"

I explained to him exactly what had happened and how we had mistakenly tied the tail to the table.

"What idiot did a stupid thing like that?" he screamed. "Didn't y'all know you were dealing with a bull worth half a million dollars?" Odd how the value increased so quickly!

By some miracle, Black Cat's tail switch grew out enough that he had some abbreviated fly-fighting weaponry that summer. But a couple of summers later, he ate a four-inch piece of baling wire and died of hardware disease. Some thought he ate the wire because his tail was too short and it caused an iron deficiency. The boys at the feed store told me he was worth a million dollars.

I'm proud to say that I have treated a bull that was a millionaire. However, I hope anyone who ever treats a million-dollar bull remembers to tie his tail to some portion of the bull's own anatomy and not a stationary object.

Twenty-nine

I t was 1968, and Choctaw County was having a 120-years-old birthday celebration, which was the cause of a lot of pride and excitement throughout the county. Those in charge of the summer event asked for all the men of shaving age to grow beards, the reason being to make things more realistic on the big day when we all dressed out in our garb from earlier times. *The Choctaw Advocate,* our weekly paper, enthusiastically did its part by regularly informing everybody of the event and encouraging participation in all aspects of it.

At first I refused to quit shaving every morning, but eventually the pressure from friends and clients became so severe that I decided to surrender and join the ranks of the great unshaven. It was the first time since being a teenager I wasn't scraping growth off my face on a daily basis.

In the 1960s beards weren't as socially accepted as they are in the

1990s, mostly because no one wanted to be labeled as a hippie. Still, it is revealing and somewhat amusing to look at old pictures of one's ancestors and see that most of the older men had big bushy beards, and nobody in their right mind would refer to those tough, stoic, straight-as-an-arrow men as hippies. But I had never liked beards, and after just two weeks of having one I knew why.

Jan and the kids thought the beard was kind of neat, and even tolerated my rubbing it on their faces during hugs, but it was giving me the itching fits! The summer weather was normally hot and humid, and in spite of trying to keep the beard shampooed daily, it itched constantly and had irritated my skin. Not only did it torment me day and night, its appearance was hideous, and not at all what I had anticipated. Instead of matching my thirty-something-year-old, plain, rusty-red hair, it was bright red on the sides, brown down on my chin, white in a couple of spots on my jowls, and had gray hairs scattered liberally throughout.

Another problem was that foul-smelling barnyard substances were constantly lodging within the whiskery mass, sometimes unbeknownst to me until I arrived home and was so informed by Jan. Her nose was unbelievably sensitive to any kind of smell, especially barnyard aromas, and still is to this very day. I discovered that after so many years of being around unpleasant barnyard smells, my nostrils had become desensitized to them. So I tried to be unusually vigilant about the washing-up process after attending a cow that had been in labor, as well as other duties involving close-up animal work. A veterinarian shouldn't be offensive to the nostrils of his family or friends.

I decided if I was going to suffer the torment of the beard through to the final day of the celebration, I would doctor it up a little. Therefore, late one night at the clinic, I took the clippers, a number-forty blade, and shaved the itchy area under my neck and chin as clean as possible. With that done, I proceeded to clip an inch space under my nose, then cleaned up an area on each cheek. What I had then was sort of a Fu Manchu–looking creation.

The new look was unique and a lot better, but I thought its multicolor aspect was still reason enough to keep me from winning the coveted prize of "best beard" on the big day. After all, that was the only thing keeping me from mowing the thing off. It was time to take drastic measures.

Lucille Skinner ran a beauty parlor on the south side of the town square and also happened to be a friend and one of my favorite clients. I had seen her dogs on several occasions, both day and night, whenever they were sick or well. She owed me a favor, and Jan suggested that I call her.

"Lucille, I need some help," I said over the phone. "But you've got to keep this quiet. I don't want Loren or Clatis or Miller Ezell or anybody else to ever hear a word about what I want you to do."

"OK, Dr. John, what is it?"

"I need to come down to your shop when you don't have any customers there, and I want you to dye my beard bright red, just like the man on that Johnnie Walker Red scotch label." His beard was rust red, but more red than rust.

"Yeah, I'll do that, if you're sure. People are gonna stare, you know."

"I really don't care, 'cause it won't be but for a few days more. I really do want to win that contest."

"Just come on down to the shop tomorrow about noon, say twelve-fifteen or so. I'll be sure there's no one here."

The next day at the appointed hour, I drove down the alley behind Bedsole's Department Store, parked out of sight behind Sparrow's Cleaners and Laundry, then, with my hands partially covering my eyes and my chin down close to my chest, I trotted the fifty feet up the back loading ramp and into the back door of Skinner's Beauty Shoppe. I hadn't needed to be so careful; everyone had gone home for lunch, so there wasn't a soul in sight of the alley.

I remembered going to a beauty parlor once before as a small child, when I accompanied my mother. It must have been a very special occasion, perhaps a church dinner or maybe when my Uncle Willis finally got married. There was little money back then for such frivolity. But I did vaguely remember the interior of a beauty shop. As I scanned the room, I saw several bucket-looking devices turned upside down on the backs of chairs. I knew they were dryers and had something to do with permanents. Over to the right, I could see chairs, tables full of various hair-treating substances, and several sinks. One particular basin had the appearance of a miniature livestock-dipping vat with a neck rest built into its side. While I was checking out the strange facility, Lucille came bounding into the room eating a Spam sandwich and drinking a Tab.

"Oh, yeah, uh huh, yep, yep," she announced thoughtfully as she examined and palpated my beard with the expertise of a Ph.D. hair stylist. "I can see why you want something done with this wreck." I always appreciated Lucille's frankness, even if it wasn't always delivered in the most diplomatic way.

"Can you fix it?" I asked nervously. "I need to get out of here before somebody sees me."

"Won't take me but a few minutes," she declared, pointing to the little dipping vat. "Go yonder and sit down in that chair, put this plastic cover around your neck and over your shoulders, then lay your head backwards in that basin." I carefully thought over what she had said, just to be sure I had heard the instructions correctly.

Moments later, Lucille was working some strong-smelling solution into my beard. It had the odor of shoe polish and hog dewormer. As she worked it in with her gloved fingers, she carried on a continuous commentary about the health of her pets, and how brilliant they all were and how much they all meant to her. I was trapped, so I uttered a lot of uh huhs and similar expressions from the throat, since I dared not open my mouth for fear of ingesting some toxic chemical. It was just like being in the dental chair, but unlike the dentist, Lucille wasn't bothering to slow down long enough to ask questions.

Minutes later, I was standing in front of a mirror admiring the handiwork of my personal hairdresser. The job she had done was fantastic, although it was a tad redder than I had called for. It was the bright red color of a Kansas City Chiefs football jersey, and after a minute or two of inspection, I reckoned that I liked it better than the color worn by the Johnnie Walker Red guy, even if it and my hair were different shades of red.

"Perfect, Lucille!" I exclaimed. "Just what I had in mind. With this color there's no way I can lose the contest."

After some important instructions about the proper care of red beards, I crept out the back door and sprinted, low to the ground, to my truck.

Jan and the kids loved the way the beard looked, and many of my clients commented favorably on its unique shape and unusually bright color. I was proud of it, too, and was doing what I could to keep it fit for the upcoming celebration the following Saturday night at the national guard armory. Every morning I would run my dog clippers lightly over it to whack down out-of-place straggly hairs.

When the hour of the long-awaited contest arrived, at least five hundred unshaven men were milling about on the armory floor, going through an unusual ritual of shaking hands, then peering intently at each other's beards, from several angles. Each man would then reach up and lovingly stroke his own beard as his comrade studied every detail of the hairy mass. Then the roles would be reversed.

There were beards and goatees of all styles, sizes, and colors. I thought to myself what a great event this had turned out to be. It was something we were all proud of, and it built community relationships. But it was a shame that there could be only one winner, and after seeing all the others, it was my opinion that none of the beards present could compare to mine. It was undoubtedly the classiest one there. I was totally confident that I would be called forward to accept the first-prize trophy.

"Our panel of female judges will select four finalists from this mob," the Chamber of Commerce man announced over the loudspeaker. "Each of you will be given a slip of paper with a number on it. Please pin this number to the front of your shirt or overalls. After the judges make their decision, they will call out the number of four finalists. If your number is called, please come up to the stage." I recall that my number was 220.

We all marched around the floor in clockwise fashion, preening ourselves like strutting roosters and playing to the large crowd. Many in the audience were clapping and yelling out encouragement to their bearded relatives and friends while the judges were making their decisions. I could see them pointing out individuals and making various hand movements to their own chins and the sides of their faces. After five minutes or so, a lady's voice made the announcement.

"This has been a difficult decision," she cooed, "but we have reached a consensus. Will numbers 86, 112, 220, and 390 please report to the stage." Much applause followed, and the shouts of encouragement became louder. I could hear Tom, Lisa, and even little Paul calling, "Yea, Daddy, yeaaa!"

When I got a close look at the other three, it was no contest! Not even close! They hadn't even combed their beards out or clipped off the stray hairs. Jack Barber, the telephone man, exhibited an ugly unkempt thing that even showed mustard stains in the chin area. I saw no way I could lose.

As the others were introduced, polite applause could be heard. But when my turn came, the applause, whistling, and yelling erupted into a crescendo several decibels louder than the others. I smiled and waved, all the while wondering whether I should put the trophy on the mantel at the house or in the waiting room at the clinic. Maybe I would donate it to the county so they could put it in the courtroom at the courthouse.

When quiet was restored, I noticed the Baptist preacher striding purposefully toward the judge's table. I smelled trouble. After a few moments of heads-together whispering, they all looked straight at me, lips pursed. They continued to stare, with lips now moving, then a couple of them started to shake their heads the wrong way. I knew there was a problem and I knew it had to do with my beard.

I was wondering if it had anything to do with my visit to Lucille's beauty parlor.

"Your attention, please," the purse-lipped head judge announced. "Your attention please! I am sorry to report that number 220 has been disqualified from the contest."

An embarrassing hush descended upon the throng, except for a few gasps and several loud yells of approval from supporters of my opponents. Then there was a scattering of boos and numerous calls of "Why?" Finally, after the initial shock wore off, I was able to speak.

"Why? What's the reason?" I yelled. There was no answer from the judges' table, so I again yelled, this time much louder. The Chamber of Commerce man finally answered.

"Because it's against the rules to wear a fake beard in this event. It says so right here in the rules and regulations. A beard that perfect has got to be fake," he said, pointing right at me. I was furious.

"This is no fake beard!" I exclaimed. "I've been cultivating this thing for weeks! Here, feel it. Try to pull the hairs out."

"No, we're not allowed to touch them," the judge lady said, recoiling in horror from the thought of it. "Besides, we've already decided on a winner."

"Who?" I asked with nostrils flared. I was really steamed now.

"The winner is number 390, Mr. Jack Barber." She smiled, leading the polite applause.

"He's a Baptist, Doc," contestant number 86 whispered to me. "That's why the preacher came up to talk to the judges. He don't want us Methodists beatin' one of his flock." Sure enough, when I checked, the three nonwinning contestants were all Methodists.

"That Baptist preacher has quit preaching and gone to meddling," I said.

But soon I was shaking Jack's hand and offering him my congratulations, and he bragged on my beard. "Why is it so red, Doc? It's different from the hair on top of your head."

"Only my hairdresser knows for sure, Jack," I replied. We all had a good laugh, then dispersed into the night, most without trophies.

Within an hour, I was clipping my face clean. It was such a relief to have a cool-feeling face once again. I have never grown another beard and have no plans to do so.

Many of my friends, clients, and colleagues wear beards, and they seem mighty proud of them, saying they are extensions of their personalities. But not many of them around here are Methodists.

Thirty

D oc, you act like you don't feel good. What's wrong with you, boy?" asked my friend Clatis Tew, the world's greatest pickup truck salesman and all-around good guy. I had stopped by the drugstore that early morning for a store-bought cup of coffee.

"Nothing wrong with me," I told him with a smile. "I'm about the luckiest feller in the world. If there's anything wrong, it's just that I've got too much work to do. I ought not even be in here with this crowd telling lies and drinking coffee."

"Yeah, I've noticed it, too," replied Loren Caudle, the town pharmacist and my main man and golfing partner. "Joe Cowan came into the drugstore yesterday telling me that you didn't even honk your horn at him when you passed by his house yesterday."

"Horn's broke. Besides, I don't even remember going by Joe's place yesterday."

"Uh huh! Didn't you go down Ararat Road about dinnertime? You went to Tiny Sample's catch pen down by the river and tested his cows again, didn't you?"

"How in the heck did you know that?"

"When I went to the bank to make a deposit yesterday, I asked Tiny's wife what he was doing. She told me that you were coming to retest the herd for Bang's disease. Shoot, I could ask anybody who lives down that road. They see that old worn-out truck of yours hauling that squeeze chute. It don't take a genius to figure out where you're going," Loren replied.

"Tiny told me you weren't in a good mood," declared Clatis.

"How come everybody knows so much about my business?" I asked.

"'Cause it's a small town maybe?" someone said.

"No, it's because of the BIS," answered Harry Moore, one of the town's two dentists. He was the broken jaw specialist, known for wiring up the jaws of state-line drunks who, after a few cans too many, challenged the wrong person. He even came to my office from time to time to help me pull teeth and repair fractured dog jaws.

"What's the BIS?" everybody said, looking at Harry.

"The barbershop information system. If you don't believe it, go around to Chappell's barbershop and just sit down for thirty minutes. I guarantee you'll pick up information the FBI doesn't have," Harry replied.

Everybody knew that Harry was right. Not only did Chappell and his associate, Myatt, know everything, on any given day at least half their customers were equally as gifted. It was impossible to pay them a visit without having to suffer through an exhibition of their information-delivery prowess, but when you walked out the door you felt totally updated about affairs local, regional, international and even extramarital.

In addition, when I was there, each person present made sure that I understood he was himself sort of a veterinarian, and a regional expert on some specialty branch of veterinary medicine. Some were poison experts, others were just specialists on poisonous plants, while others claimed to be unequaled as equine colic treaters. When I first moved to Choctaw County, I was often intimidated, as they quoted treatments that sounded foreign to my ears, which caused me to rush home and search through my up-to-date textbooks for even a hint of the barbershop therapy of which I had just been advised.

As my practice and I matured, I began to enjoy my trips to the barbershop more and more, even dropping in occasionally on a rainy day in the hope of learning a few outlandish veterinary remedies.

On that day, though, the drugstore crowd was interested in their perceived state of my mild depression. When I rose from the table and headed for the door, Clatis caught up with me.

"I think I know what the problem is," he said, his hand on my shoulder. "Let me show you something parked outside."

Seconds later we stood peering at a brand-new, shiny Chevrolet pickup. We slowly walked all the way around the white beauty, admiring the perfect paint job and the gleaming chrome. It had tinted windshield, tan seats, and was loaded with optional amenities not usually seen in a truck of the mid-sixties era. It was the most beautiful vehicle I had ever seen.

"Just came in yesterday," Clatis allowed, pulling a large, white handkerchief from a rear pocket and lightly rubbing the areas where my hands had been. He even bent over and moved his head from side to side, trying to identify the location of the finger-defiled spots he was sure I left, then wiped the smudges away. There wasn't the slightest evidence of a smear when he finished with his ever-present truck hankie.

"Your truck around the corner?" he asked. I knew what was coming next. He was now entering phase two of his prize-winning truck sales technique. No doubt he was working on another selling award, probably something like an all-expenses paid, weekend-long trip to the dog racetrack in Pensacola, all meals included at the local cafeteria. I snickered to myself just thinking about Clatis and Betty Jo in the clubhouse jumping up and down, screaming their favorite dog on to victory.

"Been a good one, hasn't it?" he stated, checking out my beloved old pickup. "But it's beginning to look a little ragged, with all the wear and tear." He lightly touched a spot or two on the hood, then looked down, starting at the fender, then all the way back to the rear bumper. He uttered sort of a "tsk, tsk" sound with his mouth and shook his head.

"What's wrong? Why are you shaking your head?" I asked.

"Well, it's just . . . I don't know how to say this, exactly, but you need to think about the image you're portraying around town with this truck."

"Well, you're the one who sold it to me, and you sure bragged on it then."

"Yeah, but that was what, two or three, maybe five, years ago? You're all over the country with this vehicle, and what people think of you has a lot to do with the truck you drive and the condition it's in. You don't go to preaching in old dirty coveralls, do you?"

"'Course not, but—"

"Of course you wouldn't. And you ought not be driving this older truck up to nice farms. What do Stink Clark and Mr. W. J. Landry think about that? And how about that crowd of big ranchers up at Livingston Stockyard?"

"Well, I don't know if I can afford to—"

"John, you can't afford not to trade up. Even though you think this one right here is in good driving shape, it has nearly a hundred thousand miles on it, and some major repairs are just down the road." When he slapped the side of the fender for emphasis, a big clod of mud fell from somewhere underneath. Now he had finished phase three and was into phase four, where the dreaded "major repair" declaration was commencing. "There's the transmission to worry about, the rear end—" But he was cut off in mid-sentence by the blasting of the two-way radio.

"Base to mobile one, do you read?" It was Sue calling from the office. I was saved by the radio!

"Go ahead."

"Someone is here with a dog that's been hit by a car. He's scraped up and has a broken femur, but not shocky."

"I'll be right there," I replied.

"John, wait just a second before you go," Clatis said. "You may not realize it, but you are having a little sinking spell right now and it's probably caused by something called the pickup truck blues. Think about it." I laughed aloud as I turned the starter, hearing the louder than usual grinding, followed by sputtering and a little too much blue smoke billowing out the rear end.

"Remember what I said." Clatis coughed. "Looks like you need new rings, maybe an engine overhaul." I waved, then turned around in the middle of the street and headed toward the clinic, hoping Walter, the policeman wasn't watching.

Later that day, after the clinic cases were treated, the dog's broken leg was pinned, and several lacerations had been sutured, I headed east on afternoon calls. When I passed McPhearson Chevrolet Company on the town square, Clatis was out front showing a customer his truck selection. He covered his ears against the noise as I blasted by. The hole in my muffler was creating more racket than I remembered before seeing his new demo truck that morning. Maybe the noise just seemed to echo louder since it was bouncing off the tall two-story buildings in downtown Butler.

Driving an old truck after being exposed to a brand spanking new one is like trying on new shoes. When you go back to the old ones they seem terribly worn and shabby. Suddenly, my truck was rattling in places that I hadn't noticed before, it ran rough, and the uncomfortable seats seemed to have springs gouging me in all the wrong places. It was roaring a little too loud, and the transmission didn't shift as crisply as it had in the past. Maybe Clatis was right about it being trading time. He might even have been right about the pickup truck blues' being responsible for my failure to wave at Joe and the fact that I hadn't joked around with Tiny Samples when testing his cows.

After thinking about the pickup truck blues affliction, I remembered reading somewhere that it was a very real disease, affecting people of all vocations and professions. One would think that farmers would be the first affected, but since pickups were becoming so popular among those who don't even need them, it was just as likely that doctors, preachers, and downtowners would also exhibit the symptoms. It is primarily a disease of males, and probably is more prevalent in the southern United States. Fortunately, it is easily cured by purchasing a new truck. Of course, there is the chance for a relapse every three to five years. I remembered observing the condition in many of my friends in the past, but until Clatis jogged my memory I was unaware of its cause.

The symptoms of the disease are essentially the same, whether the victim is a first-time sufferer or a veteran of multiple attacks. Usually the first-stage signs include depression, a sense of loneliness, and feelings of inferiority. "Everybody has a nice pickup but me!" the sufferer is frequently heard to utter.

As the condition progresses into the second stage, the sufferer is plagued by a painful neck and jittery nerves caused by the sudden jerking and twisting of the head around to observe new trucks he meets on the road. The nervousness comes about because of near accidents when the victim takes prolonged stares at coveted vehicles to the rear, not only on the road but in dealers' lots as well.

The third stage is denial. As the disease escalates, the bundle of nerves now adamantly refuses to admit in public how affected he really is. In fact, he utters antitrading phrases.

"Why, this truck is plenty good for me. It's got only a hundred and forty thousand miles on it. Besides, new trucks are just out of sight. It's ridiculous what they are asking for them," he might avow while at the feed store. "I'll just get this ole trap's transmission fixed and then paint it," he might tell his spouse. "I don't need a new one, 'cause we can't afford it right now." When the conversation contains such denials, an astute observer should know that trading day is near.

Now comes stage four, the period of shopping and shock. Visiting the truck dealer takes place in this fourth stage. The initial visit usually occurs late at night or on a Sunday afternoon when the lot is devoid of smiling and aggressive salesmen.

"Oh, man, ain't this one pretty." The victim sighs, kicking at tires and rubbing his calloused hands over the tailgate of a shiny red truck.

But seconds later, a choking sound can be heard. He has just seen the price of the thing and has succumbed to "sticker shock." This initial sticker shock wears off in forty-eight to seventy-two hours. The victim then returns for further shopping, and this time he is somewhat immune to the shock of leg-weakening high prices.

Another curious symptom is a darkening of the fingertips during this phase. These marks can be traced to a sudden interest in handling the newspaper's classified ad page and multiple dialings of the phone in order to get the selling prices of trucks throughout the region.

Stage five is the period when the trade is actually made. Individuals react differently during this stage, some returning to "good ole boy" status, while others go through a mean and insulting period, trying to squeeze out the world's best deal.

When a sufferer exhibits these symptoms, it is a sure sign that he loves the new truck and won't draw an easy breath or sleep a sound wink until it is parked outside his bedroom window.

Stage six is when all papers have been signed. There are absolutely no remaining signs of the depression or other symptoms, and the new owner's self-confidence has been restored. The elated buyer is even certain he can easily make the monthly payments. Now the boasting and gloating commences.

According to the buyer, no one has ever received a better deal on such a dynamite truck. To hear some tell it, the dealer actually paid them to take the truck off the lot. The fuel mileage is so outstanding the vehicle has to be stopped periodically to let gasoline out, and the heater is hotter and the air conditioner colder than any other. It pulls the biggest load, never uses oil, and the entertainment center picks up good country music from a station far away over the mountain.

That night when I eased into the driveway, I spied a hubcap in the carport. Tom was playing football in the front yard with his buddy Joe. His football helmet was too big for a first grader, and sometimes when he took a hard hit it got so askew he found himself peering out the ear hole.

"Daddy, you lost a hubcap from your wheel. We found it over there by the mud hole," Tom yelled as he crossed the goal line, an imaginary line drawn between two rocks.

"Thanks, Roy, I'll put it back on." One of my clients had started calling him "Roy" when we were on a farm call, because Tom enjoyed wearing his toy Roy Rogers pistols in their holsters. I still call him "Roy."

"Jan, I've been thinking," I said a few minutes later. But before I could continue, she surprised me with a response.

"Yeah, I know, you need to get a new truck," she stated, stirring the grits.

"Just how do you know that?"

"Lucille down at the beauty parlor saw you and Clatis looking at that new one this morning. Plus, the way you've not exactly been yourself lately, I figure you've got the trading fever." Women's intuition has always amazed me!

Later that night I called Clatis and asked him to get some figures together for a new truck. I reckoned I was in stage four of the pickup truck blues.

Thirty -one

A few days later, tired and still suffering from the pickup truck blues, I was driving north at a reasonable speed in my old truck, trying to make an appointment at Moore's cattle farm. But as I started up the hill near the Sumter County line, the truck suddenly lost its will to make it to the top. The engine was running as if it were in neutral, and I detected the aroma of transmission fluid.

"Aw, man!" I lamented. "The transmission is gone and I've got all this work to do. What am I gonna do?" When the county vet's truck croaks, it is panic time. I knew Mr. Moore would have several hundred cows corralled and waiting, several cowboys on horses, and a couple of good neighbors over to assist in the testing. I hated to keep clients waiting, because I knew they were just as busy as their vet, but by the time the truck was off the road and had come to a stop, I had a plan.

"Mobile one to base, do you read?" I said into the two-way microphone. Sue answered in thirty seconds.

"Sue, my transmission has gone out, right here at the county line, just down from Ralph Sherrill's place. Get a hold of Jan and have her bring me the station wagon. Then call McPhearson Chevrolet and ask them to send the wrecker, tow this thing in, and get it fixed as soon as they can. Then call Clifford Moore's house and ask them to get him word about my truck, 'cause I'll probably be two hours late getting to the ranch."

"OK, one, I'll call you back in a minute." I just hoped Jan was home and not involved in some of her civic work.

While waiting for Sue to radio back, I did what everybody always does when their vehicles conk out. I looked under the hood, but I saw nothing except dirty truck parts.

"Base to mobile one."

"Go ahead."

"Dr. John, Jan said she'd be there in about thirty minutes. But she wants to know how she's supposed to get home." I hadn't even thought about that!

"Tell her she can ride back with the wrecker, and she can get Clatis to loan her a car to get home in." Then I remembered what he had said about potential breakdowns. "Sue, call Clatis and tell him about this and it's all his fault! I think he put a hex on me and this truck!"

"Ten-four, I have him on the phone right now. The wrecker is on the way."

"What did he say, base?"

"He laughed and said "I told him so!' Also said he has those figures you asked him about, but that pretty truck is sold. Said he could have what you wanted in here in five working days."

While I was waiting for Jan to arrive on the sparsely traveled Highway 17, several travelers stopped and offered help. Some were clients, some were acquaintances who recognized my truck, and others were total strangers, just offering assistance to someone in trouble.

When Jan and Paul arrived, I transferred the basic things I would need for my work for the next few days. Even at the age of three, Paul seemed to be vehicle oriented, expressing an unusual interest in trucks. He recognized all the makes of trucks, their various classes, and their intended usages, and truly thought he was ready to drive one.

"I'm gonna get Clatis to order that new truck, Jan. I can't put up with this sort of carrying on," I declared.

"You want me to tell him when I get back?"

"Yep. He has all the specs. I'll figure out how to pay for it later. Maybe Clifford will write me a big check today, and I can collect some from Happy Dupree and some of those other big outstanding bills."

"You wouldn't have any problem if you'd just go to cash only, like that expert on practice management said at the conference. I know how to run an office," Jan said.

"The man's an idiot! How can a farmer pay every month when he only sells cattle and cotton once a year? It might work in the big city, but it won't work here." At that point, we decided to call a halt to the previously discussed "cash only" practice. I was not going to be convinced by some practice management consultant from Kansas City who had never even delivered a calf.

Later, the wrecker pulled away, dragging my old truck behind, mud clods dribbling from its undercarriage. Paul was sitting on Jan's lap, waving his hand wildly with a little help from her, as if he wouldn't see me again for several years. I felt a surge of happiness and pride, momentarily forgetting about the truck breakdown.

I was only an hour and a half late when I turned into the Moore Ranch driveway and headed for the corral. Clifford and his crew of Sumter County cowboys were sitting on the front bumper of a pickup truck, whittling, spitting, and for certain, lying about everything from football to foot rot. I knew Jan's long, white station wagon with whitewall tires was giving them new material to razz me about. I hadn't even stepped out of the car when it started.

"You gonna work cows or take chaps to kindergarten, Doc?" one said.

"Looks to me like he's gonna haul dead folks to the cemetery. That's the longest car in Sumter County. Doc, where you gonna turn that thing around at? You need forty acres," said another.

"I broke down a while ago. Everything was OK until I saw the Sumter County line, and then my truck's transmission blew up," I complained.

"Did you bring your golf clubs?" Clifford asked. I indicated that I had not.

"I thought we were gonna play in York after we got through pregnancy checking," Clifford said. "There's some folks over there who heard about that good round you shot the other day with Loren Caudle and that bunch, and they want to see how good you really are."

"How can I play with all this work to do? You must have three hundred cows penned."

"Can't you do one a minute? That's not but five hours," he said, consulting his watch. "We could be on the first tee by three."

"Let's do it after my new truck gets here. I need to get on back closer to home in case Jan needs this car."

"OK, whatever you say. Let's get going. I need a load of open cows to go to the sale this week. All these town merchants are startin' to holler for their money."

"Put me high up on that list. I gotta have some money for Clatis and that truck." Clifford didn't answer, just walked off and started yelling orders to the hands.

Like other cattle owners, Clifford wanted to go through the herd and find out which of his cows were not pregnant. The nonpregnant, or open, ones would then be sold. Pregnancy examination consists of putting the cows through a squeeze chute, then with the protection of a long glove and sleeve, making a rectal examination to detect the presence or absence of a fetus. This exam is usually done by the veterinarian or some other qualified individual. It is a dirty job and not for the squeamish. But it is a helpful procedure for the rancher, and it allows him to keep only the calf-producing cows, and dispose of the others. At Clifford's ranch, the open cow's number was taken, then the bottom part of the tail switch was scissored off to be doubly sure of her identification and condition.

Sure enough, five quick hours later I was cleaning up, while thinking about how tired my arm was and being thankful that I didn't have to play eighteen holes of golf for the next four or five hours.

"Tell me how much today's bill is, and I'll write you a check for the whole thing," Clifford said. "You better get that car back to your wife. I know how things are around my house when a car is not available."

Four nights later, Clatis, my family, and I were standing in the service area of McPhearson Chevrolet Company, casting our eyes on a beautiful new Chevy truck.

"What do you think?" he said. "Will it do?"

"Well, it's even prettier than I had envisioned," Jan declared. Paul followed Tom and Lisa around the periphery of the white beauty, softly caressing the glossy paint job. Paul was more thorough; he gave all four tires swift kicks, then looked underneath. Clatis followed right behind, mopping off phantom fingerprints.

"You know I'm gonna take care of y'all. You are my valued friends and customers." I was sure that was a slogan he had learned in truck-selling school. But I knew he was right.

All the kids piled into the cab, each taking a turn under the steering wheel, then each making some new discovery of an option lacking on the old truck. "Don't get those dirty feet on my new seats," I asserted.

"Don't worry, Doc. I put some plastic over them, 'cause I knew they'd be crawling around everywhere." Clatis always thought of everything.

"We want to ride home with Daddy," they chimed.

The truck was white as snow, with a long wheelbase and big tires that made it sit high off the ground, and it was fitted with a utility box on the back. The seats and interior were a baby blue color, which gave a softness to the country music that kicked in when Tom found the ignition switch. It was my dream truck, and I dreaded the thought of hitting a mud hole with it.

The next morning I drove through town several times, first going north to south then east to west, just showing it off, honking the horn and blinking the headlights. People I met waved, but not with their usual enthusiasm, since they thought it was a stranger just passing through. But when I peered in the rearview mirror, they had turned around and were staring as if to say, "Was that Doc in that new truck? I bet he'll start chargin' even more now!"

On my last show-off pass through town square, I parked right in front of the barbershop, so the professional communicators there could pass judgment on the truck before they passed the news on to their customers.

"I wished you'd look a' yonder, Chappell! Supervet's done drove up in a big ole new truck," Myatt yelled as I opened the door. "What's that thing on the back, a place to haul dogs around in?"

"Couldn't you afford a real truck, Doc?" one of the waiters asked.

"It is a real truck," I answered, puzzled.

"Well, I don't see F-O-R-D wrote on it nowhere," he replied. He was obviously no fan of General Motors products. But good-natured arguing about the different makes and models is one of the real pleasures of getting a new truck. Sometimes buying a truck just comes down to the person that's doing the selling, or how serious a case of the pickup truck blues you have!

Thirty-two

After a few years as the only vet in the county, I discovered that it didn't seem to matter what time I left the clinic in the evening, there was nearly always someone who needed veterinary service later that night.

Occasionally this wasn't too bad, especially if the evening called for a dull bridge party or one of those kitchenware demonstration deals. I admit that once I even claimed to have a three-hour emergency rather than attend one of those encounters. But after-work appointments and nighttime calls often get in the way of kindergarten performances, music recitals, and Little League ball games.

People who had regular jobs in Choctaw County didn't seem to understand why some of us who were self-employed were routinely tardy at these events. I could hear those "normal" people snorting and harrumphing as they stared daggers in the direction of the repeat offender, who was usually sneaking late into a hushed auditorium.

"I JUST DEHORNED A GOAT!" I wanted to say right into their ears, but then my family would have been mortified beyond words. So I refrained. My livestock-owning clients never seemed to notice late arrivals, because they too were frequently delayed because of farm emergencies.

~

"Doc, I've got a bunch of calves that need to be vaccinated, castrated, and implanted," Sonny Brewer told me over the phone one Monday evening in April.

"Well, you've called the right place, because we're running a special on those items this week," I joked.

"Good, good," he said. "I'll have 'em penned and ready to go tomorrow evening about six."

"Uh, wait a minute, Sonny," I said, hesitating. "I think Lisa is in that piano recital about seven-thirty."

"Aw, Doc, we'll easy be through by seven. It won't take but an hour to run through those thirty calves," he declared convincingly.

I knew it was a mistake when I agreed, but I consented. Sonny did have an extra-nice corral and squeeze chute, and if everything went well it wouldn't take long. On the other hand, if he had trouble getting them in from the pasture, or if one excitable calf got himself turned crossways in the alleyway or upside down in the squeeze chute, then we'd be held up and I'd be late again. If I didn't get the job done on Tuesday, it would be into the next week before we could get there, and by then he might have decided to forget the whole thing.

"Daddy, don't forget my recital tomorrow night," said Lisa as she hugged me good-night not long after Sonny's call. "I've been practicing real hard on my solo just so it will be perfect for you!" What daddy wouldn't make an extra effort to be at his little girl's first recital?

"Don't you worry, Lisa Bug, I'll be right there," I said, knocking on wood. "I may not be there right at seven-thirty, but I'll be there for your part. I'll probably be standing in the back by the door."

Tuesday went real well. I was on time for all my appointments, all the patients behaved, and there was a minimum of emergencies. There was no doubt in my mind that the new truck and being rid of the dreaded truck-buying fever had much to do with the fine way the practice was going. Since things were going so well, I felt confident that I would make Lisa's recital on time. Nevertheless, I hung my recital-going clothes in the truck just in case I wasn't able to get home to change.

It was five before six when I pulled up in front of Sonny's pasture gate, but the corral some fifty yards away was empty, its gate standing wide open. Sonny' s truck was out in the pasture, its door open, but neither he nor the calves were to be seen. Getting those wild calves penned had been my concern.

As I began to stomp, spit, and nervously twiddle the growth implants in my pocket, I heard Sonny yell.

"Yo! Yo! Yo!" he was saying to the beasts in his normal voice as he crested the hill carrying a Maxwell House coffee can under his arm. He was teasing the calves by offering them an occasional protein cube from the can while walking slowly toward the corral. Then he stopped for several minutes and exchanged pleasantries with the cows at random while they sniffed and tongued the precious cube container. My watch read six-ten. I couldn't take it any longer!

"Sonny, please hurry up!" I pleaded diplomatically. "I don't have all night!"

"Shhh!" he said, putting his finger to his lips.

I sat down on the ground on the off side of the truck and fumed. For several minutes I heard him talking cow talk, but at least the sounds were getting nearer. It was six-twenty.

"Whoap! Whoap!" I heard him say, in a louder voice, just as he entered the corral gate. A second later, I heard a shuffling, earth-gouging commotion and the dull sounds of hot bovine hide and hair bumping heavily into creosoted two-by-tens. The gate slammed shut loudly and then I heard the depressing sounds of numerous galloping hooves slowly fading away.

"Got half of 'em, Doc!" Sonny chirped proudly. "It won't take but ten minutes to get the others back up. They're just a little nervous with your new white pickup parked there. Is that a four-wheel-drive diesel or what, Doc? Sure is nice, with that telephone body and all . . ." He seemed to have no concept of the word *hurry* as he stopped and surveyed the spotless and eye-catching vehicle.

"Sonny, I'll just be dogged. I'm in a huge hurry, so get those calves in here and let's get it done. I told you I had to go to the schoolhouse tonight!" It was six-twenty-three.

Suddenly, as if a higher power had intervened, the group of calves that had escaped started loping back toward the gate. They seemed to be racing.

"Open the gate! Open the gate!" I exclaimed in a loud whisper.

While keeping an eye on the penned group, Sonny unlatched the gate, and within seconds the others had, for some strange reason, bolted into the pen. To this day, I do not know why.

"Fill the alleyway full, Sonny!" I ordered. "I'll just walk down the side, vaccinate all of 'em, implant the bulls, then we'll catch bull heads."

I was carrying my syringe and implant gun in makeshift holsters strapped to my sides so I could make quick work of the vaccination process. The time was six-thirty-five when I jabbed the first patient, so I knew I'd have to work fast.

When all the shots had been given to the first group, I jumped in among them and started pushing the heifers out as Sonny opened and closed the headgate. Later, when I finished castrating the last bull, it was seven-twenty-two.

"Sonny, I'm gone," I yelled, streaking for the truck. Even then was I beginning the undressing process. "I'd help you clean up and all, but I'm already late."

"Well, I wanted you to look at that knot on that horse's leg," he drawled, "but I reckon we can do that another night. And those deer dogs over yonder in the pen need rabies shots and deworming. And I wanted to talk to you about the best time for me to buy some steers to feed out . . ."

His lips were still moving as I cranked the powerful V-8 engine and roared away. I knew he was still unconcerned about time and trying to think up more things for me to do.

Driving back to town, I wondered how many people in the world had ever tried to change from dirty coveralls while driving a truck and keeping it between the ditches. I would not recommend this difficult procedure, but I carried it out that night as the truck rocketed toward the school and my belated appointment. I drove right up to the auditorium, left the truck blocking the driveway, bolted up the steps four at a time, and hit the door just as the audience was applauding Molly Jackson's solo.

Lisa was next. As she marched pertly across the stage toward the piano, I felt a thrill of pride.

"Isn't she the prettiest little thing I've ever seen?" I thought to myself. Her hair was back in a ponytail, and she was wearing a pretty, fluffy, little yellow dress and those funny, little black patent leather shoes with the strap over the top. Jan always had her fixed up so pretty.

She sat down on the bench, adjusted it, then began to play with concentration and great confidence. The piece was just a starter tune, but as proud and emotional as I was at that moment, she could have been a world-renowned concert pianist up there thrilling a throng of music lovers. All her hours of home practice, the numerous times she hit the wrong key, the times she became frustrated and started over, all faded into oblivion as she now fingered every ivory with just the right touch and proper timing. I could see Jan down front with Tom and Paul, her head moving in time, up and down, as Lisa deftly fingered the keys.

"This is what life is all about!" I thought to myself. I was glad it was dark in the back of the auditorium so that the other late arrivals standing just inside the back door couldn't see my glistening eyes. There was no way Lisa could know how fidgety her father had been or how proud he was of her.

When she finished, I could see Jan leading the applause, literally wearing her hands out. Lisa stood, curtsied, and briskly headed for the stage exit. But just before she went behind the curtain she looked toward the back door where I was standing and waved discreetly. She knew I was there!

When it was all over, she was the first one to come down the steps from the stage, and she beelined it toward me. "How did I do, Daddy?" she asked excitedly.

"Aw, you did great, honey. And I am so proud of you for practicing so hard and doing so well," I replied.

"I missed a couple of notes right at the end. You know, right there at the hard part."

"I didn't know. I thought it was perfect." And I really did.

A few hours later, alone in the darkness of the front porch steps, I thought about all the good fortune that had been showered upon me. The practice was still growing, and I worked daily with good and honest, down-to-earth people. By big-city standards, our income was unimpressive, but my commute to the animal clinic took all of two minutes, except late at night, when it took a minute and a half, because I didn't see the need to stop for the traffic light. Butler was almost crime-free, and like many citizens, we never locked the doors of the house.

Then I thought about my friend Carney Sam Jenkins, Choctaw County's own dirt road philosopher and expert on international policy. He was always saying, "There ain't but three things in life that really matter. That's your family, your reputation, and your health. Everything else is chaff." Later, he added friends and pickup trucks to his list of important things.

Carney Sam was right about family being number one. I was

blessed to have the love of a good woman, who was not only my wife but my best friend, my most honest critic, and a fine mother to our three children. Her support for me and our practice was unwavering. Even Missy, our springer spaniel, and our cat, Jinx, seemed genuinely pleased to be members of the McCormack household. When I reclined on the cool concrete of the porch to peer at the wonder of the stars, Missy and Jinx were suddenly in my face, licking, rubbing and making animal noises. I was forced to sit up to avoid being slurped to death.

I was truly lucky that, as a country veterinarian, I could take my children along on farm and house calls. Tom had started riding with me when he was three or four years old, helping to carry the stethoscope or medications, plus other light duties. One of his first calls was to visit a cow down with milk fever at John Dillon's dairy. While I made an examination of the patient, he stood on a turned-up bucket holding the jug of calcium high as it "glug-glugged" into the cow's jugular vein. Later, Lisa and Paul had their turns, and they too enjoyed learning about animals and their ailments.

"Why don't you bring them young 'uns with you?" a farmer occasionally suggested when calling for service. That meant his "young 'uns" wanted my "young 'uns" to come along and play while the work was being done by the adults.

I'm glad I was able to do that. Not only was it a pleasure for me, but it was educational for them. We just had to caution them about which veterinary procedures were off-limits for discussion during show-and-tell time!